THE GUARDIAN
OF BOSTON

William Monroe Trotter

STEPHEN R. FOX

STUDIES IN AMERICAN NEGRO LIFE
August Meier, General Editor

New York   ATHENEUM   *1970*

Frontispiece photograph reproduced by courtesy of *Ebony* magazine

Copyright © 1970 by Stephen R. Fox
Library of Congress catalog card number 78–108822
Published simultaneously in Canada by
McClelland and Stewart Ltd.
Manufactured in the United States of America by
Kingsport Press, Inc., Kingsport, Tennessee
Designed by Kathleen Carey
First Edition

For my parents

Preface

WHILE WRITING this book I was considerably assisted by three historians and by more librarians than I can recall, and their contributions helped me and the book immeasurably. Professor Arthur Zilversmit and Professor August Meier provided suggestions and close criticisms at different stages of the manuscript's composition. I am especially grateful for the generosity of Professor Louis Harlan, who helped me find a publisher, permitted me to read an unpublished paper of his on Booker T. Washington, and finally gave a critical reading to my manuscript in its penultimate form. Among the many librarians who lent assistance, I owe particular thanks to Mrs. Thomas V. Lape of Hancock House, Ticonderoga, New York; Mrs. Virginia E. Potts of Fisk University; Miss Elizabeth Duvall of Smith College; Donald Gallup of Yale University; Mrs. Dorothy Porter of Howard University; Maynard Brichford of the University of Illinois at Urbana-Champaign; Miss Lillian Miles of Atlanta Uni-

versity; Mrs. Nancy MacFadyen of Williams College; and
the staffs of the Schomburg Collection of the New York
Public Library, the Manuscript Division of the Library of
Congress, the Houghton Library of Harvard University,
and the Microtext Room of the Boston Public Library.

Herbert Aptheker graciously let me see the correspondence from 1903 to 1907 in the W. E. B. Du Bois Papers,
which are in his custody. Charles M. Storey and William H. Lewis, Jr., allowed me to consult their fathers'
papers at their homes. Mrs. James Weldon Johnson and
Mrs. Walter White gave me permission to see the papers
of their late husbands in the James Weldon Johnson Memorial Collection at Yale, and Professor George Cabot
Lodge made it possible for me to use the Henry Cabot
Lodge Papers at the Massachusetts Historical Society.

John Broesamle directed me to Trotter materials in the
papers of Woodrow Wilson and William McAdoo at the
Library of Congress. Eugene Gordon of New York shared
recollections of Trotter and referred me to an article of his
that commented significantly on Trotter as a journalist in
the 1920s. In Boston a number of people provided information and research suggestions, and I would like to note my
special gratitude to the late Dr. Charles G. Steward, the
late Mrs. Malcolm Banks, Ralph J. Banks, Mrs. Noel Day,
the Reverend St. Clair Kirton, Walter J. Stevens, and
Gerald Jackson.

For other kinds of assistance I would thank some ex-
ploited friends of mine: Ramon Powell and Charles
Puttkammer in Washington, James P. F. Cole and Dale
and Maggie Anderson in New York. James Cole typed
the manuscript when it was a thesis. Barbara Hopgood
prodded me into finishing the revised version and then
typed the final manuscript.

The biggest debt comes last. For their acceptance of
Monroe Trotter's company, and for other reasons, I dedi-

cate this book to my parents, Kenneth Russell Fox and Eleanor Pihl Fox.

Stephen R. Fox

Boston, Massachusetts
August 23, 1969

Contents

THE GUARDIAN
OF BOSTON

William Monroe Trotter

From Hyde Park to
the Guardian

MONROE TROTTER always insisted that he fell into the business of racial agitation by chance. He "did not seek a career of agitation and organization for equality for his race," he once wrote, lapsing into the third person. "The burden was dropped upon him by the desertion of others and he would not desert the duty." [1] Certain forces in his background, however, did point him toward the career of protest leader. In particular, there was his father, James Monroe Trotter.

I

James Trotter was born in Mississippi in 1842, the son of a slave named Letitia and her owner, Richard S. Trotter, a white man. This "family," which produced a total of three children, lived in the hamlet of Grand Gulf, twenty-five miles south of Vicksburg, on the Mississippi River.

[1] *Guardian*, December 28, 1918, p. 4, William Monroe Trotter Papers

Around 1854 Letitia and her children either escaped or were freed and went to live in the free city of Cincinnati. There the children attended a famous school for Negroes that had been started by Hiram Gilmore, an English clergyman. Later the family moved to nearby Hamilton, where James continued his education in a local academy, concentrating in music and art. Afterward he taught school for a short time.[2]

Then the Civil War gave him the chance to strike directly at the peculiar institution into which he had been born. For two years of the conflict Negroes were not allowed to enlist in the Union Army. But as the war of attrition dragged on, leaders such as Massachusetts' Governor John Andrew urged the use of black troops. The Emancipation Proclamation clinched the case. Soon after the Proclamation took effect in January 1863, Secretary of War Edwin Stanton authorized Andrew to raise an unspecified number of volunteer regiments that could include "persons of African descent." Andrew's recruiters spread across the North, and James Trotter was soon on his way to Boston to enlist.[3]

He joined the Fifty-fifth Massachusetts, an all-black regiment with white officers headed by Colonel N. P. Hallowell. One of those officers was George Garrison, a son of William Lloyd Garrison, and through him Trotter met the family of the great abolitionist and became friendly with the teenaged Francis Jackson Garrison. In his regiment Trotter showed unusual ability: he enlisted as a private,

[2] MS sketch of James M. Trotter's life in the George W. Forbes Papers; William J. Simmons, *Men of Mark: Eminent, Progressive and Rising* (Cleveland, 1887), p. 837; Arna Bontemps and Jack Conroy, *They Seek a City* (Garden City, N.Y., 1945), p. 61; Ruth Worthy, "A Negro in Our History: William Monroe Trotter, 1872–1934" (M.A. thesis, Columbia University, 1952), pp. 1–2.

[3] Luis F. Emilio, *A Brave Black Regiment: History of the Fifty-fourth Regiment of Massachusetts Volunteer Infantry, 1863–1865* (second revised edition, Boston, 1894), pp. 2, 8–12.

was quickly made a first sergeant, then sergeant major in November 1863, and second lieutenant the following April. He was one of only four Negro commissioned officers in the regiment. For fifteen months, however, the War Department refused to approve these commissions on the ground that no law specifically permitted a black officer to receive a commission. To which Trotter replied, in an angry letter to Francis Garrison, "Do you know of any law that *prohibits* it?" [4]

In the same letter Trotter described race relations within the regiment:

I am sorry to have to tell you also that most all the line officers give us the *cold shoulder*. Indeed, when our papers returned the other day disapproved those who have all along claimed to be our best friends, the line officers, seemed to feel the most lively satisfaction at the result. O how discouraging! How maddening, almost! A few, however, are *sensible* enough and kind hearted enough not to deny a poor oppressed people the means of *elevating themselves*. An officer told me that it was "too soon," that time should be granted white officers to *get rid of their prejudices*, so that a white Lieutenant would not refuse to sleep in a tent with a colored one. Of course he *supposed* that an objection of this kind would be made always by the white Lieut., and that an educated decent colored officer would never object to sleeping with the former whatever might be his char-

[4] Oswald Garrison Villard to W. E. B. Du Bois, April 18, 1905, Oswald Garrison Villard Papers; Charles Barnard Fox, *Record of the Service of the Fifty-fifth Regiment of Massachusetts Volunteer Infantry* (Cambridge, Mass., 1868), pp. 33, 44, 108, and insert facing p. 1; James M. Trotter to Francis J. Garrison, August 2, 1864, Francis J. Garrison Papers.

Most of the last letter is printed in Jack Abramowitz, "A Civil War Letter: James M. Trotter to Francis J. Garrison," *Midwest Journal*, IV (1952), 113–22.

acter. Yes, Franky, there is really more turning up
the nose on account of the commissions, *in our very
midst* than else where; and *no other reason is given
except color*. . . . because the soldiers are so *blam-
able as to have their skins dark*. Most awful crime!

Forty-three years later Garrison sent a copy of this letter to
his friend Booker T. Washington. "I am very glad to have
had the privilege of reading the letter from Mr. Trotter,"
Washington replied. "It throws a good deal of light upon
the queer make-up of his son." [5]

"In the noble stand of his regiment for full pay," Monroe Trotter wrote of his father, "he took a leading if not
the leading part, going among the men and seeking to
make them realize the full significance of holding out or
giving in." When the regiment was being recruited, Governor Andrew, acting on assurances from the War Department, had promised the Negro recruits that they would be
treated in the same manner and paid on the same scale as
white troops. The only law authorizing wages for Negroes
in the army, however, was an 1862 militia act which had
anticipated that Negroes would be used only as common
laborers and paid accordingly. The two black Massachusetts regiments—the Fifty-fourth and Trotter's Fifty-fifth
—refused to accept the laborer's wage.[6]

At Governor Andrew's urging, the Massachusetts legislature appropriated funds to bring the black troops' wages
up to the level paid white soldiers. Two men from Massachusetts came to the Fifty-fifth's encampment in South
Carolina and announced to the assembled troops that they
had brought the money. Trotter and several other black

[5] Booker T. Washington to Francis J. Garrison, December 3,
1907, Booker T. Washington Papers.
[6] W. M. Trotter to Ray Stannard Baker, October 5, 1907, Ray
Stannard Baker Papers; James M. McPherson, *The Negro's Civil
War: How American Negroes Felt and Acted During the War for
the Union* (New York, 1965), pp. 196–199; Fox, *Fifty-fifth Regiment*, p. 17.

soldiers replied, and Trotter's comments, one observer noted, were "especially good." They told the Massachusetts men that, although they were grateful for the offer, they could accept nothing but full pay *from Washington*. Otherwise it would seem that they were refusing the laborer's wage merely for the sake of the money involved. In fact they were acting on a principle: equal pay would be an implied recognition that the black soldiers were as good as the white ones. The Massachusetts men took their money and left.[7]

Shortly thereafter Stanton asked Congress to equalize the pay, and Representative Thaddeus Stevens introduced an appropriate bill. But the bill made slow progress, and by June 1864 the two Massachusetts regiments had served for a year without any pay. The financial strain was oppressive for many of the soldiers' families; in the regiments morale and discipline were declining. In mid-June a few soldiers in the Fifty-fifth refused to go on fatigue duty, but yielded under further prodding. A few days later there was a near-mutiny when a private forcibly resisted an order from a white lieutenant. The soldier was court-martialed and executed. "Had justice been done the enlisted men in regard to their position as soldiers," the regimental historian noted, "no such example would have been needed." Finally, on June 15, Congress granted equal pay, and by October most of the soldiers had received their back wages. Without the stubborn leadership of Trotter and others, even this overdue recognition might not have been granted.[8]

After the war Trotter was mustered out in Boston and

[7] Fox, *Fifty-fifth Regiment*, pp. 17–18; and see also Charles P. Bowditch, Folly Island, South Carolina, to his father, December 15, 1863, in *Proceedings of the Massachusetts Historical Society*, LVII (1924), 454.

[8] Emilio, *Brave Black Regiment*, pp. 190–91; Fox, *Fifty-fifth Regiment*, pp. 29, 34–37; McPherson, *Negro's Civil War*, pp. 201, 203.

decided to settle there permanently. Boston had the reputation of being a good place for Negroes to live. The city's
black community, numbering about 2,350 at the end of
the war, sent its children to integrated schools and was
granted the rights to intermarry, vote, hold public office,
sit on juries, and testify in court. State legislation in 1865
improved conditions further, as the new law prohibited
racial discrimination on public conveyances and at licensed
inns, public meetings, and public places of amusement. It
was no racial utopia, but it was the most enlightened area
in the North. Trotter, along with several other Negro war
veterans, was appointed to a clerkship in the Boston Post
Office.[9]

In 1868 he returned to Ohio to marry Virginia Isaacs,
whom he had met in Chillicothe during his schoolteaching
days. Her mother, Anne Elizabeth Fawcett, or Fossett, had
also been born in slavery, at Thomas Jefferson's Monticello plantation. According to an oral tradition passed
down in the Trotter family, Anne Elizabeth Fawcett was
the daughter of a male mulatto fathered by the Sage of
Monticello himself; thus Monroe Trotter would be a
great-great-grandson of Thomas Jefferson. In any event,
Tucker Isaacs, a free man of Negro and Jewish extraction,
married Anne Elizabeth and bought her freedom. On occasion Isaacs apparently forged "free papers" for escaped
slaves, a practice that put him under suspicion and
prompted him to move his family to Ohio. There, on a
farm seven miles outside Chillicothe, Virginia Isaacs grew
up.[10]

[9] John Daniels, *In Freedom's Birthplace: A Study of the Boston
Negroes* (Boston and New York, 1914), pp. 85, 94–96, 98–99;
Leon F. Litwack, *North of Slavery: The Negro in the Free States,
1790–1860* (Chicago, 1961), pp. 110–111, 149–151.

[10] Worthy, "Trotter," p. 1. Most of the speculation on Jefferson's
Negro children has involved the offspring of the favored Monticello
slave Sally Hemings. One of her children, Madison, recalled in
1873 that he and four others were the only Negroes fathered by
Jefferson. Monroe Trotter's ancestor Joseph Fossett, putatively also

James Trotter and his bride returned to Boston, where
they lived at first in the South End as he continued to work
in the Post Office. Their first two children died in infancy,
because, it was thought, of the rigors of city life. Accordingly, Virginia Trotter returned to Ohio to bear her third
child, who was born on April 7, 1872, and christened
William Monroe. When he was seven months old and
judged strong enough to make the trip, mother and child
came back to the family home at 105 Kendall Street. At
that time most of the black community lived in the West
End, on "Nigger Hill"—the north side of Beacon Hill,
below the State House, only a short distance from the
fashionable Brahmin homes on the south side of the hill.
After two years at their Kendall Street home the Trotter
family moved to suburban Hyde Park, thereby anticipating
the Negro shift to the South End and the suburbs that
would come in the 1890s. Two daughters, Maude and
Bessie, were born in 1874 and 1883.[11]

Though he lived in a white neighborhood and worked at

---

fathered by Jefferson, was not included among the five offspring
mentioned by Madison Hemings. Winthrop Jordan, in the most
authoritative recent account of the matter, apparently accepts Madison Hemings' word that there were only the five children born of
Sally Hemings. Nonetheless the question cannot be answered with
any finality. To my knowledge Monroe Trotter never took notice in
writing of his possible Jefferson ancestry. But there was an oral
tradition to that effect in the Trotter family. In 1954 Maude
Trotter Steward said that she and her brother had not publicized
their ancestry; "but we knew about it all our life," she added. The
only conclusion must be tentative: Monroe Trotter probably was
not descended from Jefferson, since Joseph Fossett, despite the oral
tradition, probably was not fathered by Jefferson. See the Waverly,
Ohio, *Pike County Republican*, March 13, 1873 (reference kindly
supplied me by August Meier); Winthrop D. Jordan, *White over
Black: American Attitudes Toward the Negro, 1550–1812* (Chapel
Hill, N.C., 1968), pp. 464–469; "Thomas Jefferson's Negro
Grandchildren," *Ebony*, X (November 1954), 78–80.

[11] *Guardian*, November 5, 1949, p. 1; Adelaide Cromwell Hill,
"The Negro Upper Class in Boston, Its Development and Present
Social Structure" (Ph.D. thesis, Radcliffe College, 1952), pp. 50,
107–108; Daniels, *In Freedom's Birthplace*, p. 143; Worthy,
"Trotter," p. 6.

a "white" job, James Trotter was still race-conscious. In 1878, for example, he drew on his musical training and published a book, *Music and Some Highly Musical People*, which was essentially a tribute to black musical achievements in the United States. In the preface he remarked that "the haze of complexional prejudice has so much obscured the visions of many persons" that they do not see that musical abilities "are not in the exclusive possession of the fairer-skinned race." Therefore the book was written in the hope "of contributing to the formation of a more just opinion, of inducing a cheerful admission of its existence, and of aiding to establish between both races relations of mutual respect and good feeling. . . ." The book was well received and sold over seven thousand copies—among which were two that Wendell Phillips and Francis Garrison gave to the Boston Public Library. It also played a role in James Weldon Johnson's musical development.[12]

At the Post Office, however, Trotter's ability was not being recognized. In 1882 a white man was promoted over his head to a chief clerkship. His own job was still secure and provided an adequate income (his son called it "a good clerkship"), but he could not abide the racial insult in being overlooked and so resigned in protest. Over the next few years he supported his family with a variety of enterprises—musical promotions, a real-estate business, the local agency for a telephone company competing with the Bell system—and was a respected citizen of white Hyde Park, giving a Fourth of July oration there in 1884.[13]

[12] James M. Trotter, *Music and Some Highly Musical People* (Boston and New York, 1878), p. 4; Simmons, *Men of Mark*, pp. 836–837; *New York Freeman*, October 17, 1885, p. 4; inscriptions on the title pages of two of the three copies of Trotter's book in the Boston Public Library; *Along This Way: The Autobiography of James Weldon Johnson* (New York, 1933), p. 51.

[13] Worthy, "Trotter," p. 6; W. M. Trotter to Ray Stannard Baker, October 5, 1907, Baker Papers; *New York Globe:* March 3, 1883, p. 1; January 26, 1884, p. 2; July 12, 1884, p. 4; *New York Freeman*, August 7, 1886, p. 1.

His greatest interest lay in politics. Characteristically independent, he was a black Democrat in an age when most Negroes were fervently loyal to the party of Lincoln. But President Hayes, a Republican, had withdrawn the last federal troops from the South in 1877, and Trotter considered it a betrayal of the black man. His rebuff in the Post Office, a Republican domain, probably clinched his decision to change to the Democrats. In the fall of 1883 he worked for Benjamin F. Butler's Democratic campaign for governor, and celebrated Butler's victory in an open letter to the *New York Globe*, the most influential black newspaper of the day. "Although it cannot be fairly claimed that the colored 'break' from the so-called Republican party has been general," Trotter wrote, "yet it has been of proportions so large as to occasion surprise and delight, and to be without a parallel in any of the states." We did not go over to the Democrats, Trotter asserted: the Democrats came to us. As for the future, "The writer (while not claiming for himself superior goodness) would appeal now to our men as he has often done in the past, to cease from this degrading practice of annually hiring themselves out for political work. . . . Our race is yet so far 'in the woods' that it cannot afford to imitate these Caucasian vices. Let us not contaminate our holy cause by baseness of any kind." [14]

Three years later New England's black Democrats— they preferred the term "Independents"—held a conference in Boston. Trotter served as temporary chairman of the meeting and was elected permanent chairman when the old black abolitionist George Downing of Rhode Island declined the post. In addressing the conference Trotter again stressed the importance of the ballot and of political independence. Then, according to the report in the white *Boston Evening Transcript*, he exhorted blacks to greater

[14] Simmons, *Men of Mark*, pp. 837–838; James M. Trotter to editor, November 9, 1883, in *New York Globe*, November 17, 1883, p. 2.

resistance of white oppression: "We have not, said the
speaker, much real reason to complain of the treatment of
the white people, but the manner in which we allow ourselves to be treated is the fundamental cause of our present
condition." As the *Transcript* reported it, Trotter added
that Negroes had not been "thoroughly in earnest in this
matter." [15] Allowing for the predictable bias of the white
reporter, this moderate criticism of black meekness fits in
with Trotter's general position as a race leader: militant
but a trifle distant, speaking down to the race from the
comfortable life in Hyde Park. He was sincerely concerned
for the race. But, having pulled himself up, he expected
others to do the same through protest and work.

His eminence among Negro Democrats led to a lucrative
political job, the recordership of deeds in Washington,
D.C., the highest federal office held by Negroes in that era.
Frederick Douglass had been the first black recorder of
deeds. He was appointed by President Garfield and served
until President Cleveland's Democratic administration
took office. Douglass then resigned and Cleveland nominated James C. Matthews, a Negro Democrat from New
York, to replace him. But the Senate twice refused to
confirm Matthews, and so, in late February 1887, Cleveland nominated Trotter, whose prospects for confirmation
looked no brighter. "The Democrats and Republicans in
Congress are almost equally perturbed by it," the correspondent of the *Boston Evening Transcript* observed, "the
former objecting to Mr. Trotter's color, and the Republicans objecting to his politics." [16]

On the morning of March 2 the Senate Committee on
the District of Columbia met and, with only one dissent,
agreed not to recommend Trotter's confirmation. This

[15] *New York Freeman*, September 25, 1886, p. 1; *Boston Evening Transcript*, September 15, 1886, p. 5.
[16] Philip S. Foner, *Frederick Douglass* (New York, 1964), p.
341; *Boston Evening Transcript*, March 1, 1887, p. 8.

seemed to doom the case. Trotter would not get his job; the post held by Frederick Douglass would not go to *any* Negro. In Boston Trotter's friends rallied what support they could. "God bless you all," he wrote to one Bostonian, "for being true to the race in this great race crisis. I care not for myself, except to try to do my duty. An unseen but mighty Providence is using me for some good purpose." Providentially, March 3 was the final day of the Congressional session. The two Massachusetts senators, both Republicans, unexpectedly endorsed Trotter on the Senate floor. Late that night he was confirmed by a vote of 32–10, with Republicans making up two thirds of the affirmative vote.[17]

He served as recorder for two financially rewarding years. His salary was a percentage of the transactions recorded by his office, and business was heavy. While in office he refused to take part in any outside protest activities. "A number of attempts have been made to induce me to take hold of other things," he told a testimonial dinner in Boston in 1887, "but I have uniformly replied that I was on duty for the colored race where I was, and if I discharged those duties properly I would reflect pride enough upon my people." In 1889 the Republicans returned to Washington and Trotter returned to Boston, where his family had remained and where his son, then a junior in high school, was making an impressive academic record.[18]

II

From the time he was five years old, Monroe Trotter once recalled, he was "dedicated to work for race equality"

[17] James M. Trotter to Charles L. Mitchell, received by Mitchell on March 4, 1887, in *Boston Evening Transcript*, March 5, 1887, p. 4; *New York Times*, March 5, 1887, p. 2; *Boston Evening Transcript*, March 4, 1887, p. 4.

[18] Worthy, "Trotter," pp. 4–5; *New York Freeman*, August 27, 1887, p. 1.

by excelling white people. Virtually all of his playmates—
and competitors—in Hyde Park were white, and his father
warned him that if he were beaten in a fight with one of
them another beating would follow when he came home.
He was the only son and the favored child among three
children. Brought up in a well-organized atmosphere of
love and discipline, he developed a precocious earnestness
that was reflected in everything he undertook. Thus when
taking piano lessons he would rise early in the morning
and practice for two hours while the rest of the household
was still in bed (though not, one may imagine, still
asleep). His lifelong wariness of alcohol also made an
early appearance. He had a serious case of pneumonia at
the age of fourteen, and the doctor prescribed whiskey.
But the invalid overheard and refused to take the remedy:
"Rather let me die." [19]

James Trotter, a demanding patriarch, set high standards for his children. The Trotters were good friends with
the family of Archibald Grimké, also residents of Hyde
Park. Grimké, a nephew of the abolitionist Grimké sisters
(and, by marriage, of the abolitionist Theodore Weld,
who spent his last years with the family in Hyde Park),
was a Negro lawyer and journalist in Boston. Like Trotter
a political independent, he served as consul at Santo Do-
mingo during President Cleveland's second administration.
Other black families came out from Boston to visit the
Trotters on weekends and holidays. But they had to measure up to James Trotter's stern ideas on racial militancy.
William H. Dupree, for example, had been a fellow officer
in the Fifty-fifth Massachusetts, a fellow employee in the
Post Office, and had married a sister of Virginia Isaacs
Trotter. For a time Trotter and Dupree had been very
close, but they collided over some issue of racial policy,

[19] W. M. Trotter to Harry C. Smith, n.d., in Cleveland *Gazette*,
March 19, 1932, p. 1; Worthy, "Trotter," p. 7; *Guardian*, August
23, 1952, p. 6, and August 18, 1952, p. 5.

perhaps the matter of political independence. Thereafter the Duprees were not welcome in the Trotter home. The Duprees doted on the youngest Trotter child, but her father would not allow her to accept any presents from them.[20]

Given his father's expectations and his own talent, young Monroe was perforce a good student, leading both his grammar and high school classes. His twenty-one white high school classmates elected him president of the senior class. He gave some thought to becoming a minister, and was urged toward such a course by the pastor and deacons of the white First Baptist Church of Hyde Park, where he spent most of every Sunday. "His father disliked so strong a religious tendency," one of his sisters later recalled, "fearing he might not like to go out in the world and fight the world's problems." Further, the father argued, a black minister would end up serving a segregated congregation. So the son left the ministry notion behind. After graduating from high school he worked as a shipping clerk in Boston for a year and then entered Harvard College in the fall of 1891.[21]

[20] Angelina W. Grimké, "A Biographical Sketch of Archibald H. Grimké," *Opportunity*, III (1925), 44–47; Worthy, "Trotter," pp. 7–8. The Duprees and Trotters were later reconciled. In 1893, after James Trotter's death, Virginia Trotter and her daughters went to live with the Duprees on Northampton Street in Boston; Monroe Trotter was at Harvard then (*Guardian*, November 12, 1949, p. 1).

[21] Worthy, "Trotter," pp. 7–8; Daniels, *In Freedom's Birthplace*, p. 122 *n;* Eda F. Wheeler to Maude Trotter Steward, April 12, 1934, in *Guardian*, April 21, 1934, p. 4, Trotter Papers; *Guardian*, March 6, 1948, p. 1, and May 24, 1952, pp. 1, 4.

On Trotter's religious faith at this time, see especially W. M. Trotter to John A. Fairlie, August 18, 1892, John Archibald Fairlie Papers: "I have finally given myself *wholly* to Christ to be led entirely by God. To abide in Christ is the secret of power and peace, to honor the Son *even as* I honor the Father. I have laid all, my life, my business, my career, in the hands of Jesus and am to live and move in Him. I now go to work because He wants me to. I chop the wood or empty the ashes because He wants me to. Everything I do in Him. . . . Now, Fairlee, I want you to give up yourself. . . . Trust in Christ and then do what He tells you to at

Harvard had admitted a black student to its medical
school as early as 1850. After the war Negroes were
enrolled in all branches of the university on an equal basis
with whites, a fact that, according to Samuel Eliot Morison, prompted some white southerners to send their sons
elsewhere. The first black undergraduate, Richard T.
Greener, graduated in 1870. During the thirty years after
the war Harvard trained a number of Negroes who went
on to prominence in their fields: George F. Grant in the
dental school, Samuel E. Courtney in the medical school,
W. E. B. Du Bois in the college and graduate school, and
George Ruffin, Clement G. Morgan, and William H.
Lewis in the law school.[22]

Monroe Trotter had no trouble making the transition
from shipping clerk to Harvard undergraduate. His lowest
mark as a freshman was a B in English. That year had an
interlude of sorrow, however, as his father died in February, at the age of fifty. A severe case of pneumonia during
his recordership in Washington had destroyed James Trotter's health, leading to tuberculosis and a slow decline. His
son was now the head of family for his mother and two
younger sisters. Money was no particular problem—the
family owned considerable property in Boston, thanks
mostly to the income from the recordership. Over the next
three years Trotter won a total of $800 in Harvard schol-
arships. He supplemented that with jobs during his vacations. In the summer of 1892, for example, he sold desks
from door to door in towns near his home (and remarked
of this experience, with a touch of condescension, that "I
sell more among the laboring people than among the better
class. . . . No house is too poor for me to call"). At

any cost. Don't trust in yourself, but in the power and help of God.
You then have the secret to efficiency."
    [22] Folder on "Negroes at Harvard," Harvard Archives, Widener
Library, Harvard University; Samuel Eliot Morison, *Three Centuries of Harvard 1636–1936* (Cambridge, Mass., 1946), pp.
416–417.

Harvard he lived in a single room in College House, the cheapest student dormitory, and, with tuition only $150 a year, he paid for most of his education himself.[23]

He worked hard at his studies, taking extra courses, and continued to be active in church work. Not that he was *always* so serious: he enjoyed playing tennis and wheeling around Cambridge and Boston on his bicycle. He also cheered on Harvard's athletic teams, and once jestingly considered going out for crew "in order to break Yale's long chain (two or three links) of victories." But in general he indulged in few of the frivolities of college life, at least on an organized basis. His formal extracurricular activities reflected a no-nonsense earnestness: the Wendell Phillips Club, the Young Men's Christian Association, and the Prohibition Club. In addition, he helped organize and was president of the Total Abstinence League, a group of about thirty ascetic undergraduates. He was a teetotaler all his life and, his brother-in-law once remarked, "believed that beer-drinking students were headed straight for Hell." [24]

Like most Harvard students of the day, he took a great variety of courses without going deeply into anything and had no major subject. His first two years he concentrated in English, foreign languages, and mathematics, and then moved into history, philosophy, government, and political economy. In his introductory philosophy course he heard

[23] Record of Class of 1895, Harvard Archives; sketch of James Trotter's life in Forbes Papers; Worthy, "Trotter," pp. 1–2; *Harvard University Catalogue 1892–93* (Cambridge, Mass., 1892), pp. 212, 492; *Catalogue 1893–94* (1893), pp. 221, 529; *Catalogue 1894–95* (1894), p. 568; W. M. Trotter to John A. Fairlie, August 18, 1892, Fairlie Papers; *Harvard Index 1891–2* (Boston, 1891), pp. 236, 250; *Index 1892–3* (1892), pp. 242, 256; *Index 1893–4* (1893), pp. 254, 270; *Index 1894–5* (1894), pp. 268, 289.

[24] W. M. Trotter to John A. Fairlie, August 10, 1893, Fairlie Papers; *Harvard College Class of 1895 Secretary's Report, No. 1* (Cambridge, Mass., 1898), pp. 80, 82, 83; *The Autobiography of W. E. B. Du Bois* (New York, 1968), p. 138; interview with Dr. Charles G. Steward, quoted in Worthy, "Trotter," p. 9.

lectures by George Herbert Palmer, Josiah Royce, George Santayana, and William James. Senior year was probably the most rewarding, highlighted by Francis Peabody's social ethics course, Edward Cummings' sociology course, and American constitutional and political history under Albert Bushnell Hart and his young assistant, Oswald Garrison Villard.[25]

Trotter's academic performance was a confirmation, if he needed it, of his father's claims for the black man's intellect. Competing with some of the best white students in the country, he stood third in his class of 376 as a freshman and never ranked lower than eighth. He was especially good at foreign languages. His worst marks were a C and a C+ in English composition courses. (Though he would spend a career in journalism, his life-long quarrel with the English language remained at best a stalemate. "It's" was his characteristic spelling of the neuter possessive pronoun.) He was the first Negro at Harvard to be elected to Phi Beta Kappa, gaining that honor in his junior year.[26]

Being a Harvard student was no protection from white America's peculiar mores. In the spring of 1893 a Negro at Harvard Law School named William H. Lewis—a brilliant scholar and later an All-American football player as well—was twice denied service at a Harvard Square barbershop. Within the Yard, though, there seemed to be remarkably little prejudice. Trotter of course could not have joined the exclusive clubs, but probably he had no interest in them anyway. His friendships were cosmopolitan, including white students from Europe and the United States. Later in life he would cherish the memory of his college years, for a greater reason than the usual nostalgia

[25] Record of Class of 1895, Harvard Archives; Oswald Garrison Villard to W. E. B. Du Bois, April 18, 1905, Villard Papers.
[26] Record of Class of 1895, Harvard Archives; Worthy, "Trotter," p. 8.

of the old alumnus. "The democracy which I had enjoyed
at dear old Harvard" was a tangible affirmation of the
possibilities for racial justice in this country. As he wrote
in 1923, a little wistfully:

> Harvard was an inspiration to me because it was the
> exemplar of true Americanism, freedom, equality,
> and real democracy. Harvard was a place where all
> races, proscribed in other sections, could find carried
> out in a practical way the policies and ideals that all
> beings want. Each individual was taken on individual
> worth, capability, and ambition in life.

In June 1895 he received the A.B. degree *magna cum
laude.*[27]

III

Three and one half months later, a thousand miles and
several worlds from that Harvard commencement, Booker
T. Washington stood up and made a speech at a trade
exposition in Atlanta. It was a blandly phrased but desperate attempt to halt recent trends in southern race relations.
Since the end of Reconstruction the Negro's condition had
steadily declined. Southern legislatures, purged of all but
token black representation, made legal a system of segregation and, ultimately, Negro disfranchisement. Extra-
legally, lynching was an accepted procedure of southern
justice. Virtuosos such as South Carolina's Pitchfork Ben
Tillman were refining the art of Negro-baiting demagog-
uery. In the North, Republicans during the 1880s showed
occasional interest in what was happening to the Negro in

[27] *Boston Daily Globe*, May 26, 1893, clipping in William H.
Lewis folder, Harvard Archives; Worthy, "Trotter," pp. 8–9;
Guardian, August 18, 1952, p. 5; *Harvard College Class of 1895:
Fourth Report* (Cambridge, Mass., 1910), p. 199; *New York
Times*, January 13, 1923, p. 5.
  Trotter took extra courses and received an M.A. in 1896 after
writing a thesis "on Kidd's Social Evolution" (W. M. Trotter to
John A. Fairlie, October 29, 1895, Fairlie Papers).

the South. After 1891 this Republican concern abruptly stopped, amid a growing consensus that the race problem was the South's problem and could only be handled there.[28]

So under that Georgia sun in September 1895 Washington set forth a plan. He humbly admitted the mistakes of Reconstruction—"we began at the top instead of at the bottom . . . a seat in Congress or the state legislature was more sought than real estate or industrial skill. . . ." Now we must start from where we are, at the bottom, for "No race can prosper till it learns that there is as much dignity in tilling a field as in writing a poem." Of the white man we ask only that he employ us instead of immigrant laborers, "those of foreign birth and strange tongue and habits." We shall not agitate for political or social equality. Living separately yet working together, both races will determine the future of "our beloved South." [29]

The genius of this "Atlanta Compromise" speech lay in its studied ambiguity. Thus the most famous passage of the address: "In all things that are purely social we can be as separate as the fingers, yet one as the hand in all things essential to mutual progress." Was a school "purely social" or "essential to mutual progress"? Washington did not say, and consequently all shades of racial opinion could find much in the speech with which to agree. It had no original ideas, but it was a smooth articulation, in a public forum, of what was coming to be the conventional wisdom in the South. Whether the speech ultimately helped improve conditions remained unclear. It did have one obvious immediate effect. Given wide publicity and all but unanimous approval, it made the rather obscure principal of

[28] Rayford W. Logan, *The Negro in American Life and Thought: The Nadir 1877–1901* (New York, 1954); C. Vann Woodward, *The Strange Career of Jim Crow* (revised edition, New York, 1965); Stanley P. Hirshson, *Farewell to the Bloody Shirt: Northern Republicans & the Southern Negro, 1877–1893* (Bloomington, Ind., 1963).

[29] E. Davidson Washington, ed., *Selected Speeches of Booker T. Washington* (New York, 1932), pp. 31–36.

Tuskegee Institute the national spokesman for his race.[30]

For the next twenty years Washington was the most powerful Negro in the United States. It was an incredible success story, from slavery and the coal mines of West Virginia to honorary degrees from Harvard and Dartmouth, summer homes in Massachusetts and New York, friendships with the great and powerful, tea with Queen Victoria, and a celebrated dinner with Theodore Roosevelt at the White House. Roosevelt called him "the most useful, as well as the most distinguished, member of his race in the world" and consulted him on political matters. "I am not sorry that I found myself part of a problem," Washington wrote in 1911; "on the contrary, that problem has given direction and meaning to my life and has brought me friendships and comforts that I could have gotten in no other way." [31]

IV

For a few years Washington's race leadership and the condition of American Negroes were of peripheral concern to Monroe Trotter. He left Harvard with the expectation that he could make a career in white America. He was also one of the young luminaries in Boston's polite Negro society, then at its height. Prestigiously educated, talented, handsome, and heir to a small fortune amounting to perhaps $20,000, Trotter was an exceptionally attractive figure. He was a man of compact stature and regular features, about five feet eight inches and 140 pounds, with small hands and feet and an olive complexion. "His skin

[30] August Meier, *Negro Thought in America, 1880–1915: Racial Ideologies in the Age of Booker T. Washington* (Ann Arbor, Mich., 1963), pp. 117, 99; Logan, *Negro in American Life,* p. 286; Samuel R. Spencer, Jr., *Booker T. Washington and the Negro's Place in American Life* (Boston, 1955), pp. 99–105, 108–09.

[31] Spencer, *Washington,* p. 135; Booker T. Washington, *My Larger Education: Being Chapters from My Experience* (New York, 1911), p. 20.

was fine grained," one who then knew him later remembered, "and the shade was made lighter by what appeared to be a white inner layer shining through giving it a sort of silvery tinge." He was a member of the Omar Khayyam Circle, an exclusive Negro literary group that met at the home of the Cambridge schoolteacher Maria Baldwin, and he enjoyed the activities of the Boston Bachelors.[32]

That last affiliation, however, was in jeopardy. He was courting Geraldine Louise Pindell, known to her suitors as Deenie. She too came from a tradition of racial militancy: her uncle, William Pindell, had been a leader in the fight that integrated Boston's schools in the 1850s. Six months Trotter's junior, she grew up in Boston, attended grammar school in Everett, then went to a business college and worked as a bookkeeper and stenographer. She was petite, vivacious, and very fair; a few years later the white journalist Ray Stannard Baker observed that "she would ordinarily pass for white." W. E. B. Du Bois dated her for a time and remembered her as "a fine forthright woman, blonde, blue-eyed and fragile." [33]

Trotter knew her as a child and saw her occasionally when he was in college. She nearly died of pneumonia in 1895 and was still frail that spring when she attended his Class Day. Soon he was pursuing her in earnest. One night he escorted her home from a lawn party in Revere, and on her doorstep she yielded for a goodnight kiss. "And that night," he later wrote, "Monroe Trotter found his love for once and for all time." They were married on June 27,

[32] Hill, "Negro Upper Class in Boston," pp. 107–108 and facing p. 145; *Guardian*, April 13, 1946, p. 4, and August 23, 1952, p. 6; *Harvard College Class of 1895: Second Report* (Cambridge, Mass., 1902), p. 113.

[33] Worthy, "Trotter," pp. 13, 16; Donald Martin Jacobs, "A History of the Boston Negro from the Revolution to the Civil War" (Ph.D. thesis, Boston University, 1968), pp. 257–260; Ray Stannard Baker, *Following the Color Line: American Negro Citizenship in the Progressive Era* (Harper Torchbook edition, New York, 1964), p. 225; *Autobiography of Du Bois*, p. 138.

1899, and moved into a house at 97 Sawyer Avenue in
Dorchester, on top of a hill in a previously all-white neighborhood. Trotter and his bride loved their new home;
"from the sitting room window," he later noted, one could
see "over all the country as far as Blue Hill and from my
bed-room window over all the bay down to the red buildings on Deer Island." Happily settled on their hilltop, they
had a good marriage from the start. A few days after the
ceremony Trotter wrote a friend his first impressions of the
union, and the friend, a man of poetic inclination, replied
in verse:

> I rather like the cheerful way
> You look at married life;
> And though unskilled, think all you say
> Is true—with such a wife.
> * * *
>
> A good beginning then you make,
> Embarking on life's river:
> A charming wife, sweet home, good bake,
> Warrant a perfect liver.
>
> I, Celebs, hope no other life
> Than taste Pieria's Fountain;
> But your joys are a happy wife,
> Your home, Parnassus' Mountain.
>
> Not only in these, but otherwise,
> Dear friend, do you surpass us;
> So hope naught else in Paradise
> Better than your "Parnassus." [34]

Life was pleasant, and yet his racial awareness was
deepening. When he had looked for a job after college he
had found racial discrimination blocking his way for the

[34] *Guardian*, December 28, 1918, p. 4, Trotter Papers; W. M.
Trotter to John A. Fairlie, June 15, 1902, Fairlie Papers; *Guardian*, February 12, 1949, p. 4.

first time. "I was practically offered a place to teach in Washington, D.C., salary $1000.00 a year to start with," he wrote his white college classmate John Fairlie a few months after their graduation. "But I desired a business career, and besides the place is too far South and the school a separate one. So I did not take it." He also considered applying to a banking house. "One idea was to work up to be the foreign agent of the firm, in Europe, where I would be recognized as a man." But that plan fell through when, despite his Harvard Phi Beta Kappa key, he could not find an opening. He thought of taking over the local newspaper in Hyde Park, "but I decided that I did not want to carry that load on my back yet, especially as I should be a 'green hand' at the business." Finally he settled on a real-estate career, but was torn between applying to an established firm in Boston and starting his own practice in Hyde Park, as his father had done. "I should prefer to take my chances in an established firm," he told Fairlie, "but there is in the way of *high* preferment for me one large impediment that other men do not have to hinder them." Moreover, "business is a hard field in which to work, the prizes go to comparatively a few, and only the pickings are left for the great majority; and the more I see of business, the more I lean to a profession. I have not, however, yet given up hope, and still aim at a business career." [35]

For the time being he took a temporary job as a clerk for an industrial fair, where his hours were from eight-thirty in the morning until ten o'clock at night. After the fair was over he continued to mark time "clerking around," as he put it, working as a shipping clerk for a Boston bookseller, then as an indexing clerk for the Boston Book Company, and finally as a statistical clerk for a

[35] W. M. Trotter to John A. Fairlie, September 8, 1895, Fairlie Papers. Fairlie went on to a career of some distinction as a political scientist at the University of Illinois. He was managing editor of the *American Political Science Review* from 1916 to 1925 and president of the American Political Science Association in 1929.

genealogist. Then, with the help of a white man who had been an officer in his father's regiment, he gained a position in the Boston real-estate firm of Holbrook and Company. In 1899 he went into business for himself in Boston as an insurance agent and mortgage negotiator. Dealing mostly with white clients, he established a good reputation and prospered, eventually buying several pieces of property on his own.[36]

His life was falling into a pattern much like his father's —working with white people, living in a white neighborhood, keeping a strong but somewhat aloof interest in the race's welfare, and dabbling in politics. He was already into politics on a rudimentary level, working for Republican Congressional and municipal candidates and serving as an alternate delegate from his ward at several conventions. For a while he was an assistant registrar of voters in Boston; a few years later he made a jocular reference to one day sitting on the Boston City Council. He also spent some time on explicitly racial activity. On Lincoln's birthday in 1899, for example, at a commemorative dinner he presented a paper on "Higher Education for the Negro." Presumably the paper argued that black students should try to go to college: a perfectly valid point, especially in light of the industrial education for blacks then in vogue in the South, but a point that still involved only a tiny portion of black Americans.[37]

His elitist militancy was characteristic of the upper crust of Boston's Negro society. From 1865 to 1900 the city's black population grew more than twice as fast as the

[36] W. M. Trotter to John A. Fairlie, October 29, 1895, Fairlie Papers; Trotter to Ray Stannard Baker, October 5, 1907, Baker Papers; *Harvard College Class of 1895: Second Report*, p. 113; Worthy, "Trotter," p. 14; Charles W. Puttkammer, "William Monroe Trotter: An Evaluation of the Life of a Radical Negro Newspaper Editor, 1901–1934" (senior thesis, Princeton University, 1958), pp. 4, 71.

[37] *Harvard College Class of 1895: Second Report*, p. 113; W. M. Trotter to John A. Fairlie, June 15, 1902, Fairlie Papers.

total population. At the top of this expanding group was a small leadership class, perhaps two percent of the whole, well educated and of northern antecedents, oriented toward white society and white values, and proud of Boston's relative freedom. In the late 1890s Trotter found this group's views congenial with his own. Cherishing the enlightened air of Boston, they were dismayed by the worsening conditions for Negroes in the South and could not accept Booker T. Washington's rise to prominence through his reassuring public statements of optimism and good cheer. Washington saw a threat to his role as national spokesman for the race and arranged a reconciliation dinner with his Boston critics at Young's Hotel in Boston in the spring of 1898. After the meal several of the local elite spoke for the group. "Each of the speakers," an observer friendly to Washington recalled, "launched into a tirade against Dr. Washington and his policies and methods, many of them in lofty flights of speech they had learned at Harvard University." One of those Harvard men, the Law School graduate William H. Lewis, told Washington to go back to the South and leave politics in the hands of others. An unruffled Washington absorbed the criticism, then rose and talked about Tuskegee for half an hour, making no reference to the preceding speeches. There was no reconciliation.[38]

A year later the local black leaders held an anti-lynching meeting on the ninety-ninth anniversary of John Brown's birth. In the evening's principal address Archibald Grimké took note of Washington's failure to speak out in public against the southern mob murders. "I have kept silent," Washington replied to Grimké, in private, "because I wanted to wait until I knew the white people of the South

[38] Hill, "Negro Upper Class in Boston," p. 131; Meier, *Negro Thought*, pp. 154–155; I. D. Barnett's recollection of the Young's Hotel dinner, *Guardian*, July 15, 1911, p. 7; Emmett J. Scott and Lyman Beecher Stowe, *Booker T. Washington: Builder of a Civilization* (New York, 1916), pp. 314–315.

were in that frame of mind where they were willing to listen to what I had to say." No such sensitivity to white opinion hampered the Bostonians. They drafted an open letter to President McKinley, again hammering at conditions in the South. "We ask you for what belongs to us," they wrote, "the high sanction of Constitution and law, and the Democratic genius of our institutions and civilization. These rights are everywhere throughout the South denied to us." And though "the silence of death reigns over our people and their leaders at the South, we of Massachusetts are free, and must and shall raise our voice to you and through you to the country." It was, Washington conceded to Grimké, a "straightforward and manly" letter.[39]

Such public protests were one response. By degrees Trotter came to see them as being only of limited usefulness. Gradually, at some point around the the turn of the century, he decided to become more actively involved in racial matters. In bringing about this change of mind there were principally three external factors: the worsening conditions in the South, the fact that white southern racial attitudes seemed to be spreading north, and Booker T. Washington's apparent acquiescence in both developments. "The conviction grew upon me," he recalled a quarter century later, "that pursuit of business, money, civic or literary position was like building a house upon the sands, if race prejudice and persecution and public discrimination for mere color was to spread up from the South and result in a fixed caste of color." Of what value, he asked himself, would a comfortable living and the home in Dorchester be if he were treated like a social pariah even

[39] *Boston Evening Transcript*, May 10, 1899, p. 4; Booker T. Washington to Archibald Grimké, June 5, 1899, Archibald Grimké Papers; Herbert Aptheker, ed., *A Documentary History of the Negro People in the United States* (New York, 1951), pp. 787–791; Washington to Grimké, November 20, 1899, Grimké Papers.

in Boston? Further, there was an internal factor, a kind of
noblesse oblige sense impressed upon him by his father.
James Trotter, in refusing half pay in the army and in
resigning from the Post Office, had shown contempt for
what he described in 1883 as "that despicable selfishness
that cares far more for one's own mere bodily comfort than
for not only its own liberty and high aspiration of spirit,
but also that of the race. . . ." Less concerned for bodily
comfort, and more concerned for the race, after 1900
Monroe Trotter started taking a new direction in his life.[40]

In March 1901 he helped organize the Boston Literary
and Historical Association, a group that became a forum
for militant race opinion. It was founded by Boston's black
elite, as he wrote a prospective speaker, in order "to improve and quicken the intellectual life of the Colored people of Boston and to have a body to represent their best
interests." Archibald Grimké was the first president, and
Trotter was on the executive committee. The Literary met
every week or two at a school in the white Back Bay area
and heard lectures by such Negro intellectuals as W. E.
B. Du Bois, the novelist Charles Chesnutt, Kelly Miller of
Howard University, and Maria Baldwin, and by such out-
wardly sympathetic whites as B. O. Flower of the *Arena*,
the author George Washington Cable, N. P. Hallowell of
James Trotter's regiment, Oswald Garrison Villard of the
New York *Evening Post*, and William Lloyd Garrison,
Jr., son of the abolitionist. The Literary provided a sense
of local solidarity and occasionally brought the proud black
man's case to a wider public.[41]

Trotter also joined a local group of a more political
orientation, the Massachusetts Racial Protective Associa-

---

[40] *Harvard College Class of 1895: Thirtieth Anniversary Report*
(Cambridge, Mass., 1925), p. 303; James M. Trotter to editor,
November 9, 1883, in *New York Globe*, November 17, 1883, p. 2.
    [41] W. M. Trotter to Charles W. Chesnutt, April 3, 1901,
Charles W. Chesnutt Papers; Hill, "Negro Upper Class in Boston,"
pp. 142–143.

tion, an organization led by William H. Scott, a black minister from Woburn. Trotter headed the group's committee on business and finance and gave one of his first public addresses of a protest nature before the group in October 1901. His speech that day was, significantly, an attack on Booker T. Washington. "He advised his race to keep out of politics and has criticised what use they made of the franchise," Trotter declared. "In Boston he said that the Negro should wait for the franchise until he had got property, education and character. Washington's attitude has always been subservient to the white people of the South." On the question of social equality "his attitude has ever been one of servility." In short, said Trotter, Washington was concerned only for his school and was "sacrificing the interests of his race to his own special scheme." [42]

At about this time Trotter, Scott, and another member of the Protective Association, George W. Forbes, discussed the feasibility of starting a new weekly newspaper in Boston. Trotter could provide the money needed at the outset. Forbes, who had worked for an earlier black newspaper venture in Boston in the 1890s, could provide the technical expertise. Scott urged the two men to go ahead. The agreement was worked out, and the new paper was christened *The Guardian*. "With its establishment," Trotter wrote a few years later, "my decision to enter the lists against discrimination because of color took tangible form." [43]

Trotter's partner in the new enterprise was an outspoken man with literary aspirations. Eight years older than Trotter, Forbes had grown up in Mississippi and Ohio and had attended Wilberforce University and then Amherst College, where he worked his way through and was a classmate and close friend of William Lewis. For a few

[42] *Guardian*, November 9, 1901, p. 3, Trotter Papers; *Boston Traveler*, October 25, 1901, p. 3.

[43] Worthy, "Trotter," p. 20; *Harvard College Class of 1895: Third Report* (Cambridge, Mass., 1905), p. 142.

years after college he edited the Boston *Courant*, and since
1897 had been an assistant librarian in the West End
branch of the Boston Public Library. Well read and cynical, he had a flair for vivid polemical language. (At a
protest meeting in 1900 he lamented "the pitiable farce we
are making of our 'sacred constitution' here at home, while
we are running all over the globe trying to force it upon
other peoples as a model badge of free citizenship.") At
first he wrote most of the *Guardian*'s editorials—long,
graceful essays crammed with literary allusions.[44]

The first issue of the *Guardian* appeared on November
9, 1901, and promised its readers "an organ which is to
voice intelligently the needs and aspirations of the colored
American." The editors vowed to pay special attention to
citizenship rights and to the task of presenting the Negro
fairly to public opinion. "We have come to protest forever
against being proscribed or shut off in any caste from
equal rights with other citizens, and shall remain forever
on the firing line at any and all times in defence of such
rights." Trotter, listed on the masthead as Managing Editor, was embarked on his lifework.[45]

[44] *Libraries*, XXXII (1927), 236–237; "George Forbes of Bos-
ton," *Crisis*, XXXIV (1927), 151–152; W. E. B. Du Bois, *The
Ordeal of Mansart* (New York, 1957), p. 304; *Boston Daily Globe*,
May 10, 1900, p. 5; William H. Ferris, *The African Abroad: or
His Evolution in Western Civilization; Tracing His Development
Under Caucasian Milieux* (2 vols., New Haven, 1913), II, 797.

[45] *Guardian*, November 9, 1901, p. 2, Trotter Papers.

The Challenge to Booker T. Washington

T H E *Guardian* is an up to date journal," declared W. Calvin Chase, a veteran Negro editor. "Editor Trotter is a man." The *Guardian* is "putrescent," announced the *New York Age*, the most influential Negro newspaper; "Editor Trotter of the Boston Skunk makes himself smelt if not felt." The anti-Washington spokesman L. M. Hershaw, writing in *Charities*, called Trotter's paper "the foremost race journal in advocating equal and identical civil and political rights for Negroes." The *Guardian* may be "carrying its cases too fast and too far," said another black newspaper, the Indianapolis *Freeman*, and, somewhat later, Trotter should "take 'something' for his mental malady lest it become chronic—perhaps fatal." [1]

Even readers who detested the *Guardian*'s editorial pol-

[1] Washington *Bee*, November 29, 1902, p. 4; *New York Age*, August 31, 1905, p. 4, and January 26, 1905, p. 2; L. M. Hershaw, "The Negro Press in America," *Charities*, XV (1905–1906), 68; Indianapolis *Freeman*, February 1, 1902, p. 4, and November 11, 1905, p. 7.

icy admitted the paper's journalistic competence. In general it was, as Trotter immodestly described it, "a clean, manly and newsy race paper." [2] Appearing every Saturday, in most respects it was a typical black newspaper, its eight pages filled with local and national news of the Negro, mostly culled from other black papers and the white press. Social correspondents reported the local gossip from as far away as New York, Chicago, and Washington, D.C.—and thus provided the necessary enticement for readers outside New England to subscribe to the paper. Church news, serialized fiction, and some fashion and sports notes completed a typical issue, all for a nickel a copy or $1.50 for a year's subscription.

The editorials on page four made the *Guardian* notorious among the black journals of the day and prompted its readers to spirited and divergent opinions on the paper's usefulness. Week after week in his editorials Trotter mounted an extended attack on the person, prestige, and racial policies of Booker T. Washington.

I

Personally the two men could scarcely have been more different. Washington was born in slavery, never knew his father (some white man) or even his date of birth, and was raised by his uneducated and overworked mother. Trotter was born in freedom and was raised in a stable household dominated by a remarkable patriarch. Washington grew up in penury and struggled through Hampton Institute, where Samuel Chapman Armstrong was "more and dearer than a father." Trotter grew up in Hyde Park and won scholarships at Harvard. Washington presented himself as a man of patience, optimism, and humility;

[2] For examples of readers who admired the *Guardian* but disliked its editorials, see Bradley Gilman to Booker T. Washington, December 31, 1904, Booker T. Washington Papers, and Francis J. Garrison to Oswald Garrison Villard, December 23, 1904, Oswald Garrison Villard Papers; *Guardian*, July 2, 1904, p. 4.

Trotter operated from a continuing sense of crisis and was impetuous, volatile, and sometimes arrogant. Washington read history and found cause for hope: "merit, no matter under what skin found, is in the long run, recognized and rewarded." Trotter read the same history and discerned a continuity in the Negro's treatment by white Americans: "a spirit of ruthless and rapacious domination of his interests by them from the foundation of the republic." Washington urged the importance of "actual achievement in constructive work" instead of "mere denunciation of wrong." "There is no hope for any man or woman," he warned, ". . . who is continually whining and crying about his condition." Trotter declared himself temperamentally "unsuited to playing the part of the timid, or the cowardly" and demanded "the spirit of protest, of independence, of revolt." There is no cause for despair, said Washington, and "I like to belong to a race that has hard, knotty problems to be solved." "The policy of compromise has failed," Trotter insisted. "The policy of resistance and aggression deserves a trial." [3]

Their disagreement on matters of public racial policy was comprehensive. Washington spoke primarily to and for the 90 per cent of American Negroes who lived in the South, and he urged them to stay in Dixie. The black man is "at his best in the country districts," Washington wrote, and too often "at his worst in the cities, and especially in the cities of the North." Trotter, with his northern background, spoke to a different audience. There was undeniably prejudice in the North, Trotter conceded, but it was "not nearly so virulent" as in the South, and Boston was

[3] E. Davidson Washington, ed., *Selected Speeches of Booker T. Washington* (New York, 1932), p. 23; Booker T. Washington, *Up From Slavery* (New York, 1901), p. 41; *Guardian*, February 6, 1904, p. 4; Booker T. Washington, *My Larger Education: Being Chapters From My Experience* (New York, 1911), p. 65; E. D. Washington, *Selected Speeches*, p. 207; *Guardian*, April 9, 1904, p. 4, and April 30, 1904, p. 4; E. D. Washington, *Selected Speeches*, p. 153; *Guardian*, October 22, 1904, p. 4.

particularly enlightened, "the most liberal city on the color line." The North's relative freedom gave its Negroes the opportunity, and the responsibility, to demand justice for all black Americans. "The north is the battle ground," the *Guardian* declared, "and the northern Negroes are the soldiers." [4]

No such bellicose rhetoric came from Washington. Ever the realist, he made a point of dealing with conditions as they were: by the early 1900s the southern Negro generally could not vote and had to contend with a legalized Jim Crow system in all areas of life. Washington welcomed neither development, but tried to make the best of them. Thus on the matter of segregation he hid behind ambiguities such as "separate as the fingers, yet one as the hand" and preferred to discuss other issues. As for the ballot, he wrote to the Negro author Charles Chesnutt, "There is something deeper in human progress than the mere act of voting; it is the economic foundation which every race has got to have." Political rights, in Washington's view, would be conferred after a black man had shown that he could be a law-abiding, productive citizen. [5]

In the citadel of Boston, Trotter was witnessing a slow deterioration of the rights that he and other local blacks had formerly taken for granted. "A few years ago," Ray Stannard Baker reported in 1908, "no hotel or restaurant

[4] Booker T. Washington to Mary White Ovington, January 24, 1905, James Weldon Johnson Memorial Collection; *Guardian:* June 11, 1904, p. 4; July 18, 1903, p. 4; May 23, 1903, p. 4.

[5] Booker T. Washington to Charles W. Chesnutt, December 6, 1907, in Helen M. Chesnutt, *Charles Waddell Chesnutt: Pioneer of the Color Line* (Chapel Hill, N.C., 1952), p. 205.

My general treatment of Washington, here and elsewhere, owes a great deal to the following accounts: August Meier, *Negro Thought in America, 1880–1915: Racial Ideologies in the Age of Booker T. Washington* (Ann Arbor, Mich., 1963); Jacqueline James, "Uncle Tom? Not Booker T.," *American Heritage,* XIX (August 1968), 50–54, 95–100; Emma Lou Thornbrough, ed., *Booker T. Washington* (Englewood Cliffs, N.J., 1969). At the same time, of course, none of these scholars should be held responsible for any statement I make on my own authority.

in Boston refused Negro guests; now several hotels, restaurants, and especially confectionary stores, will not serve Negroes, even the best of them." So long as Washington, the foremost race spokesman, did not condemn such a deterioration, Trotter made him an accomplice in the crime. Borrowing from the language of the Dred Scott decision, the *Guardian* charged that "the northern Negro has no rights which Booker Washington is bound to respect. He must be stopped." [6]

An increasingly popular Bookerite idea, to which Trotter particularly objected, was the doctrine of industrial education. Both men agreed that education was crucial for the black man. But their emphases were quite different: for one it would be practical training leading to a good job, for the other it was a necessary right that could prove the quality of the black man's brain. To a degree this was the difference between the Hampton man and the Harvard man. At times Washington showed traces of anti-intellectualism. His college-educated critics, he once wrote, "know books but they do not know men"; they "understand theories, but they do not understand things." Conversely, Trotter was sometimes an intellectual snob, referring to "a fourth-rate school like Georgetown university" and noting that a Bookerite "should be forever cursed by all college men." The argument over education went deeper, however. "Education in itself is worthless," said Washington; "it is only as it is used that it is of value." Since most Negroes must stay and work in the South as farmers and artisans, their schooling should "meet the needs of conditions." In short, industrial education.[7]

[6] Ray Stannard Baker, *Following the Color Line: American Negro Citizenship in the Progressive Era* (Harper Torchbook edition, New York, 1964), p. 120; *Guardian*, May 23, 1903, p. 4.

[7] Washington, *My Larger Education*, pp. 123, 120; *Guardian*, April 23, 1904, p. 4; W. M. Trotter to George A. Towns, October 28, 1903, George A. Towns Papers; E. D. Washington, *Selected Speeches*, pp. 39–40; Booker T. Washington, *The Future of the American Negro* (Boston, 1899), p. 48.

Trotter granted that industrial schools such as Tuskegee did have some value, and occasionally the *Guardian* carried advertisements for them (though never one for Tuskegee). Characteristically, his objection was more of a symbolic nature. He opposed industrialism because "the idea lying back of it is the relegating of a race to serfdom." That underlying idea, the innate mental inferiority of Negroes, "must be admitted to be the reason why industrial education is more popular with the general white public than advanced or classical education." To prove their equality Negroes must seek and succeed at the highest forms of education—Trotter had done it himself. And Washington, "this apostle of industrialism," was doing great harm by soliciting in the North for his "practical" school.[8]

On education Washington stressed the short-range advantages while Trotter saw the long-range implications; on the issues of politics and the suffrage these positions were reversed. Once disfranchisement was in effect, Washington treated the right to vote as an eventual luxury, not necessary for present endeavors. Trotter reasoned in the opposite direction, arguing that intelligent political activity would force progress in other areas. The ballot, in Trotter's view, was "a sacred right" as well as a hardheaded source of power, the absolute *sine qua non* "without which nothing satisfies us." The Republican party was no longer responsive to black interests, but it still had the support of most Negroes. Consequently the black vote, in Trotter's opinion, was like a chained elephant, "perpetually in motion, swaying its vast body now to one side, now to the other, but it never makes any progress." Therefore independence in voting should be "the new war cry of Negro freedom." Functioning as an independent bloc, in close

[8] *Guardian*, April 2, 1904, p. 4, and March 19, 1904, p. 4; "The Industrial Threat," *Guardian* editorial enclosed with letter from Charles Alexander to Booker T. Washington, May 31, 1905, Washington Papers.

elections northern Negroes could "control the presidency and easily determine the political complexion of Congress." As for the South, Congress should either invalidate all elections or reduce the region's Congressional delegations in retaliation for the disfranchisement of the black voter.[9]

The substantive differences between the two men over the questions of agitation, the acceptance of segregation, education, and politics were the basic framework for a struggle that became extraordinarily bitter with the addition of crucial factors of manner and style. Washington came up from the black mass and Trotter was from a favored "white" background, and yet Trotter seemed to have more outward pride in his color and in Negroes. Washington liked to warm up his audiences with darkey stories, homely tales about rural southern Negroes. In his writings he would refer to the Negro's "naturally cheerful and affectionate disposition," and he once wrote that the black man is "naturally a farmer, and he is at his very best when he is in close contact with the soil." Washington also was quick to apologize for what he characterized as the race's past mistakes, especially during Reconstruction. Trotter could not tolerate what he called Washington's "crime of race ridicule and belittlement." One capable black man, the *Guardian* countered, if given only a fair chance to prove himself, "is worth more to the race than a half dozen Tuskegees which must exist on the belittlement and exaggeration of the race's shortcomings." [10]

Further exacerbating the debate was an amorphous force, later summed up in the phrase "the Tuskegee Machine" by W. E. B. Du Bois, which made it seem to

[9] *Guardian:* April 30, 1904, p. 4; February 27, 1904, p. 4; January 16, 1904, p. 4; December 26, 1903, p. 4; October 22, 1904, p. 4; April 30, 1904, p. 4; January 9, 1904, p. 4.
[10] Thornbrough, *Washington,* p. 30; Washington, *My Larger Education,* p. 67; *Guardian,* February 6, 1904, p. 4, and September 13, 1902, p. 4, William Monroe Trotter Papers.

Trotter that there was a conspiracy against him and anyone else who disputed Washington's leadership. Part of this could be traced to admirers of Washington who could not understand why any Negro should quarrel with Bookerite ideas; thus, for example, it seemed to Trotter that some of the Boston daily newspapers were "smothering all those who wished to condemn" the Tuskegeean. Washington had little directly to do with this kind of hindrance, though presumably he would not have disapproved of it. He did take various steps on his own to discredit and minimize the dissents by his black critics. Once he admitted to Francis Garrison that he did seek "to keep the race in harmony" with his program. "But," he added, "I have tried to do this in a manly, open manner and pursuing methods that all of my friends would approve." That is, such methods as planting spies, pressing libel suits, subsidizing reliable newspapers, and extending the lure of political and financial advancement through his white friends. The humble educator was a consummate power broker.[11]

"Our trump card on Booker," Trotter once confided to Du Bois, "is his corrupt methods." Those "corrupt methods" gave Trotter a superb opportunity to gain a rhetorical advantage over Washington by presenting himself as the prey of great and malevolent forces bent on his destruction. "The real issue as to Washington," Trotter declared in the *Guardian*, "is his lust for power, his desire to be a political leader, to be a czar, his clandestine methods of attempting to crush out all who will not bow to him. . . ." Again, another time, "it is plain Mr. Washington seeks to be uncriticized, and if it is within his power he will get where there will be no Negro paper to oppose his leadership, and no Negro will dare to do so. Then he can rule the

[11] This paragraph draws generally from the works listed in note 5, above, and from W. M. Trotter to John A. Fairlie, June 15, 1902, John Archibald Fairlie Papers; Booker T. Washington to Francis J. Garrison, May 17, 1905, Washington Papers.

race with an iron hand. . . ." [12]

A final complicating factor was the nature of the *Guardian*'s attack on Washington: personal, vituperative, and occasionally vicious. At its most basic it was simple name-calling: Pope Washington, the Black Boss, the Benedict Arnold of the Negro race, the Exploiter of all Exploiters, the Great Traitor, the Great Divider, the miserable toady, the Imperial Caesar, the heartless and snobbish purveyor of Pharisaical moral clap-trap. Late in 1902 Washington made a speech in Boston, and a man from the *Guardian* brought back a description.

> His features were harsh in the extreme. His vast leonine jaws into which vast mastiff-like rows of teeth were set clinched together like a vice. His forehead shot up to a great cone; his chin was massive and square; his eyes were dull and absolutely character-less, and with a glance that would leave you uneasy and restless during the night if you had failed to report to the police such a man around before you went to bed. But those eyes along with an enormous nose and mouth seemed huddled together in the centre of his face. Add to this the physique of a man of medium size, bearing every evidence of high living. . . .

The *Guardian* gleefully reported in the fall of 1902 that Washington's daughter Portia had flunked out of Welles-ley College. His children, the paper observed, "are not taking to higher education like a duck to water, and while their defect in this line is doubtless somewhat inherited, they justify to some extent their father's well known an-tipathy to anything higher than the three Rs for his 'people.' " When he bought a comfortable summer home

[12] W. M. Trotter to W. E. B. Du Bois, March 26, 1905, W. E. B. Du Bois Papers; *Guardian*, March 5, 1904, p. 4, and July 30, 1904, p. 4.

in South Weymouth, Massachusetts, the *Guardian* printed
a sarcastic report and advised its readers that the house
"gives the great surrenderer a full and close view of many
wealthy neighbors." Tuskegee Institute was "the monument to the short-lived liberty of the Negro in America.
. . ." "It's bad enough to be enslaved by white men,"
said Trotter, "without being put under thraldom to a
Negro." [13]

The *Guardian*'s vitriolic assault was a risk, because
while it brought the paper fame and gave Trotter's case
against Washington a wider circulation, in its freewheeling excesses it could alienate readers who were sympathetic to basic ideas of protest. Charles Chesnutt wrote to
Trotter praising the *Guardian* as "interesting and instruc-
tive" and complimented "its uncompromising stand on all
questions pertaining to the rights of the Negro." But,
Chesnutt wondered, "are you not likely, with your strong
feelings and impulsive disposition to make the matter too
much a personal one and thereby injure your own influence?" In the same fashion, John S. Durham, a prominent
black lawyer in Philadelphia, advised a Bookerite friend
that he did endorse Trotter's insistence on "the assertion of
absolute human equality, with no compromise or eva-
sions." However, Durham explained, "Trotter and I disagree absolutely both as to his methods and as to his attacks
on Dr. Washington and Fortune. This I have made perfectly clear to Trotter." T. T. Fortune, editor of the *New
York Age* and one of Washington's closest lieutenants, had

[13] *Guardian*, December 27, 1902, p. 4, and October 4, 1902, p.
1; *Guardian* article reprinted in Cleveland *Gazette*, September 6,
1902, p. 1; *Guardian*, February 28, 1903, p. 4, and February 27,
1904, p. 4.

According to a letter from Wellesley's president, Caroline Haz-
ard, to the *Boston Evening Transcript* (reprinted in Cleveland
Gazette, November 29, 1902, p. 1), Portia Washington did not
flunk out but left "entirely of her own accord"; see also T. T.
Fortune to Booker T. Washington, November 3, 1902, Washington Papers. The probability is that she did not do well during her
one year at Wellesley, 1901–1902, and so it was suggested that
she leave.

a drinking problem and was duly called "Teetotaller, Truthful Fortune" in the *Guardian*. That sort of gratuitous abuse probably hurt Trotter's case.[14]

And there was a further, more basic problem: most Negroes, even most of the intellectuals, supported Washington and the broad outlines of his program. The Bookerites endorsed their leader for different reasons—often from genuine sympathy with his ideas, sometimes from personal ambition or fear of the Tuskegee Machine—but the consensus was impressive in the early 1900s. "The evil days upon which the race has fallen," the *Guardian* lamented, "have made us appear like the voice of one crying in the wilderness." The first task was to convert the race. Washington was warned: "The colored people see and understand you; they know that you have marked their very freedom for destruction, and yet, and yet, they endure you without murmur!" Trotter aimed to change that.[15]

II

The initial battleground was in Boston, the principal northern stronghold of the anti-Bookerites. Though a strong tradition of racial militancy had come down from the abolitionist era, some of the most influential members of the city's black community supported the Tuskegee program. Washington's best friend in Boston was probably his former protégé, Dr. Samuel E. Courtney. The two men had known each other since the 1870s, when Courtney had attended the first school taught by Washington back in West Virginia. Later Courtney went to Hampton Institute, taught mathematics at Tuskegee for four years, and then took medical courses at Harvard and opened a

[14] Charles W. Chesnutt to W. M. Trotter, December 28, 1901, Charles W. Chesnutt Papers (this is apparently a first draft of Chesnutt's letter that may have been toned down later, but the original is probably a truer indication of his attitude); John S. Durham to Whitefield McKinlay, September 5, 1902, Carter G. Woodson Papers; *Guardian*, February 6, 1904, p. 4.

[15] Meier, *Negro Thought*, p. 102; *Guardian*, July 26, 1902, p. 4, and September 13, 1902, p. 4.

practice in Boston. The *Guardian* contemptuously referred
to him as a "southern man." In 1900 his home in Boston
was the site of the founding of Washington's National
Negro Business League ("the sole and only business of
which," Trotter observed, "is to belittle political rights,
which are all important, and to magnify small trade, which
is of little consequence"). Treasurer of the Business
League was Gilbert C. Harris, also a Bostonian of southern
background and the owner of a prosperous wig-making
concern. Frank Chisholm, a Tuskegee graduate and northern field representative for the school, lived in Cambridge.
Other active black Bookerites in the area included the
attorney Clifford Plummer, a manufacturing chemist
named Philip J. Allston, and Peter J. Smith, a job printer
and sometime handyman. Smith briefly published a newspaper to compete with the *Guardian*, and was constantly
seeking favors from Tuskegee. Thus he would warn
Washington about the operations of the Trotter circle:

> Those fellows are working like trojans to influence
> people white and black against you North and South,
> and Trotter has said he will spend all his own money
> and everybody's else he can get to kill you. I feel and
> I am sure thousands of others do that it is the pigmy
> striking at the giant, but it is well to watch the little
> fellow and never be caught napping. Those fellows
> have some following you know, and all Negroes are
> not thoughtful. . . .

Smith added that Trotter had two men "in the field working against us" and, offering himself, "It does seem as if
we might have one." [16]

[16] Booker T. Washington, *The Story of My Life and Work*
(Cincinnati, 1900), p. 67; W. N. Hartshorn, ed., *An Era of
Progress and Promise, 1863–1910* (Boston, 1910), p. 416; *Guard-
ian*, December 20, 1902, p. 4, and June 18, 1904, p. 4; Peter J.
Smith to Booker T. Washington, February 11, 1903, Washington
Papers.

The local anti-Washington men were more active and more vociferous, and, generally speaking, better educated and more articulate than their Bookerite adversaries. They called themselves "radicals," in the old abolitionist sense of the term, that of demanding full equality and civil rights for the black man without making explicit criticisms of the basic American economic and political system. The best-known and most widely respected of the "Boston radicals" at first was Archibald Grimké. But the principal impetus came from younger men of college training, Trotter, George Forbes, and two lawyers, Clement G. Morgan and Butler Wilson. Beneath them in a loose orbit was a host of others—teachers, domestic servants, waiters, housewives. The *Guardian* was their mouthpiece and the Boston Literary was their club. "The whole affair is conducted on a basis of exclusion," a disgruntled Bookerite wrote of the Literary; "only sympathizers whether capable or incapable of addressing an audience are given an opportunity to say a word." Actually, on occasion such uncommitted race men as Kelly Miller were invited to speak. In the fall of 1902 Miller lectured to the group on higher education for the Negro and took his usual middle course, including some praise for Washington and calling him the most influential black man since the end of slavery. Even measured praise for the Tuskegeean was too much for the radicals in the audience, who one after the other stood up and argued with Miller. A witness recalled, "To say that he was surprised and astonished would be putting it mildly." In this case the disagreement was on a genteel intellectual plane. On the following evening the Trotters gave Miller a party at their home in Dorchester, and agreeable relations were preserved.[17]

[17] Charles Alexander to Booker T. Washington, June 13, 1904, Washington Papers; *Guardian*, November 22, 1902, pp. 4, 5; William H. Ferris, *The African Abroad: or His Evolution in Western Civilization; Tracing His Development Under Caucasian Milieux* (2 vols., New Haven, 1913), I, 373.

Trotter was the most forceful and insistent of the radicals, and to some observers he seemed to be an ever-vigilant watchdog, ready to pounce on any deviation from militant ideas. The Reverend Bradley Gilman, a white minister friendly to Tuskegee, spoke at the Literary and later reported to Washington, with relief, that "our friend Trotter was not drawn from his lair in a ferocious mood. . . ." In his rebuttal to Gilman's lecture Trotter referred indirectly to the Tuskegeean, and Gilman thought he saw "that most persons present took his words 'with a grain of salt,' smiles went around, and an air of . . . toleration seemed to be general." Other speakers were not so intimidated. At one meeting Trotter asked his former Harvard professor Edward Cummings if he believed that the Negro's disfranchisement in the South derived from the southern white man's conclusion, from "bitter experience," that the black vote was "irresponsible." Cummings replied that many friends of the Negro conceded that the South during Reconstruction suffered from an ignorant electorate. "All colored?" Trotter demanded. "No, not by any means," Cummings replied. "That is the point," said Trotter. "If that was the point," said Cummings, gaining the advantage, "then it was not evident in the question." (Laughter at Trotter's expense.) [18]

The most talented black Bostonians considered themselves radicals, but Washington did carry off one outstanding coup by 1903: the "conversion" of William H. Lewis, one of the brightest militants. At Amherst and Harvard Law School he had been a football star and an exceptional student. After his law degree he settled in Cambridge, started a legal practice, and was elected to the City Council. At the Young's Hotel dinner in 1898 he delivered a memorable anti-Washington speech in the Tuskegeean's presence. A few years later W. E. B. Du Bois, then

[18] Bradley Gilman to Booker T. Washington, December 31, 1904, Washington Papers; *Guardian*, June 18, 1904, p. 8.

wavering between the camps, brought the two men together, and Lewis came to realize how much Washington's favor could do for his political ambitions. "I cannot
tell you," Lewis wrote Washington in October 1901,
"how pleased I am to know of your continued interest and
good will." A month later Lewis was elected to the state
legislature from his mostly white neighborhood. The
Guardian, in its first issue, offered congratulations but
added that Lewis "is a young man of some parts and
possibilities as long as fortune enables him to take the tide
at the flood, but if for any reason the tide is out, or seems
setting the other way, much assistance must not be expected from him in stemming it." During 1902 Lewis did
some legal work for Washington and late that year, after
being defeated for reelection to the legislature, went to the
White House for an interview with President Roosevelt.
They talked for forty-five minutes, and, Lewis reported to
Washington, the President said that "he was very glad
that I was more in unison with you than formerly. I told
him . . . that we had the same aims and the same ends in
view." With Washington's help Lewis was then appointed
an assistant district attorney in Boston. He continued on
occasion to sound like a radical ("There can be no compromise of human rights," he thundered in 1903) and ration-
alized his professional aspirations in terms of helping the
race. "If I could get a chance in Washington in the Department of Justice," he wrote Tuskegee in 1909, "I feel
certain that I could 'make good,' and put race prejudice to
flight. . . ." [19]

Even with the loss of Lewis, Boston remained a bastion

[19] *Guardian*, July 15, 1911, p. 7; W. E. B. Du Bois to George
Foster Peabody, December 28, 1903, enclosed with letter from Du
Bois to Oswald Garrison Villard, March 24, 1905, Villard Papers;
William H. Lewis to Booker T. Washington, October 14, 1901,
December 29, 1902, January 28, 1903, Washington Papers;
Guardian, November 9, 1901, p. 2, Trotter Papers; *Guardian*,
January 3, 1903, p. 8; Lewis to Washington, July 2, 1909,
Washington Papers.

of anti-Washington militancy. But Trotter saw the limitations of the citadel approach—radical declarations and petitions emanating from the relative safety of Boston—and so in 1903 he started to coordinate the efforts of the Bostonians with those of radicals elsewhere. In the spring he helped organize a protest meeting for New England Negroes in Boston, and in June he and Clement Morgan attended a similar affair in New York for Negroes from southern New England, New York, and New Jersey. His real hope was to infiltrate a race organization of national importance, the Afro-American Council.[20]

III

The Council's history illustrated the shift in Negro thought from protest to accommodation. At its first meeting in 1890, T. T. Fortune—who himself reflected the shift—urged the black man to "fight fire with fire" and "face the enemy and fight inch by inch for every right he denies us." At first the group urged a militant protest approach. But toward the end of the decade the Council came under the influence of Washingtonian ideas and personalities, and its annual conventions became forums in which the most prominent leaders within the race argued and labored their way toward a comprehensive program for racial advancement. Thus, in preparation for the St. Paul convention in the summer of 1902 there were rumors that the radical forces were planning a *Putsch* and would try to turn out the dominant Bookerites. Peter Smith warned Tuskegee that "the 'Guardian' folks are going to use every effort to have the Afro-American Council *Denounce* you at their meeting . . . and purpose to capture the convention for that end." As it turned out, the Washington men had their way at St. Paul virtually without opposition. "It was wonderful," Emmett Scott, Washing-

[20] *Boston Evening Transcript*, March 31, 1903, p. 14; *Guardian*, April 4, 1903, pp. 1, 2, 4, and June 13, 1903, p. 1.

ton's private secretary and alter ego, exulted to his mentor, "to see how completely your personality dominated everything at St. Paul." In rejoinder the *Guardian* claimed that the Council misrepresented the Negro people and had betrayed their trust, because "the race looked to this organization as practically the only national organization it had which was formed to guard its political interests," and such interests were no longer vital to the group's leadership.[21]

Still, it was the only available vehicle for agitation on a national scale, so in the spring of 1903 the two camps prepared for another confrontation at the Louisville convention in July. "Do you think that I ought to go to Louisville?" William Lewis asked Washington. "Can I be of service there?" Lewis was not anxious to spend the travel money, but he told Washington that "Of course if it is the President's wish it is a command." Perhaps at the urging of Washington and Roosevelt, Lewis joined the Boston delegation of Trotter, Forbes, William H. Ferris, and one other radical. Ferris, a recent graduate of Yale, was nominally based in Boston and had recently spent several months working around the District of Columbia, according to the Indianapolis *Freeman*, "with a trunk heavily laden with copies of the Guardian and a mouthful of specious talk, both of which he distributed with a prodigality bordering upon recklessness."[22]

In Louisville the Boston radicals joined with the attorney F. L. McGhee of St. Paul and a few others and tried to give the council a more radical orientation. Trouble began

[21] Meier, *Negro Thought*, pp. 128–130; Peter J. Smith to Booker T. Washington, July 3, 1902, Washington Papers; Emmett J. Scott to Washington, July 17, 1902, in Emma Lou Thornbrough, "The National Afro-American League, 1887–1908," *Journal of Southern History*, XXVII (1961), 504; *Guardian*, July 26, 1902, p. 4.

[22] Meier, *Negro Thought*, p. 176; William H. Lewis to Booker T. Washington, April 23 and 15, 1903, Washington Papers; Indianapolis *Freeman*, February 14, 1903, p. 1.

at once, during the first evening's discussion with the committee on resolutions. Trotter, Forbes, and Ferris secured the approval of a resolution asking Roosevelt to urge Congress to reduce southern representation. Other radical proposals—a statement declaring that "agitation is the best means to secure our civil and political rights" and another saying that the revised southern state constitutions were "a diabolical political crime"—were rejected. The next morning Fortune, as presiding officer, refused to allow Forbes and Trotter to rebut a paper on Negro literature which effusively praised Washington. That afternoon Ferris caused an uproar by objecting to a huge picture of Washington that loomed over the meeting hall.

The radicals picked up a few crumbs, and the Washington men rolled over the opposition. "These young men who come from Boston," said J. C. Napier, a Bookerite politician and businessman from Nashville, "with their high notions of life, with their blood-thirsty speeches, would make it better by visiting the South, knowing something of the conditions of their people and preaching to them a gospel of peace." Washington addressed the convention and asked for "positive, constructive action" and "patience, self-control, and courage." "An inch of progress," Washington declared, "is worth more than a yard of complaint." The convention approved an address to the country, and it read about as expected; Trotter asked for some changes but was denied. Fortune, who at one point was provoked to calling Trotter a liar, was reelected president and happily told Washington that "The Boston gang, at least, know that I know how to boss their sort where brains and nerves are needed. . . . I was out for scamps all the time, with blood in my eyes and a chip on both shoulders." Emmett Scott thought that "the Boston idiots" were treated "in delightful fashion." It was an impressive display of power by the Tuskegee forces.[23]

[23] *Guardian*, July 11, 1903, p. 1; Washington *Bee*, July 11, 1903, p. 1; Cleveland *Gazette*, July 11, 1903, p. 1; E. D. Wash-

And it was a conspicuous defeat for the radicals. "There was never a clearer case of being dominated to death by one man," the *Guardian* lamented. The Council's address to the country was "the feeblest utterance outside of a prayer ever put on paper." The would-be insurgents had been crushed. In a few weeks Trotter's frustrations exploded in the most famous incident of his career.[24]

IV

He knew he had some legitimate objections to Washington's leadership. The problem was to acquaint the public, white and black, with those objections. Louisville, despite being a radical debacle, was a beginning. In its aftermath the *New York Times* and the *Literary Digest*, two oracles of white opinion, took note of the anti-Washington movement.[25] Louisville was enemy territory, though, and Trotter hoped for better results by confronting Washington in Boston. Late in July the Boston branch of the National Negro Business League gave him the chance. The League announced plans for a public meeting to be held on July 30 in the Columbus Avenue African Methodist Episcopal Zion Church. William Lewis would preside, Harry Burleigh would sing, and Fortune and Washington would deliver the principal addresses. It would be Washington's first appearance before a Negro audience in Boston in some time.

In the *Guardian* office at 3 Tremont Row the editors drafted nine questions—challenges, actually—that Trotter would attempt to ask from the floor.

1. In your letter to the Montgomery Advertiser you said: "Every revised constitution throughout the

---

ington, *Selected Speeches*, pp. 92–99; Indianapolis *Freeman*, August 13, 1904, p. 1; T. T. Fortune to Booker T. Washington, July 13, 1903, Washington Papers; Emmett J. Scott to Whitefield McKinlay, July 27, 1903, Woodson Papers.

[24] *Guardian*, July 11, 1903, p. 4, and July 25, 1903, p. 4.
[25] *New York Times*, July 3, 1903, p. 1; *Literary Digest*, XXVII (1903), 37–38.

southern states has put a premium upon intelligence, ownership of property, thrift and character." Did you not thereby indorse the disfranchising of our race?

2. In your speech before the Century club here in March you said: "Those are most truly free who have passed the most discipline." Are you not actually upholding oppressing our race as a good thing for us, advocating peonage?

3. Again, you say: "Black men must distinguish between the freedom that is forced and the freedom that is the result of struggle and self-sacrifice." Do you mean that the Negro should expect less from his freedom than the white man from his?

4. When you said: "It was not so important whether the Negro was in the inferior car as whether there was in that car a superior man not a beast," did you not minimize the outrage of the insulting Jim-crow car discrimination and justify it by the "bestiality" of the Negro?

5. In an interview with the Washington Post, June 25, as to whether the Negro should insist on his ballot, you are quoted as saying: "As is well known, I hold that no people in the same economic and educational condition as the masses of the black people of the south should make politics a matter of the first importance in connection with their development." Do you not know that the ballot is the only self-protection for any class of people in this country?

6. In view of the fact that you are understood to be unwilling to insist upon the Negro having his every right (both civil and political), would it not be a calamity at this juncture to make you our leader?

7. Don't you know you would help the race more by exposing the new form of slavery just outside the gates of Tuskegee than by preaching submission?

8. Can a man make a successful educator and

politician at the same time?

9. Are the rope and the torch all the race is to get under your leadership?

Trotter later denied there was any plan to break up the meeting. Ideally, Washington would be forced to respond, in public, to the questions. Even if he turned them aside, the questions would be published in the newspapers.[26]

Others, perhaps including Trotter, had something more spectacular in mind, and as the night of the meeting approached there were rumors of a possible disruption. The stage was set: on the night of July 30 the church was packed with some two thousand spectators. After an opening prayer by the Reverend J. H. McMullen, Lewis introduced Fortune and made some kind references to Washington in passing. The mention of Washington's name brought hisses from the audience. "If there are any geese in the audience," Lewis warned, "they are privileged to retire." And if they did not, he added, they would be arrested. Fortune spoke for about a minute and made a derogatory comment about the Boston delegation at Louisville. Forbes, out in the crowd, protested and called the remark slanderous; Fortune retreated and said he was not referring to Forbes. A few minutes later Granville Martin, a Negro butler and *Guardian* stalwart, tried to interrupt Fortune with a question. Ushers came forward, Martin resisted, and so Lewis had him removed by the policemen in attendance. Fortune tried again, coughing and wheezing from the cayenne pepper someone had tossed up to the platform, and managed to finish his speech. Things quieted down during a song by Burleigh and a short talk by a local Bookerite, Edward Everett Brown.

Then Lewis, pleading for the right of free speech, introduced Washington and brought on chaos. Martin came back into the church and bellowed a question. Lewis or-

[26] *Guardian*, August 1, 1903, p. 1, and August 15, 1903, p. 4.

dered five policemen to arrest him, and as he was removed the shouting crowd disintegrated into a confusion of scuffles and fist fights. In the front of the hall one of the fighters, Bernard Charles, was stabbed, then arrested. Trotter stood on a chair and started reading from the list of questions—pointlessly, since no one could hear him over the din. Samuel Courtney shouted a suggestion: "Throw Trotter out the window!" The police took Trotter and his sister Maude out of the church and booked them at the East Dedham Street station; a short while later their mother bailed them out. Back at the church, Washington finally was able to give his speech. The disturbance, he said, was caused by only a few individuals, and he knew that most of his audience believed in the principle of free speech. Then he delivered one of his homily-laden sermons: "the world cares very little for what you or I know, but it does care a great deal about what you and I do. An educated man on the street with his hands in his pockets is not worth one whit more than an ignorant man with his hands in his pockets." We must teach our children "the dignity and beauty of labor" and the "disgrace of idleness." We must be more frugal. Boston's Negroes listened in silence, with the exception of one last outburst, and the meeting ended quietly.[27]

The evening did not go quite as planned. Trotter evidently had no desire to be arrested. Nonetheless the incident, soon given the hyperbolic title of "the Boston Riot," had its intended effect. The Boston daily newspapers gave it sensational and exaggerated coverage. The *Boston Post* reported three stabbings (including two policemen), sev-

[27] *Boston Evening Transcript*, July 31, 1903, p. 12, and August 5, 1903, p. 2; *Guardian*, August 1, 1903, p. 1; Elliott M. Rudwick, *W. E. B. Du Bois: A Study in Minority Group Leadership* (Philadelphia, 1960), pp. 73–74.

Maude Trotter was at first charged with stabbing a policeman with her hatpin; decades later she told a meeting that she had done nothing of the sort, that in fact she held hands with her fiancé all through the uproar (*Guardian*, April 13, 1946, p. 4).

eral other injuries, and dozens of ejections from the church. Newspapers all over the country picked up the story. The white reaction was a mixture of condemnation and astonishment that Negroes could disagree with Washington. Said the *Boston Evening Transcript*, "In no case is the old text, that a prophet is not without honor save in his own country, better exemplified than in the case of Booker T. Washington, whose work is appreciated and applauded even by the Negroes' hereditary oppressors, and whose person is persecuted only by his own race." The *New York Times* called the riot "a most disgraceful and lamentable episode" perpetrated by individuals who were "all for war and for a rush into full equality of every kind, deserved or undeserved." A Buffalo newspaper discerned "an atavism suggestive of the Congo forests." "If the Boston negro is not capable of understanding so able a representative of his race," asked the *St. Louis Post-Dispatch*, "what is to be expected of other Afro-Americans?" Evidently, remarked a Chattanooga journal, "razor carrying is popular with the darkey in the effete East." The *Milwaukee Sentinel* said that Washington "will hereafter believe that, however tractable and receptive the average negro may be, the Boston negro is not to be fooled with." [28]

Radical spokesmen, already acquainted with Washington's methods, reacted differently. "The revolt at Boston was the first that has reached the public," said the Reverend Reverdy Ransom, an anti-Washington minister then living in Boston. "There would be others if Mr. Washington did not control the strong papers conducted by colored men and if they expressed the sentiments of the people." The Washington *Bee* reminded its readers that "the politi-

[28] *Boston Post*, July 31, 1903, p. 1; *Boston Evening Transcript*, July 31, 1903, p. 12; *New York Times*, August 1, 1903, p. 6; and these clippings in Box 1036, Washington Papers: Buffalo *Courier*, August 2, 1903; *St. Louis Post-Dispatch*, August 2, 1903; Chattanooga *News*, August 1, 1903; *Milwaukee Sentinel*, August 2, 1903; and others.

cal dictatorship and methods of Booker Washington are at the bottom of the whole affair. . . . There is only one way to get rid of trimmers and apologists." Another radical paper found the same villain: "Booker T. Washington has become such an autocrat lately that he absolutely refused to answer these questions which are of vital importance to the Negro." White men may support him, this newspaper added, "but they can never ram him down the throats of the Afro-Americans as their new Moses, for he believes in building up his own popularity by walking over the dead bodies of his black brothers." [29]

Washington's supporters were just as caustic. "What is the matter with those Boston Negroes?" asked the Indianapolis *Freeman*. "Has much learning made them mad?" The Washington *Colored American*, echoing the *Times*, described it as "one of the most disgraceful and riotous scenes in the history of Boston" and demanded that the race repudiate "such crazy, desperate characters as Trotter." One of the most interesting, if unpublicized, comments came from Washington himself. "You will be glad to know," he wrote a friend, "that Trotter, Forbes, Grimke and two or three others, have by their actions completely killed themselves among all classes, both white and colored, in Boston. Trotter was taken out of the church in handcuffs, yelling like a baby. They are to be tried in Court tomorrow, and every effort is being exerted by the citizens of Boston to secure their conviction." [30]

Charges against Maude Trotter were dropped, but the Bookerites pressed the charges against Martin, Charles,

[29] Ransom quoted in *Literary Digest*, XXVII (1903), 188; Washington *Bee*, August 8, 1903, p. 4; Chicago *Broad Ax*, August 8, 1903, p. 1.

[30] Indianapolis *Freeman*, August 8, 1903, p. 4; Washington *Colored American*, August 22, 1903, p. 6; Booker T. Washington to Whitefield McKinlay, August 3, 1903, Woodson Papers.

Washington later discussed the riot in Chapter v, "The Intellectuals and the Boston Mob," in *My Larger Education*, pp. 112–127.

and Trotter: trying to discredit the *Guardian* people further, the Washingtonians succeeded in giving the riot greater significance. On July 31 the three defendants were arraigned in municipal court and pleaded not guilty to the accusation that they disturbed a public meeting, "making loud and indecent noises and tumults . . . to the great injury, insult, interruption and disturbance of the quiet and orderly people then and there assembled. . . ." Trial was set to begin on August 4. Trotter was surprised at this development. Two days before his trial he sent out a form letter to his most respectable acquaintances: "At a racial meeting last Thursday I was unlawfully ejected while maintaining my rights of free speech. I am to be tried Tuesday morning at 10 o'clock. . . . it would be a very great favor to me if you would be present to say what you think of my reputableness if you are called upon. It is solely the importance of the cause that induces me to ask this rather extraordinary request." At the trial the prosecution hired an expensive white lawyer (the *Guardian* surmised that Tuskegee was paying his fees). Lewis, the main witness for the prosecution, said that Trotter and Martin interrupted him during his introductory remarks, that Trotter made such a disturbance when Washington began speaking that the Tuskegeean had to sit down, and that there was no further trouble after Trotter was removed. Under cross-examination Lewis denied that he bore the *Guardian* editor any ill will because of certain remarks about him in the paper ("His is a real case," the *Guardian* had just declared, "of being colored for leadership and revenue only"). McMullen also testified against Trotter, and Archibald Grimké led the witnesses in his defense. The judge decided that Charles acted without premeditation, but that Trotter and Martin, "from their persistent and repeated attempts to interfere with the programme . . . went there for the purpose of preventing Mr. Washington from speaking, if not for the purpose of preventing the meeting." He fined Charles $25 and sentenced Trotter and Martin to thirty days in jail. All three appealed and were granted a jury trial to begin in Superior Court in October.[31]

"Trotter & crowd are getting worse," Courtney wrote to Washington on September 10, "they still feel confident of getting off. We must act and and at once." At first McMullen pressed the case, no doubt spurred on by the *Guardian*'s comment that he was "hiding his own sudden flop to Booker Washington by trumping charges on others." But as the second trial approached he told Lewis that he was willing to let the matter drop. "I advised him strongly against that," Lewis reported to Washington, "unless and until Trotter and Martin both came to him in person and ask[ed] forgiveness and were willing to apologize, and then it would be time enough *to consider what ought* to be done. He agreed with me, and so the matter stands as before." Shortly thereafter Forbes asked his college classmate "to agree to call off the dogs." Lewis refused, since "if I did anything without their personal request . . . they would be gloating over it as a triumph for them." Trotter and Martin made no apologies, so the week-long trial began on October 2.[32]

Trotter's attorneys, Clement Morgan and Edgar Benjamin, produced no surprises. A series of witnesses testified to the defendant's good character: the commander of his father's regiment, N. P. Hallowell, real-estate associates, a

[31] Superior Court Vol. 2261 (October 1903, Vol. 471), Case 2543, in Room 712, New Court House, Boston; W. M. Trotter to "Dear Sir" (form letter), August 2, 1903, Fairlie Papers; *Guardian*, August 15, 1903, p. 4, and August 1, 1903, p. 4; *Boston Evening Transcript:* July 31, 1903, p. 12; August 5, 1903, p. 2; August 6, 1903, p. 12; August 7, 1903, p. 3.
[32] Samuel E. Courtney to Booker T. Washington, September 10, 1903, Washington Papers (here and elsewhere the ampersand has been substituted for a writer's use of the plus sign for the word "and"); *Guardian*, August 1, 1903, p. 4; William H. Lewis to Washington, September 16, 1903, Washington Papers.

Harvard classmate, Grimké again, other friends. Courtney, Lewis, Edward Everett Brown, and other local Bookerites testified for the prosecution. The only issue was
whether the defendants, in trying to ask questions, intended to disrupt the meeting. The jury acquitted Charles
but found such intent on the part of the other two and
affirmed their jail sentences. On October 8 the judge denied further appeals, said it was disgraceful that Negroes
should have caused such a disturbance in Boston, where
"we try to give them their rights," and sent Trotter and
Martin to the Charles Street Jail. And thus, said the
Guardian, "the first victims in the cause for redemption
from Booker Washington went forth to martyrdom." [33]

While they were in jail Trotter's friends put out the
Guardian and planned a public meeting to greet the martyrs on their liberation. J. Solomon Gaines, a black waiter
in the Trotter circle, wrote various spokesmen outside
Boston urging them to attend the meeting. "It would cheer
the heart of Monroe," Gaines wrote to Charles Chesnutt,
"and it would also be an attestation of the fact that educated men of our race like yourself are unitedly opposed to
Bookerism in politics." In prison Trotter continued to
write for the *Guardian* and worked on the speech he would
deliver on his release. "I don't know just what I shall say,"
he wrote a friend from jail, "but I am so full of wrath at
the men who did this piece of dirty work and so mad about
the arrogant, white pro-Washington sentiment that I
hardly dare trust myself." As for Lewis, "He is the dirtiest
cur in this case." "Study to lay Booker out," he concluded.
"Yours jailed but not extinguished, Trotter." [34]

The liberation reception on November 7 was anticlimac-

[33] *Guardian*, October 10, 1903, pp. 1, 4; *Boston Post*, October 9,
1903, p. 2.
[34] J. Solomon Gaines to Charles Chesnutt, October 11, 1903,
Chesnutt Papers; Gaines to Harry C. Smith, October 8, 1903, in
New York Age, October 17, 1903, p. 1; W. M. Trotter to George
A. Towns, October 28, 1903, Towns Papers.

tic. The leaders invited from out of town were not present
as two hundred Negro Bostonians heard short talks by
Trotter, Martin, and Grimké. By then, though, the riot
had performed its main function, that of attracting publicity for the anti-Washingtonians. Even such a southern
apologist as Thomas Nelson Page, writing in *Scribner's
Magazine* a year afterward, could not ignore the dissent
from "a considerable element among the more advanced
Negroes." The Boston Riot, Page noted, was caused "by
an educated element who believe in agitation rather than in
Principal Washington's pacific and rational methods. . . .
And to prove their case they use red pepper and razors."
Few white men at this time agreed with the radicals' case,
but at least they knew of its existence after the riot.[35]

V

Within the race the Boston Riot made relations between
the camps even more hostile, led to the retirement of
Forbes from the *Guardian*, and—most important—was the
final nudge that brought the radicals the considerable talents of W. E. Burghardt Du Bois.

Like Trotter, Du Bois had grown up in Massachusetts
in an atmosphere of relative toleration. After high school
he went south for three years, attending Fisk University
and teaching in the rural areas of Tennessee during his
summers. Upon graduation from Fisk he entered Harvard
as a junior in the class of 1890; eventually he earned three
degrees there. During his last year in Cambridge he met
Trotter, whom he remembered as "thick-set, yellow, with
close-cut dark hair. He was stubborn and straight-laced
and an influential member of his class." The doctoral
candidate and the freshman saw little of each other,
though in the spring both joined a party of Negro students

[35] *Boston Sunday Post*, November 8, 1903, p. 10; Thomas
Nelson Page, "The Disfranchisement of the Negro: One Factor in
the South's Standing Problem," *Scribner's Magazine*, XXXVI
(1904), 16.

that traveled to Amherst to see the graduation of Forbes and Lewis. Over the next decade Du Bois published two scholarly books and, as a professor of sociology at Atlanta University, began turning out annual monographs on the American Negro. A man of great brilliance and intensity, shy and difficult in many of his human relations, he kept to the black college community in Atlanta as much as possible, avoided the indignities of being black in Georgia, and dedicated himself to the task of uplifting the race through the establishment of scientific truth. "I put no special emphasis on special reform effort," he later wrote of himself at this time, "but increasing and widening emphasis on the collection of a basic body of fact concerning the social condition of American Negroes, endeavoring to reduce that condition to exact measurement whenever or wherever occasion permitted." [36]

In the late 1890s his racial philosophy was much like Washington's, and he nearly took a job at Tuskegee. Gradually his thinking became more radical as he realized that "one could not be a calm, cool and detached scientist while Negroes were lynched, murdered and starved. . . ." He read the shrill radical newspaper from Boston: "I did not wholly agree with the *Guardian*, and indeed only a few Negroes did, but nearly all read it or were influenced by it." In 1902 he attended the St. Paul conference of the Afro-American Council, was revolted by the steamroller tactics of the Bookerites, but made no public protest. The *Guardian* pounced on his silence and concluded that, "like all the others who are trying to get into the band wagon of the Tuskegeean, he is no longer to be relied upon." This conclusion was not final, however. A few months later the *Atlantic Monthly* published a Du Bois essay, "Of the Training of Black Men," a firm brief for the higher education of Negroes. The *Guardian* called it a "remarkable

[36] *The Autobiography of W. E. B. Du Bois* (New York, 1968), pp. 138, 214.

article by a very remarkable Negro," "beyond all praise," virtually "the very best thing that has been said by a Negro on the question of Negro education in America." Approval was granted again the following January after a Du Bois speech at the Boston Literary.[37]

That spring he published *The Souls of Black Folk*, one of the classics of black literature. In this collection of lyrically written essays, one controversial piece, "Of Mr. Booker T. Washington and Others," announced his formal break from Tuskegee. It was a temperate but explicit criticism of Washington's public positions on education, voting, and civil rights. Either out of tactfulness or out of a limited understanding of Washington's methods, it made no direct attack on the operations of the Tuskegee Machine. He still occupied a precarious middle ground, critical of Washington but reluctant to assume an active role among the radicals. In the summer of 1903 he sent his wife and daughter to board with the Trotters in Dorchester while he lectured at Tuskegee's summer school. The arrangement epitomized his ambivalence: after teaching at Washington's school he would join his family and the Trotters in August.[38]

But then came the Boston Riot, which he remembered in his autobiography decades later as "a new and surprising turn to the whole situation which in the end quite changed my life." He arrived in Boston shortly after the riot and at first was furious with Trotter: "I thought that he had been needlessly violent, and had compromised me as his guest. . . ." At a meeting in Trotter's home Du Bois stressed the difference between disagreeing with Washington's policies and attacking him personally. Given this first

[37] *Ibid.*, pp. 222, 238; W. E. B. Du Bois to Oswald Garrison Villard, March 24, 1905, Villard Papers; *Guardian:* July 26, 1902, p. 4; September 6, 1902, p. 4; January 10, 1903, p. 1.
[38] W. E. Burghardt Du Bois, *The Souls of Black Folk* (Chicago, 1903), Chapter III; *Guardian*, July 4, 1903, p. 5; W. E. B. Du Bois to Oswald Garrison Villard, March 24, 1905, Villard Papers.

close contact with Trotter, however, Du Bois found himself increasingly attracted to the *Guardian* editor's "unsel-
fishness, pureness of heart and indomitable energy." And
when Trotter was imprisoned, as Du Bois recalled it, "my
indignation overflowed. . . . to treat as a crime that which
was at worst mistaken judgment was an outrage." [39]

Black friends of Tuskegee had helped put Trotter in
jail; soon white friends of the institution were leaning on
Du Bois, and he began for the first time to feel the weight
of what he would later call the Tuskegee Machine. Atlanta
University's financial health depended on the support of
northern white philanthropists, nearly all of whom were
admirers of Washington. The school's teachers were therefore expected to adhere to the Bookerite orthodoxy. Nonetheless a junior member of the faculty, George A. Towns
of the Harvard class of 1900, sent an unmistakably radical
letter to the jailed Trotter and was duly admonished by
Atlanta's white president, Horace Bumstead: "The publication in the Guardian of your letter to Mr. Trotter is
making serious trouble for me and I fear will work considerable injury to the University and its cause." Again, a
little later: "When you told Mr. Trotter that he was going
to jail for a principle, you obscured the fact that he had

---

[39] The quotations in this paragraph are from *Autobiography of
Du Bois*, p. 248; W. E. B. Du Bois, "William Monroe Trotter,"
Crisis, XLI (1934), 134; Du Bois to George Foster Peabody,
December 28, 1903, enclosed with letter from Du Bois to Oswald
Garrison Villard, March 24, 1905, Villard Papers; *Autobiography
of Du Bois*, p. 248.

Du Bois described the Boston Riot's effect on his thinking in
essentially similar terms at widely scattered points in his long life:
in the 1903 letter to Peabody, in his *Crisis* obituary of Trotter in
1934, in *Dusk of Dawn* in 1940, and in the posthumous *Autobiography*. See also Rudwick, *Du Bois*, p. 72, on the effect of the riot:
"It was this incident which finally brought Du Bois into active
leadership of the radicals." For some reason, both in *Dusk of Dawn*
and the *Autobiography* Du Bois dated the riot in the early summer
of 1905. In his memory it was the immediate jolt that prompted
him to organize the Niagara Movement. Actually, the Movement
was founded nearly two years after the riot.

done anything worthy of punishment." The school's trustees then recorded "their great astonishment and profound regret" at Towns's action. Trotter learned of the matter and wrote the chastened heretic, ". . . I heard Booker was setting the white millionaires onto Bumstead to get after you for your letter to me." Hereafter, Trotter suggested, the *Guardian* could print Towns's writing as anonymous editorials, "and no one shall be the wiser." He added, "Don't mind of course if I 'Trotterize' them." [40]

Du Bois felt the same pressure. In October he sent his college classmate Clement Morgan a cautious appreciation of Trotter, praising his "single hearted earnestness & devotion to a great cause" and saying he was more inclined to state his respect in public "when I see him the object of petty persecution & dishonest attack." The letter was published in the *Guardian* and marked the first time Du Bois had publicly endorsed Trotter. Du Bois notified Kelly Miller of the letter's publication and expressed his regret that Miller could not write a similar letter. "I was both glad and sorry to see your Guardian letter," Miller replied to Du Bois, "—glad for the sympathy expressed for as sincere a man as there is in the race; but sorry that I feel sure your expression will be misjudged." [41]

Predictably enough, Du Bois's *Guardian* letter once again brought "the white millionaires" down on Bumstead. Du Bois took his case directly to one of the most prominent of the philanthropists, George Foster Peabody, a New York banker with extensive charitable interests in southern Negroes. At the end of the year Du Bois wrote a long letter to Peabody which was intended for circulation

[40] Horace Bumstead to George A. Towns, November 5, 14, December 5, 1903, and W. M. Trotter to Towns, January 2, 1904, Towns Papers.
    [41] W. E. B. Du Bois to Clement G. Morgan, October 19, 1903, in the Francis L. Broderick notes on the W. E. B. Du Bois Papers; Du Bois to Kelly Miller, November 2, 1903, and Miller to Du Bois, November 4, 1903, Du Bois Papers.

and which probably understated his tightening alliance
with Trotter. Du Bois told Peabody that he abhorred the
violence of the riot—but also objected strongly to the jail
term. He admired Trotter as a man and agreed with most
of his ideas.

> As between him and Mr. Washington, I unhesitat-
> ingly believe Mr. Trotter to be far nearer the right in
> his contentions and I only pray for such restraint and
> judgment on Mr. Trotter's part as will save to our
> cause his sincerity and unpurchasable soul, in these
> days when every energy is being used to put black
> men back into slavery and when Mr. Washington is
> leading the way backward.

"I was grateful for the frank expressions in your letter,"
Peabody replied, "but I was deeply sorry to note the
unfrank and vague words of depreciation of others and
think you too largely endowed and in too important a
relation to your race to indulge them." Trotter apparently
heard about Du Bois's letter to Peabody and happily welcomed the new recruit to his ranks. "Dubois seems to be
anti-Washington at last," he wrote to Towns. "How about
it?" The next issue of the *Guardian* called Du Bois "a fine
fellow" who was not attempting "to force himself upon his
race as a leader." [42]

Thus the two most able radicals were ready to work
together. A few years later Kelly Miller proposed a conspiracy theory for the relationship. "Conscious of his own

[42] W. E. B. Du Bois to George Foster Peabody, December 28,
1903, enclosed with letter from Du Bois to Oswald Garrison
Villard, March 24, 1905, Villard Papers; Peabody to Du Bois,
January 9, 1904, Du Bois Papers, and see also Horace Bumstead to
Du Bois, January 26, 1904, Du Bois Papers; W. M. Trotter to
George A. Towns, January 2, 1904, Towns Papers; *Guardian*,
January 9, 1904, p. 4. The letter to Peabody is printed (but dated
in 1905) in Herbert Aptheker, ed., *A Documentary History of the
Negro People in the United States* (New York, 1951), pp.
881–883.

lack of attractive personality and felicity of utterance,"
Miller wrote, ". . . Trotter began to cast about for a man
of showy faculties who could stand before the people as
leader of his cause." The *Guardian* editor found his man
and "wove a subtle net" around Du Bois, "and gradually
weaned him from his erstwhile friendship for Mr. Washington, so as to exploit his prominence and splendid powers
in behalf of the hostile forces." Miller had an interesting
but dubious theory. Trotter, then or later, never expressed
any doubts about his own abilities. Du Bois's personality,
if anything, was more forbidding and less approachable
than Trotter's. With only minor influence from the *Guardian*, Du Bois was radicalizing his own point of view. Trotter did not control such factors as Tuskegee's domination
of the Afro-American Council, the jail terms after the riot,
and the white pressure on Bumstead. A general sympathy
of outlook and the normal chaos of events united the two
men. By the spring of 1904 Trotter was ready to pay Du
Bois the ultimate compliment: "If he keeps on he will even
outfoot us in true and manly statement. The iron seems to
have entered his soul." [43]

And, he might have added, it had departed the soul of
George Washington Forbes. Two days after Trotter was
released from jail the co-founders of the *Guardian* dis-
solved their partnership by written agreement. The break
was in part a matter of personality. Forbes was a gentle,
bookish man, a librarian all his life, and in the aftermath of
the Boston Riot the fight against Washington took on more
comprehensive, even frightening, dimensions. Adversity
merely stimulated Trotter's adrenalin. But he had the
strong man's flaw: his bulldog tenacity could often become
a prickly stubbornness. Particularly during these years
Trotter had a totalitarian mind. The truth was as he

[43] Kelly Miller, *Race Adjustment: Essays on the Negro in America* (New York and Washington, D.C., 1908), p. 14; *Guardian*,
April 23, 1904, p. 4.

defined it. Compromise was not flexibility, but cowardice. Other men were either manly or unmanly, with him or against him. These qualities made him an admirable spokesman for the protest tradition, but hamstrung his personal relationships. Forbes was only the first of a series of associates that Trotter worked with and then alienated.

Forbes had other reasons. During the first week of August the Reverend McMullen and four officers of his church called on Boston's mayor and asked that Forbes, a city employee, be fired. The churchmen contended that Forbes was "the head and leading spirit of the disturbers" and "gave the signals to the men who had been stationed at different places in the church." He was not fired, but he knew of the attempt. His old friend Lewis subsequently urged him to quit the *Guardian*. Tuskegee, omnipresent as ever, followed the matter closely. After Trotter was jailed Emmett Scott urged Washington, "If we could now have Forbes and the other man removed, not out of malice but simply because they deserve it, I think it will do much to aid the whole general cause." [44]

The *Guardian*'s increasingly pressing financial difficulties made bitter enemies of the former partners. When Forbes departed, the *Guardian* owed its printer some $200. A month later, on December 4, Forbes filed a petition that the paper be declared bankrupt. At about the same time Wilford H. Smith, a New York lawyer and one of Washington's most confidential friends, made the printer a standing offer to purchase the notes against the *Guardian*. Trotter sent out a circular letter describing Washington's "attempt to get the Guardian in his clutches by means of his great wealth" and asking for contributions, "as the Guardian is really a philanthropic enter-

[44] *Guardian*, August 8, 1903, p. 1, and July 30, 1904, p. 4; Emmett J. Scott to Booker T. Washington, in Samuel R. Spencer, Jr., *Booker T. Washington and the Negro's Place in American Life* (Boston, 1955), p. 142.

prise." The debts were paid, so by the time Forbes's case came up that June in bankruptcy court the matter was dropped. "Now that the Guardian can't be made bankrupt," Trotter asked, "will Dr. Washington have his standing offer for the Guardian's notes at full face value withdrawn? Small business that!" [45]

Thereafter Forbes performed occasional services for the Bookerites. In 1905 he sent a letter to the *Boston Evening Transcript* opposing the reduction of southern Congressional representation and received the congratulations of the Indianapolis *Freeman:* "Mr. Forbes has risen in mental stature and statesmanly breadth since he took his leave of the dwarfish environments of No. 3 Tremont Row." Later he offered, to Courtney, to write the Boston letter for the *New York Age*, and did some work for Washington's Committee of Twelve. He wrote occasionally for a church journal and faded into anonymity, working at the library and, according to Lewis, "always dreaming that someday he would become a writer." [46]

VI

As the post-riot factions reshuffled and polarized, Washington changed his approach to the Boston heretics. Officially he continued to belittle Trotter's importance. "Among the rank and file of our people," he wrote Bradley Gilman early in 1905, "I am sure he has no influence, especially in Boston, but he has among a certain element."

[45] *Guardian*, July 2, 1904, pp. 1, 5, and July 9, 1904, p. 4; W. M. Trotter to "Dear Friend and Co-Worker" (form letter), February 2, 1904, Towns Papers; Ruth Worthy, "A Negro in Our History: William Monroe Trotter, 1872–1934" (M.A. thesis, Columbia University, 1952), pp. 21, 31–32.

[46] Indianapolis *Freeman*, November 18, 1905, p. 2; Samuel E. Courtney to Booker T. Washington, December 8, 1905, William H. Lewis to Washington, May 25, 1908, Washington to George W. Forbes, July 31, 1908, and Forbes to Washington, August 19, 1908, Washington Papers; "George Forbes of Boston," *Crisis*, XXXIV (1927), 151–152; MS memoir by William H. Lewis, William H. Lewis Papers.

At the same time he quietly tried to destroy Trotter and the *Guardian*.[47]

Washington's secret campaign against Trotter began early in September 1903 with the espionage efforts of a New York Bookerite named Melvin J. Chisum. Chisum was a man of no particular distinction; a few years later Washington's best friend in New York remarked that Chisum "has made up his mind not to work, and expects to live by borrowing," and in 1916 the *New York Age* reported that Chisum had fled from a criminal libel conviction in Oklahoma. But in 1903 his casual unscrupulousness made him a good henchman-errand boy for Tuskegee. Somehow he gained the confidence of the Boston radicals and was admitted to a meeting in Trotter's home on the evening of September 1, 1903. There about fifty radicals organized the Boston Suffrage League and adopted a resolution: "We call upon President Roosevelt to dispense with Booker Washington as our political spokesman." That, according to the published reports, was the substance of the meeting.[48]

Washington was due to speak in Cambridge on the following evening, however, and according to Chisum the radicals concocted a plan that would make the Boston Riot seem like a polite debate. Chisum described the scheme in an affidavit submitted to Lewis: while Washington was speaking the plotters would start a bonfire in an adjacent vacant lot. Someone would shout "Fire!" The electricity would be cut off. In the ensuing darkness and confusion, said Chisum, Trotter would draw a gun and shoot Washington. If the radicals had such a plan, or even part of such a plan, they did not execute it. Washington's speech, to an

[47] Booker T. Washington to Bradley Gilman, January 9, 1905, Washington Papers.

[48] Charles W. Anderson to Booker T. Washington, March 5, 1906, Washington Papers; *New York Age*, March 16, 1916, p. 1, and April 13, 1916, p. 1; Worthy, "Trotter," p. 75; *Boston Evening Transcript*, September 2, 1903, p. 14.

audience sprinkled with plainclothesmen, was not disturbed. Lewis was skeptical of Chisum's story. ". . . I
am not inclined to believe absolutely the story of our
confidential friend," he told Washington. "I think that he
has overdrawn it somewhat, and I am not sure that he did
not himself make some of the propositions purporting to
have been made by others." So Lewis decided to keep it
quiet and "hold it as a club over their heads." The story
leaked out, though, and was published in the Indianapolis
Freeman a year later in an article signed by "a wise man
from the east." The *Freeman* suggested that Trotter be
"put up in a mad house." It was material for a libel suit,
but Trotter did not press the matter—perhaps because he
did not want to make public what had really happened at
his house that night.[49]

Libel was already a weapon in the war within the race.
In the spring of 1903 a black undergraduate at Yale
named William Pickens—later field secretary of the
NAACP—had won the school's major prize in oratory for
a speech on Haiti. But in so doing he had ridiculed that
Negro nation's erratic political history and had even inti-
mated that the island might have been better governed by
white men. Thus Pickens, said the *Guardian*, "has the
unique honor of being the first Negro ever to have won
literary oratorical honors at Yale by surrendering his self-
respect, sacrificing his pride, emasculating his manhood
and throwing down his own race." Then, when he repeated his speech in Cambridge, the *Guardian* was livid
about "the little black freak student at Yale. . . . with his
enormous lips, huge mouth, and a monkey grin co-exten-
sive with his ears. . . ." This assault did nothing but

[49] "Trotter and Trotterism," MS in Box 308, Washington Papers; *Boston Evening Transcript*, September 3, 1903, p. 10; William H. Lewis to Booker T. Washington, September 11 and 16,
1903, Washington to Lewis, October 19, 1903, Lewis to Melvin J.
Chisum, September 5, 1903, Washington Papers; Indianapolis
Freeman, August 13, 1904, pp. 1, 5.

injure Pickens' pride until after the Boston Riot, when Wilford Smith came to him and proposed a libel suit against Forbes and Trotter.[50]

Du Bois learned of it and interceded for Trotter by writing to G. W. Andrews, the head of a Negro school that Pickens had formerly attended. The *Guardian*'s editorials, Du Bois admitted, were "too radical to suit me" but were "honest and self-sacrificing." And in the libel suit, Du Bois told Andrews, Pickens was merely functioning as "a cat's paw" for Washington, who was behind the matter. Andrews reported back that Pickens denied being prodded into the suit by Washington's lawyer and would drop it if the *Guardian* apologized. Trotter, in jail, would not hear of it; he wrote George Towns that Forbes "is badly scared in this and wants me to join him in an abject apology, which I should almost rather die than agree to." From prison, though, he could not stop Forbes from printing a retraction. The case was dismissed early in November.[51]

Later that month T. T. Fortune started another legal action against the *Guardian*. Emmett Scott, of all people, urged him not to press the case, on the ground that Trotter was already in enough trouble ("I think we have got our friends on the run," Lewis had written to Tuskegee a few days earlier). Scott pointed out to Fortune that the *Guardian* people were trying to convince the public that they were being persecuted for their opposition to Washington. "You may of course expect the cry to be set up," Scott warned, "that you are being influenced by the Wizard to bring this suit, and while I believe the dirty gang needs to

[50] Worthy, "Trotter," pp. 27–28; *Guardian*, May 9, 1903, p. 1, and May 23, 1903, p. 4.

[51] W. E. B. Du Bois to G. W. Andrews, October 23, November 3, 1903 and Andrews to Du Bois, October 26, November 2, 1903, Broderick notes on Du Bois Papers; W. M. Trotter to George A. Towns, October 28, 1903, Towns Papers; Indianapolis *Freeman*, November 21, 1903, p. 1.
  Later the *Guardian* (July 30, 1904, p. 1) commended Pickens on his election to Phi Beta Kappa.

be thoroughly repressed, I think just now an inopportune time for the suit to be brought." [52]

Besides, there were other ways to repress the dirty gang. One of Washington's great sources of power was his control of the black press. News releases and canned editorials poured out of Tuskegee. Once, the *Guardian* pointed out, the same editorial appeared on the same date in at least four different Negro journals. More directly, Washington used advertising revenue and even outright ownership to influence editorial policies. In the face of this pressure, the *Guardian* noted, Fortune's *New York Age*, "which was once trumpet-voiced in public affairs . . . has died away to the almost inaudible and feeble chirp of a katydid. . . ." As early as January 1902 the *Guardian* charged Washington with subsidizing three Negro newspapers. The charge was accurate enough, but Washington always denied such reports. "If I should attempt to use money with some papers," said the ingenuous Tuskegeean, "I should soon have to use it with all. . . . So, when I have encountered opposition or criticism in the press, I have preferred to meet it squarely." [53]

Trotter's *Guardian* could not be bribed, so Washington tried to sustain a Bookerite paper in Boston to compete with it. During 1902 the *Advocate* was published by two members of Washington's National Negro Business League, Peter Smith and W. H. Moss. Smith, whom Fran-

[52] Emmett J. Scott to T. T. Fortune November 23, 1903, and William H. Lewis to Booker T. Washington, November 17, 1903, Washington Papers.

[53] *Guardian*, July 30, 1904, p. 4, and January 10, 1903, p. 4; *Guardian* article noted in Indianapolis *Freeman*, February 1, 1902, p. 4; Washington, *My Larger Education*, pp. 40–41.

On Washington's relations with the Negro press, see Spencer, *Washington*, pp. 163–166; August Meier, "Booker T. Washington and the Negro Press: With Special Reference to the *Colored American Magazine*," *Journal of Negro History*, XXXVIII (1953), 67–90; Emma Lou Thornbrough, "More Light on Booker T. Washington and the New York *Age*," *Journal of Negro History*, XLIII (1958), 34–49; Meier, *Negro Thought*, pp. 224–236.

cis Garrison once described as his protégé, was, according to Trotter, "a poor man, whose only visible means of support was the cleaning of a few down town offices. He was notoriously the agent or rather runner for Booker Washington." Smith did court Washington's approval and on one occasion asked him for a loan of $150 at 6 per cent interest. But the *Advocate* lacked distinction. The *Guardian* dubbed it the "Barroom Flyer" and reported the squabbles among its publishers. Washington evidently took little interest in its welfare and it quickly stopped appearing. In the spring of 1903 the *Enterprise* made a debut. According to the radical Chicago *Broad Ax*, the *Enterprise* was started "for the purpose of unhorsing The Guardian" and was "run for the benefit of Booker T." It carried a picture of the Tuskegeean on its front page, but could not compete with the *Guardian* and was no more successful than the *Advocate*. Toward the end of the year, though, Washington helped Smith and J. Will Cole (also "a hired hand" of Tuskegee, in Trotter's view) start yet another paper, the *Colored Citizen*.[54]

Smith, not much of a journalist, needed Tuskegee money to keep his sheet going. "The Guardian folks," he reminded Scott, would be greatly pleased to see the demise of the *Colored Citizen*. "Their friends stand by them Scott and organize their strength and each week I am told contribute something to carry on the fight against Mr. Washington." Again, "The people seem very much pleased each time the paper appears and the Guardian folks are going around crying baby all the time. I am satisfied that we are

[54] *Guardian:* July 26, 1902, p. 4; August 30, 1902, p. 5; September 13, 1902, p. 4; Francis J. Garrison to Oswald Garrison Villard, May 18, 1910, Villard Papers; W. M. Trotter to W. E. B. Du Bois, March 20, 1905, Du Bois Papers; Peter J. Smith to Booker T. Washington, June 20, 1902, Washington Papers; Chicago *Broad Ax* quoted in *Guardian*, April 25, 1903, p. 4; Indianapolis *Freeman*, April 11, 1903, p. 4; W. M. Trotter to George A. Towns, January 2, 1904, Towns Papers.

forging ahead. . . ." Washington was *not* satisfied. He
brought in a replacement for Smith, Charles Alexander, a
former resident of Boston and a Tuskegee graduate, then
teaching printing at Wilberforce University. Smith departed gracefully in mid-February, hoping that the new
Colored Citizen would be "the means of eradicating the
evil that is being done by the Guardian." The *Guardian*
said goodbye with a bit of doggerel:

> Vale! Peter Jefferson Smith.
> Vale! J. Will Cole.
> You are so soon done for
> You must wonder what
> You were begun for. Vale! [55]

Washington provided Alexander with the usual Tuskegee news service and, at first, regular letters of encouragement, suggestions for the paper, introductions to prospective Boston advertisers, and, most important, money.
"I would also get in touch with the Boston daily papers,"
Washington advised in March. "If you will read Trotter's
paper of last week, it will show you what can be done in the
way of getting help from these papers and thus keeping a
live journal before the public and at very little, if any, cost
to yourself." Alexander struggled with his task but found
the *Guardian* and its circle to be formidable opponents. He
reported being insulted by a Miss Trotter, probably
Maude ("but I paid no attention to her. I shall pay no
attention to anyone who insinuates"); he said that the
Guardian maligned him (". . . Trotter's ammunition is
about run out on you, and now he wishes to let me be
ridiculed to the Boston people, and as many of them do not
take my paper they get wrong impressions and thoughts

[55] Peter J. Smith to Emmett J. Scott, January 3, February 5, 16,
1904, Washington Papers; Cleveland *Gazette*, July 26, 1902, p. 1;
Guardian, March 5, 1904, p. 4.

among themselves to my discomfiture and to my discredit"); the *Guardian* was getting money from three
schools in the South, the *Guardian* had too many pretty
women working for it, the *Guardian* had a committee of
four hundred working against the poor *Colored Citizen.*[56]

Washington tried to keep his involvement secret, but
Trotter pieced together the circumstantial evidence and
charged him with "virtual ownership" of the *Colored Citizen.* Within a few months of his arrival in Boston, Trotter
observed, Alexander had become the secretary of the Boston branch of the Business League. Further, "Is not cor-
ruption apparent when a newspaper arises from nobody
knows what source, but [is] espoused by men notoriously
without money. . . ." Francis Garrison asked Washington about his relations with the paper. Washington replied, "I suppose I have spoken to Mr. Alexander not less
than half a dozen times against the constant use of my
name in his paper." (Which was true—Washington
wanted to keep his interest from being too apparent.) "I
do not own a dollar's worth of interest in a single Negro
publication in this country." [57]

Despite Tuskegee's efforts, the *Colored Citizen* paid
only about 25 per cent of its actual cost and was, as
Alexander admitted after a year of frustration, "a dire
failure." In April 1905 he turned it into a monthly magazine, named after himself, and subscribers to the defunct
newspaper received the *New York Age* for the balance of
their subscriptions. A jubilant Trotter told Du Bois that
Washington had "laid down" to him. As Tuskegee funds
were gradually withdrawn, *Alexander's Magazine* limped

[56] Booker T. Washington to Charles Alexander, March 9, 1904,
Alexander to Washington, March 14, December 5, 1904, February
6, 1905, Alexander to Emmett J. Scott, January 10, 1905, and
other correspondence in Box 19, Washington Papers.

[57] *Guardian,* July 23, 1904, p. 4, and July 30, 1904, p. 4;
Booker T. Washington to Francis J. Garrison, May 17, 1905,
Washington Papers.

along, taking a moderate pro-Washington line, and folded in 1909. In an ironic last attempt to keep it going, Alexander offered his periodical to the fledgling NAACP, a non-Bookerite protest group.[58]

VII

The political campaign of 1904 brought more trouble. "Trotter is making an effort to get the Guardian helped by the Republican State Committee of Connecticut," Washington wrote his New York lieutenant Charles Anderson. "I hope you will take measures to thwart his plans at once." On September 22 Trotter, according to Anderson, talked for two hours with a prominent white Republican in New York. At the end of the month there were rumors of another conference. "WHERE IS EDITOR?" Washington wired Clifford H. Plummer, a Boston lawyer who was secretly a Bookerite. "HAS HE LEFT FOR NEW YORK? SEE IF HE IS PLANNING TO LEAVE. ANSWER AT ONCE." Plummer replied on September 30, "HE LEFT AT ONE OCLOCK TODAY BLOCK HIM." Washington, in New York, reported back, "EDITOR HERE LAST NIGHT. . . . KEEP ME POSTED BY TELEGRAPH." Tuskegee did not miss this chance to return some of Trotter's criticisms. Emmett Scott wrote an editorial for the *Colored Citizen* about "this Boston pirate," the "brave, roaring make-believe lion" who goes to New York and "cringingly begs for political cash!!" Trotter, neglecting to mention his own political forays, went ahead and wrote a *Guardian* editorial criticizing Washington for meddling in the Republican campaign. "No one wants him in Negro politics," said Trotter. "Yet he has practically given up school work and gone out into Republican politics. How long will his financial backers support

[58] Charles Alexander to Booker T. Washington, February 6, 19, April 12, 1905, Washington Papers; *New York Age*, May 18, 1905, p. 2; W. M. Trotter to W. E. B. Du Bois, April 22, 1905, Du Bois Papers; Meier, *Negro Thought*, p. 226; Francis J. Garrison to Oswald Garrison Villard, June 22, 1909, Villard Papers.

him in this role?" Tuskegee did not have a monopoly on agile dissembling.[59]

Nor a monopoly on libel suits. Trotter sued Alexander, citing the "pirate" article and another which called him a "toad" and predicted that if Washington "will invite this creature to dinner, or show him any courtesy whatever, he will cease his continued meanness, and sell himself for 'recognition.' " In response Alexander started a cross-libel suit of his own. "I will want you to help me in every way possible," he wrote Scott. "If this fellow wins out in his case, he will of course kill the influence of the Boston Colored Citizen, but if he loses, the Boston Colored Citizen will be more firmly rooted in the confidence of the people and will really have a boom that will be worth while." At the trial Alexander admitted under cross-examination that Scott had actually written the libelous pieces. Trotter produced some twenty witnesses to Alexander's nine, but the judge was not impressed. He awarded $500 in damages to Alexander and only $100 to Trotter. "Of course I am glad to learn that we have won so substantial a victory over Trotter," Scott told Alexander. "I am only sorry that he gets the comfort out of having you fined at all." [60]

Meanwhile Clifford Plummer had been busy. He seemed to be a good anti-Bookerite. He contributed to the fund that sent Trotter, Forbes, and Ferris to the Louisville imbroglio and, as a favor to a family friend, served as

[59] Booker T. Washington to Charles Anderson, September 7, 1904, Anderson to Washington, September 22, 23, 1904, Washington to Clifford H. Plummer, September 30, October 1, 1904, Plummer to Washington, September 30, 1904, Charles Alexander to Washington, February 6, 1905, Washington Papers (I was directed to the Plummer correspondence cited here and below by the references in Meier, *Negro Thought*, p. 310); *Guardian*, October 8, 1904, p. 4. The *New York Age*, December 21, 1905, p. 4, charged that Trotter made a total of three trips to New York during the 1904 campaign.

[60] Cleveland *Gazette*, March 11, 1905, p. 2; Charles Alexander to Emmett J. Scott, February 6, 23, March 21, 1905, Scott to Alexander, March 23, 1905, Washington Papers.

Bernard Charles's attorney during the Boston Riot trials. At the same time he sought Washington's favor and was ready to do his bidding. Plummer's chance came when Trotter moved to unify the radicals of New England into a single organization.[61]

After the riot Trotter had founded the Boston Suffrage League. One of its first meetings was the gathering at Trotter's home that Chisum infiltrated. The following spring Trotter started to expand its membership. "Join the Suffrage League no matter what other organization you belong to," the *Guardian* urged. "Books open at Guardian office. No fee. Only race loyalty required." The League sponsored a successful protest meeting at Faneuil Hall late in April, and then made plans for a New England convention that fall. Plummer, the apparent radical, learned of the plans and told Washington about them. "WIRE ME DEFINITE AND PRECISE INFORMATION FINAL PLANS OF ENEMY," Washington telegraphed to Plummer. "ARE YOU SURE OF CONTROL?" Plummer reported back that he had fomented a quarrel among the organizers on procedural methods, and that he had been put in charge of hiring a hall and sending out the notices to prospective delegates. With the mailing list in hand, "which I am quite sure I will be able to get, I think my victory is won. . . . we have them now at a standstill." He was, he assured Washington, in a position to know what the radicals were planning: "Can't anything pass between now and the time I see you but what I shall know." On the eve of the conference, set for October 19 in Providence, the planners met in the *Guardian* office to draft the resolutions. At Plummer's insistence a reference to "beggars who come from the South" was deleted. "The suggestions in the resolutions did not by any means, please me," Plummer told Wash-

[61] *Guardian*, July 18, 1903, p. 5; Clifford H. Plummer to Booker T. Washington, June 27, July 9, 30, 1902, August 3, 1903, Washington Papers.

ington, "but I am satisfied that in my objections I did not uncover myself. . . . My associates on the committee did not have the slightest suspicion of my stand." [62]

In Providence Negroes from Massachusetts, Connecticut, and Rhode Island joined to form the New England Suffrage League. Despite its name, the group was more than a suffrage society. "The object is not to discuss how the Negro should vote," Trotter said, "but to lay the wrongs and the claims of the race before the American public." The League elected Trotter president and endorsed resolutions asking for federal antilynching legislation, federal compensatory aid to southern schools ($120 million a year until 1925), the outlawing of segregated seating on interstate carriers, and the enforcement of the Fifteenth Amendment. Trotter called the meeting "a complete success" and "the best suffrage conference we ever attended." Plummer, less enthusiastic, warned Tuskegee that "about all in it are anti-Washington men." Moreover, "You may expect a more enlived [*sic*] and active opposition than you have had for some time up here with Trotter at the head, but I can promise it shall not all be one-sided while I am there." For his diligence Plummer was given $30 and a letter of introduction to a prominent white man. [63]

Another prominent white man, Oswald Garrison Villard, was due to speak at the Boston Literary in December. Knowing he was entering a delicate situation, he asked his friend Washington what he should say. You will find,

[62] W. M. Trotter to Ray Stannard Baker, October 5, 1907, Ray Stannard Baker Papers; *Guardian*, April 2, 1904, p. 4, and April 30, 1904, pp. 1, 8; Booker T. Washington to Clifford H. Plummer, September 29, 1904, Plummer to Washington, September 30, October 1, 24, 1904, Washington Papers.

[63] *Guardian*, October 15, 1904, p. 4, and October 22, 1904, pp. 1, 4, 8; Clifford H. Plummer to Booker T. Washington, October 24, 1904, Emmett J. Scott to Plummer, October 21, 1904, Washington to Plummer, October 27, November 2, 1904, Washington Papers.

Washington replied, that many of the members of the Literary believe "that I was willing to surrender all the rights of the colored people and cater to all the unreasonable wishes of the Southern whites." Some of these men are honest in their opposition, some are not: but in either case they "have never had the opportunity of seeing what the conditions are in the South." They are restless and impatient. "I become just as impatient as they do, and wish just as much as they that I could change conditions, but you and I both know that the mere wishing will not make a change, that we have got to go through a long process of evolution which can only be brought about by development in property, education and character." We are all pursuing the same ends, albeit by different means, "and there is no necessity for quarreling." You might suggest "pretty strongly" to these people that "friendly and sympathetic cooperation" is more useful than "mere abuse." And I am willing to listen to criticism. And ". . . I am always willing to change my policy when I am convinced that I am wrong. . . ." [64]

Speaking at the Literary a few days before Christmas, Villard fashioned his talk along the suggested lines and weathered a predictable response from the audience. Plummer was there, at Washington's bidding, and advised Tuskegee that Trotter, Morgan, and the other rebutters "made no reference to what the speaker said; and I have doubts if they know what they said themselves, for the Lord knows I can't recall it now." [65]

VIII

After three years the *Guardian* had changed Trotter's life. He had started the paper as a complement to his real-estate business: while earning his livelihood at a se-

[64] Booker T. Washington to Oswald Garrison Villard, November 16, 1904, Villard Papers.
[65] Clifford H. Plummer to Booker T. Washington, December 22, 1904, Washington Papers.

cure, conventional job he could work on a part-time basis in the greater interest of the race. "It has cost me considerable money," he wrote his college friend John Fairlie, "but I could not keep out of it. In the columns of The Guardian we have at least the relief of expressing our views on colorphobia in all its forms. I can now feel that I am doing my duty and trying to show the light to those in darkness and to keep them from at least being duped into helping in their own enslavement. . . . I am henceforth on the firing line." By degrees he gave more time to helping "those in darkness" and less time to his business. At some point, probably after the Boston Riot and the departure of Forbes, he had to make a decision. Clearly he could not do justice to both his business and his race work. One would have to be relinquished. His decision—to continue with the *Guardian*—was in effect made for him as the newspaper gradually sucked in his energies and funds. He could later claim with some justice that he had not actively sought the career of race champion; rather, it slowly overtook him. "I am still running the Guardian," he wrote Fairlie in 1906, "and seem to be down to the color line question as a life work, though hardly for a livelihood." [66]

Giving himself over to racial agitation and organization meant altering his style of life. It meant putting mortgages on the home in Dorchester and eventually selling it altogether. It meant less leisure time and less social respectability. It meant losing old friends and fighting for one unpopular cause after another. All of this is ordinarily the lot of the reformer in America, and Trotter accepted it, for the most part, without complaint. The genteel affluence of the late 1890s became the genteel poverty of the *Guardian* years. Eventually he became acidly contemptuous of what he called "the high toned and salaried crowd," the class that he was born into and might have remained in through

[66] W. M. Trotter to John A. Fairlie, June 15, 1902, September 16, 1906, Fairlie Papers.

life. When someone betrayed or frustrated him he would all but invariably accuse the opponent of pursuing selfish materialistic ends. At times it would seem that poverty, sacrifice, and virtue all went together in his mind. Moneyed men, almost by definition, could not be principled men.[67]

For Deenie Trotter the decision to leave the comfortable life behind was more difficult. The man she had married was a rising young businessman, well educated and of a prominent family. She could anticipate a pleasant, comfortable life, unremarkable and respectable, perhaps distinguished by occasional good works. Then he launched the *Guardian.* She "protested, mildly," he recalled, "and complained of her husband's late coming home at night." The Boston Riot was crucial for her, as it was for many others. With her husband in jail, she started working for the paper, keeping accounts and helping with the society columns. Quietly, almost invisibly, she became his most important supporter and co-worker. By 1905 she could speak, from her own experience, on the need of making personal sacrifices in the greater interest of the race.[68]

[67] "The high toned and salaried crowd"—W. M. Trotter to Freeman H. M. Murray, September 23, 1913, Freeman H. M. Murray Papers. John E. Milholland was the most conspicuous exception to Trotter's general distrust of wealthy men.

[68] *Guardian,* December 28, 1918, p. 4, Trotter Papers; *The Celebration of the One Hundredth Anniversary of the Birth of William Lloyd Garrison, By the Colored Citizens of Greater Boston under the Auspices of the Suffrage League of Boston and Vicinity* (Boston, 1906), p. 14.

Organization by Radicals: The Niagara Movement

T HE BOOKERITES enjoyed a knack for organization. The Afro-American Council and, in particular, the National Negro Business League gave Washington an immediate tactical advantage over the radicals, who had nothing comparable to either group. An anti-Tuskegee organization could be founded and sustained essentially by one factor only: the shared convictions of the group's members. Washington, on the other hand, with his contacts among whites, could keep his groups lubricated by the judicious dispensing of financial and political favors. Such mundane and persuasive tactics were not available to the radicals. Nonetheless it was becoming evident that some kind of militant organization would be necessary before the radicals could see any reduction of Washington's power and prestige.

Trotter appreciated the need for radical mobilization. The meeting he and Morgan attended in New York in the spring of 1903 was a start. Late that year he went down to

Washington for a conference that would found a group, he hoped, to replace the "gelded" Afro-American Council. He and other anti-Bookerites launched the National Negro Suffrage League and elected a president, James H. Hayes, a Richmond lawyer of erratic allegiances but then opposed to Washington. Trotter was pleased with the new group. "It is said," the Indianapolis *Freeman* wonderingly remarked, "that Trotter actually behaved himself at the Washington Suffrage Convention." But a few months later Hayes accepted appointment as a delegate to the Republican national convention. Trotter, always wary of such political encumbrances, demanded Hayes's resignation from the presidency. Evidently Hayes would not resign, but in any case it made little difference, for the organization never attracted any considerable support even from the anti-Bookerites.[1]

A more successful union of radicals waited on two developments. One, a last attempt by Washington to reconcile the feuding camps, brought about the other, Du Bois's decision to form a new organization of anti-Bookerites.

I

In February 1903 Washington told Du Bois of his plan for a conference to unite all black spokesmen. "I am very anxious," Washington emphasized, "that the meeting be not confined to those who may agree with my own views . . . but that it shall in every way represent all the interests of the race." Lack of funds and the year's intraracial turbulence forced the suspension of further planning until that fall. Then Washington's friend Andrew Carnegie agreed to finance the meeting, and Tuskegee sent out invitations for a conference at Carnegie Hall in New York

[1] *Guardian*, December 26, 1903, p. 4, and March 12, 1904, p. 4; Indianapolis *Freeman*, January 2, 1904, p. 4; August Meier, *Negro Thought in America, 1880–1915: Racial Ideologies in the Age of Booker T. Washington* (Ann Arbor, Mich., 1963), p. 237.

during the first week of January. News of the meeting, Washington advised one Negro clergyman, should be "kept absolutely from the public for the present." And our object, he assured Du Bois, "is to try to agree upon certain fundamental principles and to see in what way we understand or misunderstand each other and correct mistakes as far as possible."[2]

Du Bois, having witnessed the Boston Riot, Trotter's imprisonment, and the harassment of Atlanta's President Bumstead, was suspicious of the Tuskegeean's intentions. He listed the twenty-eight Negroes invited to the meeting and found only six who could be described as anti-Bookerites: himself, Archibald Grimké, Clement Morgan, Kelly Miller, E. H. Morris, and F. L. McGhee. (Trotter, of course, was not invited.) Grimké was asked to the conference only on the insistence of Du Bois. Washington agreed to include Grimké, but grumbled that the Bostonian was "not at heart interested in the real condition of the South" and was "more bent on noteriety and keeping up discord than upon any other motive. . . ." Furthermore, said Washington of the distinguished lawyer and former consul, "I cannot see that Mr. Grimke has ever done anything to entitle him to be a representative in such a body." Washington also resisted the inclusion of George Forbes, but for a different reason. "Du Bois is very sensitive on the question as to who shall be invited," Washington wrote to William Lewis, and since Forbes "has made a break with Trotter . . . Du Bois will object, for he does not object to saying that we are trying to pack the conference with people who are thinking in a certain direction."[3]

[2] Booker T. Washington to W. E. B. Du Bois, February 12, 1903, Booker T. Washington Papers; Meier, *Negro Thought*, p. 177; Washington to Abraham Grant, October 28, 1903, and to Du Bois, November 8, 1903, in Herbert Aptheker, *Toward Negro Freedom* (New York, 1956), pp. 96, 99.

[3] Aptheker, *Toward Negro Freedom*, pp. 99–100; Booker T. Washington to W. E. B. Du Bois, January 2, 1904, Washington to William H. Lewis, December 3, 1903, Washington Papers.

There was, Du Bois warned Miller, danger of a "gag-law or white-wash," and the handful of radicals would have to keep it from becoming a "B.T.W. ratification meeting." "You must come," he urged Morgan. "Otherwise the other side will say we refuse to treat." In any event, "We're going to have a warm time." He drafted a confidential memorandum for the anti-Bookerites: "Bring every speech or record of Washington you can lay your hands on so that he can face his record in print. The main issue of this meeting is *Washington*, refuse to be side-tracked." [4]

Rumors of the upcoming meeting circulated through the radical grapevine. "But why not let us know who are to be invited?" the *Guardian* asked Tuskegee. "Why have it secret? And above all, let both sides be equally represented. No tricks, Mr. Washington." Trotter went to New York for the conference but could not get into the hall. It was, as Du Bois had anticipated, a warm session. Morgan presented Washington with the nine questions from the Boston Riot. At one point Lewis accused Morgan of taking notes on the secret discussions; Morgan heatedly replied that he was merely writing letters. Du Bois announced that if the conference were to hedge on the issues of suffrage, education, and public accommodations he would walk out and make his disagreement public even if he were the only conferee to do so. The radicals were permitted to speak their minds, but there was no mistaking the forces behind the affair. Most of the whites in attendance were admirers of Washington: Carnegie, the New York businessman and philanthropist Robert Ogden, Carl Schurz, George Foster Peabody, Oswald Garrison Villard, Lyman Abbott of the

[4] W. E. B. Du Bois to Kelly Miller, November 2, 1903, Du Bois to Clement G. Morgan, November 24, December 28, 1903, W. E. B. Du Bois Papers; Aptheker, *Toward Negro Freedom*, pp. 100–101; Du Bois to Francis J. Grimké, December 28, 1903, in Carter G. Woodson, ed., *Works of Francis J. Grimké* (4 vols., Washington, D. C., 1942), IV, 89–90.

Outlook, William Hayes Ward of the *Independent*, and others. The undermanned radicals and the Bookerites thrashed out a compromise platform, threading a careful line between militant and conservative positions. Washington and one of his supporters, Hugh Browne of Pennsylvania, were named along with Du Bois to appoint a permanent Committee of Twelve at a later date. Sketchy reports of the proceedings leaked out to the radical press. "Even the Bookerites are admitting privately," Trotter wrote, "that Mr. Washington called that secret conference because he was being seriously hurt by the attack of the Guardian." And a week later: "So after all the conference was called to stop the opposition. So Booker is getting tired of it. Wonder whether he is glad he jailed us last summer. . . . Washington can't settle this controversy behind closed doors, even if Abbott, Carnegie and Baldwin are there. But the conference is great recognition for us. How about it, boys?" [5]

"We are unquestionably on the right road," Browne wrote Du Bois some weeks afterward, "—let us travel it arm in arm." That contrived sense of harmony—the Washington *Bee* had sardonically called the conference "a perfect love feast"—was quickly shattered by both sides. Du Bois suggested that the Committee be given a broader base. Washington refused, arguing that "for a year at least the Committee would better consist of twelve only. If we can make that a success, it may prove the basis for a larger and more thorough organization." The conferees had called a truce on attacking each other in public, but in April Du Bois published his sharpest critique of Tuskegee yet in a symposium in the *World To-Day*. ("Is the Conference truce off for good?" Kelly Miller demanded of Du

[5] *Guardian*, December 26, 1903, p. 4; W. M. Trotter to "Dear Friend and Co-Worker" (form letter), February 25, 1904, George A. Towns Papers; Washington *Bee*, January 23, 1904, p. 1; Aptheker, *Toward Negro Freedom*, p. 101; *Guardian*, January 16, 1904, p. 4, and January 23, 1904, p. 4.

Bois. ". . . What is the use of meeting in St. Louis if
battle still rages along the same old lines.") The Committee of Twelve met in July with Du Bois unexpectedly
absent, adopted a more conservative platform than the
consensus statement from the previous January, and
named Washington its chairman, Browne its secretary,
and—as a sop to the radicals—Grimké its treasurer.
Grimké and Du Bois were so annoyed that they resigned
from their positions, but shortly thereafter were persuaded
to return. Late that summer the group met in St. Louis.
Du Bois pleaded illness and did not attend, and in his
absence the Washington men cemented their control.[6]

Clearly, Du Bois was not greatly concerned with making the Committee work. Just as clearly, the conservatives
intended to keep their control of the group. Du Bois resigned for good in March 1905, and received a scolding
joint letter from Miller and Grimké: "We are frank to say
that your sudden and unexplained withdrawal from a com-
pact of your own devising would seem to lay you liable to
the charge of bad faith; and, as you know, your opponents
are ready to exploit the charge." "I refuse to wear Mr.
Washington's livery," Du Bois fired back, "or to put on
his collar. . . . At present I propose to fight the battle to
the last ditch if I fight it stark alone."[7]

II

"Fall on me at any and all times," Trotter wrote Du
Bois when he learned of the resignation, "and I shall do

[6] Hugh M. Browne to W. E. B. Du Bois, March 1, 1904, Du
Bois Papers; Washington *Bee*, January 16, 1904, p. 4; Booker T.
Washington to Du Bois, February 25, 1904, Washington Papers;
Du Bois, "The Parting of the Ways," *World To-Day*, VI (1904),
521–523; Kelly Miller to Du Bois, April 23, July 8, 1904, Du Bois
Papers; Aptheker, *Toward Negro Freedom*, pp. 101–103; Archi-
bald Grimké to Washington, July 13, 1904, Washington Papers;
Grimké to Du Bois, August 13, 1904, Du Bois Papers.
[7] Kelly Miller and Archibald Grimké to W. E. B. Du Bois,
March 15, 1905, Du Bois papers; Du Bois to Grimké, March 21,
1905, Archibald Grimké Papers.

anything I can to assist you." Trotter had followed Du Bois's struggles with the Committee and now set out to provoke him into taking an open position of radical leadership. "My wife says you are a brick," Trotter told Du Bois, "all you need is a red head." Again, a few days later, "Harry Smith of Cleveland wants to know why you don't 'warm up' to the fellows. I don't know what he means." The two most able radicals were, for the time being, working in close harmony and trading compliments. In some quarters this development brought consternation. "Our bumptious friend Trotter," Harvard's Albert Bushnell Hart wrote his old student Du Bois, "has made a great deal of unnecessary trouble by his assaults on Mr. Washington . . . and I have actually found people who seemed to suppose that you and Trotter were working together." [8]

They *were* working together, but there was a limit to what they could accomplish as individuals. Earlier in the year Du Bois had charged in print that Tuskegee used $3,000 worth of "hush money" to subsidize Negro newspapers "in five leading cities." Oswald Garrison Villard, at that point an uncritical admirer of Washington, challenged Du Bois to prove his contention. Du Bois asked Trotter and other radicals for evidence. Trotter responded with some accurate but undocumented information on Tuskegee's relations with the Boston *Colored Citizen* and the *Colored American Magazine*. "It is necessarily of a circumstantial nature," Trotter added. "Much depends on the reasonableness of your prospective convert. Would to God I had the direct evidence." Other radicals provided Du Bois with further evidence. Du Bois sent the information along to Villard and stated his reluctant conclusion

[8] W. M. Trotter to W. E. B. Du Bois, March 26, April 1, 1905, Du Bois Papers; Elliott M. Rudwick, *W. E. B. Du Bois: A Study in Minority Group Leadership* (Philadelphia, 1960), p. 92; Du Bois to Paul V. Kellogg, May 10, 1905, Francis L. Broderick notes on Du Bois Papers; Albert Bushnell Hart to Du Bois, April 24, 1905, Du Bois Papers.

"that the methods of Mr. Washington and his friends to stop violent attack had become a policy for wholesale hushing of all criticism and the crushing out of men who dared to criticise in any way." But Villard was not swayed. "I must say frankly," he replied to Du Bois, "that it will take a great deal more than the evidence you have presented to shake my faith in Mr. Washington's purity of purpose, and absolute freedom from selfishness and personal ambition." [9]

Just to be certain, though, Villard and his uncle Francis Garrison asked Washington about the matter. Washington denied all the accusations and ascribed them to the sinister influence of the *Guardian*. "It is difficult for me to deal with a man who is so utterly wanting in truth or honor as Trotter," Washington wrote Garrison.

> He has no hesitation whatever in giving assertion to the most baseless and unreasonable falsehoods. . . . The fact is, Mr. Trotter and his few followers are trying the old game of trying to get something for nothing; they want public approval and confidence without paying the price to secure it. . . . his greatest claim to noteriety is an attempt to break up a Negro meeting. . . . Trotter cannot understand how one can differ from me without continually heaping personal abuse upon me.

This confidential letter was utterly convincing to the white men. "I agree with you that it is absolutely satisfactory,"

[9] *Voice of the Negro*, II (1904–05), 677; *The Autobiography of W. E. B. Du Bois* (New York, 1968), pp. 247–248; Oswald Garrison Villard to W. E. B. Du Bois, February 7, March 13, 1905, Du Bois to W. M. Trotter, March 15, 1905, Trotter to Du Bois, March 18, 20, April 19, 1905, C. E. Bentley to Du Bois, March 18, 1905, J. W. Cromwell to Du Bois, March 18, 1905, all in Du Bois Papers; D. R. Wilkins to Trotter, March 20, 1905, in Ruth Worthy, "A Negro in Our History: William Monroe Trotter, 1872–1934" (M.A. thesis, Columbia University, 1952), pp. 32–33; Du Bois to Oswald Garrison Villard, March 24, 1905, Villard to Du Bois, April 18, 1905, Oswald Garrison Villard Papers.

Villard wrote his uncle, "and I wish we could put it into Du Bois's hands and shut him up." [10]

There was the problem. Most of Washington's power derived from his prestige among whites. Villard and Garrison, steeped in the abolitionist tradition, were among the most racially enlightened white men of their day. Yet in 1905 even they considered Washington's detractors to be nothing more than jaundiced malcontents, not to be taken seriously by anyone genuinely interested in helping the black man. So the anti-Bookerites simultaneously had to persuade the race to greater militancy and convince sympathetic whites that Tuskegee should not receive their unanimous support.

"It strikes me," Trotter had written Du Bois in February, "you had better vouchsafe a line or two on 'developments' occasionally. The honest men must somehow get together for more concerted defence." Then, after Du Bois left the Committee of Twelve, Trotter suggested that "A national 'strategy board' for defensive and offensive and constructive action might be advisable. But no white man, especially like Ogden, can pay 'expenses.' That 'expenses paid' is fatal to the 'Committee of 12.'" F. L. McGhee of St. Paul and C. E. Bentley of Chicago were also thinking in terms of a national anti-Washington organization and broached the matter to Du Bois. Together the four men planned a secret meeting to be held that summer in western New York. Du Bois sent invitations to 59 carefully selected individuals in 17 states. They were all known to be reliable anti-Bookerites and were asked to join in "organized, determined and aggressive action on the part of men who believe in Negro freedom and growth." [11]

[10] Booker T. Washington to Francis J. Garrison, May 17, 1905, Washington Papers; Oswald Garrison Villard to Garrison, May 23, 1905, Francis J. Garrison Papers.

[11] W. M. Trotter to W. E. B. Du Bois, February 27, March 26, April 19, May 15, 1905, and Du Bois to Trotter, May 13, 1905, Du Bois Papers; Herbert Aptheker, ed., *A Documentary History of the Negro People in the United States* (New York, 1951), pp.

In the second week of July Du Bois went to Buffalo, had
trouble finding hotel accommodations there for the Negro
conference, and so crossed to the Canadian side of Niagara
Falls and hired a small hotel in Fort Erie, Ontario. The
radicals, fearing harassment from the Tuskegee Machine,
had kept the arrangements for their conference as secret as
possible. The Bookerites learned of the plans, though, and
Clifford Plummer traveled to Buffalo to check up on the
proceedings. In Buffalo Plummer looked around and happily reported that there was no radical conference there
(which was true) and that "the conference amounted to
nothing." [12]

Twenty-nine black men from all over the country gathered at Fort Erie: seven from New England, led by Trotter and Morgan, six from the South, eight from the Midwest, including Bentley, McGhee, and Harry Smith of the
Cleveland *Gazette*, four from the Middle Atlantic states,
and four from the District of Columbia. They formed the
Niagara Movement and organized an executive system of
overlapping jurisdictions that would prevent domination
by any one man. (They understood the lesson to be derived
from the Committee of Twelve.) Du Bois would serve as
general secretary, the Cincinnati lawyer George Jackson
as general treasurer, and they would act in conjunction
with an executive committee made up of the chairmen of
each state's local chapter. Work was divided among special committees; Trotter headed the most important, the
Press and Public Opinion Committee. The state committees would "cooperate with congressmen and legislators to
secure just legislation for the colored people" and carry
out educational and propaganda functions. The Movement

900–901, 904; Trotter to John E. Bruce, May 18, 1905, John E.
Bruce Papers.
   [12] W. E. Burghardt Du Bois, *Dusk of Dawn: An Essay Toward
an Autobiography of a Race Concept* (New York, 1940), p. 88;
Clifford H. Plummer to Booker T. Washington, July 12, 13, 16,
1905, Emmett J. Scott to Plummer, July 12, 1905, Washington
Papers.

would meet together annually to report on progress.[13]

The founders endorsed a "Declaration of Principles" drafted by Du Bois and Trotter which addressed white America in plain, unambiguous language. "The Negro race in America, stolen, ravished, and degraded, struggling up through difficulties and oppression, needs sympathy and receives criticism; needs help and is given hindrance, needs protection and is given mob-violence, needs justice and is given charity, needs leadership and is given cowardice and apology, needs bread and is given a stone. This nation will never stand justified before God until these things are changed." The basic solution? "Persistent manly agitation is the way to liberty, and toward this goal the Niagara Movement has started and asks the co-operation of all men of all races." More specifically, the white man must permit manhood suffrage, equal civil rights, equal economic opportunities, and full access to all types of education. "Any discrimination based simply on race or color is barbarous, we care not how hallowed it be by custom, expediency, or prejudice." The Civil War amendments to the Constitution must be enforced. The Christian Church must live up to its pretensions. We black men have our own duties: "to vote. . . . to respect the rights of others. . . . to work. . . . to obey the laws. . . . to be clean and orderly. . . . to send our children to school. . . . to respect ourselves, even as we respect others." But in doing so we shall not cease to remind the white man of his responsibility. "We refuse to allow the impression to remain that the Negro-American assents to inferiority, is submissive under oppression and apologetic before insults." [14]

It was a radical document, even without any direct

[13] *Boston Evening Transcript*, July 15, 1905, p. 14; Rudwick, *Du Bois*, pp. 94–95.

[14] Francis L. Broderick and August Meier, eds., *Negro Protest Thought in the Twentieth Century* (Indianapolis, 1965), pp. 49–52. My summary of the Declaration of Principles changes the order of the points made in the actual document.

references to Washington, and it set down the program for a radical organization. Trotter was pleased with the Niagara men, "so endowed with intellect, so imbued with high purpose, so consumed with the passion for liberty, so calmly aware of the difficulties and risks threatening, so quietly determined to persevere and faint not." Together they could confront Washington and the white man beyond.[15]

III

We have one essential quality in the Niagara Movement, wrote Du Bois: "like-mindedness." The Committee of Twelve had shown the futility of trying to embrace all viewpoints in one organization. The Movement would be a radical forum, not a debating society. For this reason, apparently, Du Bois did not invite Archibald Grimké and Kelly Miller to Niagara Falls. Miller in 1905 was a perceptive but uncommitted observer, plying a delicate middle course between the camps. Thus within a few months he could take part in a quiet conference of Bookerites in New York and co-sign a radical circular letter to Roosevelt—and feel sincere in both ventures. The case of Grimké was more perplexing. One of the earliest of the "Boston radicals," and an old friend of the Trotter family, Grimké had elected to stay on the Committee of Twelve despite his anger with some of Washington's methods. In return, the Committee had circulated, in pamphlet form, Grimké's *Atlantic Monthly* article on "Why Disfranchisement Is Bad." Apparently Grimké was offended by some of Trotter's methods, and by degrees he moved further into the Tuskegee camp. "Grimké has been 'throwing me down' for some time," Trotter lamented to Du Bois in the spring of 1905. "He told me to my face he was 'afraid of' me. I suppose you know he became a 'staff correspondent' of the

[15] *Guardian*, July 22, 1905, clipping in W. E. B. Du Bois folder, Harvard Archives, Widener Library, Harvard University.

New York Age two weeks ago. . . . I had boomed Grimké so and he is president of the Boston Suffrage League, and now an employee of Tim Fortune! It certainly is hard." So Du Bois excluded Miller and Grimké from the Niagara meeting despite their considerable importance within the race. Both men were annoyed at what they took to be an insult.[16]

Early in August Washington had a long talk with Grimké during which the former Trotterite "went over many of the details covering the devilment of the whole gang." A jubilant Washington told his secretary that Grimké "seems more than anxious now to line up with us." Miller "feels the insult very keenly and resents it in very strong language, but he is mushy and cannot be depended upon for a straight out fight." A few days later Du Bois tried to recover his loss in a recruiting letter to Miller and Grimké. "Today we have a growing enthusiastic organization of nearly 75 members, educated determined & unpurchasable men," Du Bois wrote. ". . . We are united for active work, not against persons but for principles. Will you not join us?" It was no use; they would have nothing to do with the new group. A few months later Samuel Courtney told Washington that the Boston radicals were ostracizing Grimké: "They say he too was bought and that he expects a job in Washington in return for his exchange of base." [17]

[16] Aptheker, *Documentary History*, p. 905; Meier, *Negro Thought*, pp. 215–216; Booker T. Washington to H. B. Frissell, December 30, 1904, Washington Papers; *New York Age*, March 9, 1905, p. 2; Washington to Archibald Grimké, September 20, 1904, June 5, 10, 1905, Grimké Papers; W. M. Trotter to W. E. B. Du Bois, March 26, 1905, Du Bois Papers.
This paragraph is in part conjecture: it is not clear that the "insult" was just Du Bois's failure to invite Grimké and Miller to the conference. The situation may have been exacerbated by some other breach of manners on Du Bois's part.
[17] Booker T. Washington to Emmett J. Scott, August 7, 1905, Washington Papers; W. E. B. Du Bois to Archibald Grimké and Kelly Miller, August 13, 1905, Grimké Papers; Samuel E. Courtney to Washington, December 8, 1905, Washington Papers.

The Tuskegee Machine infiltrated the Niagara Movement, tried to isolate it within the race, opposed it in a variety of ways, and all the while minimized its importance in public. Shortly after the founding conference Washington, Fortune, and Charles Anderson held a strategy meeting and agreed to keep news of the radical group out of the Negro press. And when it was mentioned, Scott later advised, loyal editors should "hammer" at the Movement. "Could you not secure a man in New York," Washington asked Anderson, "who would get right into the inner circles of the Niagara movement through the Brooklyn crowd and keep us informed as [to] their operations and plans?" "I am very anxious," the Tuskegeean wrote a friend in the District of Columbia, ". . . to know what effect, if any, the vile work which Trotter, DuBois and that gang have been doing lately . . . has had upon the colored people in Washington." [18]

Tuskegee's opposition was based on considerations both of policy and power. Washington, in a candid moment, could have agreed with virtually all the long-range goals articulated in the Niagara Declaration of Principles. He could not have agreed with the immediate means proposed: agitation, the political emphasis, the relative lack of attention to economic development, and the demand for an immediate end to all color discriminations. Further—and this was crucial—the Niagarites could not press their dissent without attacking Washington's leadership, if only by implication. In challenging his ideas, they had to challenge the man too. Consequently the Bookerites treated the Movement as an overt threat to their prestige within the race and as an assault on Washington personally. The

[18] Elliott M. Rudwick, "The Niagara Movement," *Journal of Negro History*, XLII (1957), 181; Booker T. Washington to Charles W. Anderson, December 30, 1905, Washington Papers; Washington to Whitefield McKinlay, September 1905, in Samuel R. Spencer, Jr., *Booker T. Washington and the Negro's Place in American Life* (Boston, 1955), p. 159.

"real object" of the Movement, declared the *New York Age*, is to oppose Washington. "There is nothing constructive suggested in the Niagara Movement," the *Age* complained. "Every move it makes is in the direction of tearing down some individual or some constructive force." [19]

And to prove the point Emmett Scott wrote an *Age* editorial arguing that Trotter was the Movement's "mainspring and moving spirit." The *Guardian* editor, according to Scott, "says that the Niagara Movement is the outgrowth of the Church riot. That is, he claims the two are one and inseparable, and on this basis he asks for the support and confidence of the race." The Niagara men propose nothing new, but want only "to break down the helpful influence of one member of the race. . . ." They claim to seek "free discussion of all subjects, and yet Trotter was not invited to the Columbus Avenue Church meeting, he was not on the program to speak and it was not presumed that he would speak." Reluctantly "we give to the public what we should never have divulged"—the aborted plan of the Trotterites to break up the Washington meeting in Cambridge after the riot. "This program of wrath, disorder and possibly murder" was halted only when an unnamed Negro attorney (Lewis?) burst into the final meeting of the plotters "and gave them to understand in no Sunday-School language that he had the names of every man and knew all the details of their plans. . . . At this revelation the little gang was thunderstruck and scattered in every direction; not one of them dared to show his face at the meeting. This is another sample of their bravery." If Trotter had any common sense he would, despite "his own personal dislikes and own personal mental weakness," at least not embarrass the friends who try to work with him. Trotter's followers are mostly drones who contribute nothing to the race. "They consider themselves for the most part too high to mingle with the race; too intelli-

[19] *New York Age*, August 2, 1906, p. 4.

gent and 'refined' to come into bodies where so-called common individuals are." The members of the Movement must decide between following such a man or returning to right principles. They "must now reaffirm their allegiance to Trotter and his methods or throw him overboard. There is no middle ground. They ask the race to follow them; on which platform do they ask it?" [20]

Tuskegee had backed off on its stop-Trotter campaign since the initial flurry of activity after the Boston Riot. Despite all the time and money Washington had given to the effort, Trotter and the *Guardian* seemed invulnerable. So the Bookerites confined their assault to rhetorical attacks and other more subtle techniques. For example, Anderson would proudly report from New York that "I have caused the 'Boston paper' to be removed from two other shops in this city during the past week. I am giving the matter my personal attention." Washington's friends, admirers, and sycophants in Boston kept him informed, sometimes to the Tuskegeean's confusion. Thus the reassuring news from a Boston clergyman in December 1905: "I am persuaded that the opposition spirit is waning and I believe that sentiment in favor of the general principles for which you stand is . . . gaining." But a month later Charles Alexander, still hoping for Tuskegee funds, felt it his heavy responsibility to warn that "the influence of the Guardian and of Trotter and his element, is rapidly spreading. People are beginning to think that these hotheaded fellows are right and hence they are supporting them." [21]

[20] "Trotter and Trotterism," MS with written corrections in Emmett Scott's handwriting in Box 308, Washington Papers. This editorial was probably never published in the *Age;* it does not appear in the virtually complete file of the paper for 1905 at the Schomburg Collection of the New York Public Library. The plan for a second riot had already appeared in the Washington press, in the Indianapolis *Freeman*, August 13, 1904, pp. 1, 5.

[21] Charles W. Anderson to Booker T. Washington, October 16, 1905, Henry J. Callis to Washington, December 14, 1905, Charles Alexander to Washington, January 16, 1906, Washington Papers.

The Boston Bookerites stayed on the alert and were careful to report their activities to Tuskegee. In the fall of 1905 Paul Wootton talked with the state's Republican gubernatorial candidate, Curtis Guild, before he addressed the Boston Suffrage League and "outlined to him what I wanted him to say, in which he acquiesced." ("I am very grateful to you for your visit to Mr. Curtis Guild," Washington replied; "Mr. Guild is a fine man and can be depended on to do the right and sensible thing.") In October 1905 Clifford Plummer once again infiltrated the annual meeting of the New England Suffrage League. And in January Alexander announced, a trifle prematurely, that "The backbone of the Guardian is at last broken on account of my vigorous protest." Alexander had called the *Guardian*'s attacks on Washington to the attention of the paper's printer, who then refused to do any further work for Trotter. He took his business to another printer—who was, said Alexander, less competent and more expensive—and the *Guardian*, backbone and all, survived.[22]

The divisions within Boston's Negro community surfaced late in 1905 over the celebration of the centennial of William Lloyd Garrison's birth. Trotter missed no chance to recall what he regarded as the heroic age of Negro history in America, the period of "the war of the slaveholders' rebellion." Naturally he revered Lincoln and, after him, General Benjamin F. Butler, who freed the slaves in his military district and pressed for the use of black troops and was therefore "next to President Lincoln the greatest character in the Civil War."[23] Trotter's real heroes, though, were the abolitionists, both white and black. He helped sponsor and sometimes was the main force behind affairs in Boston that honored Elijah Lovejoy, John Green-

[22] Paul L. Wootton to Booker T. Washington, September 21, 1905, Washington to Wootton, September 25, 1905, Clifford H. Plummer to Washington, September 25, 1905, Emmett J. Scott to Plummer, September 29, 30, 1905, Charles Alexander to Washington, January 25, 1906, Washington Papers.

[23] *Guardian*, April 16, 1904, p. 4, and January 4, 1908, p. 2.

leaf Whittier, Frederick Douglass, Harriet Beecher Stowe, Charles Sumner, John Brown, and Wendell Phillips. These memorials, usually consisting of speeches at Faneuil Hall, both honored the dead and reminded the living of the support white men had once given to black protest.

Garrison was the giant in Trotter's pantheon of abolitionist heroes. Prior to launching the *Guardian* he had studied Garrison's methods. A stern bust of Garrison stared down from the top of Trotter's roll-top desk. In 1907 Trotter moved the paper's office from Tremont Row to 21 Cornhill Street, where Garrison had published the *Liberator;* the *Guardian* proudly announced that it came from "Garrison's old stand." He could only have been pleased with Kelly Miller's remark in 1903 that "Mr. Trotter possesses considerable independent means, and is as uncompromising as William Lloyd Garrison." [24] In fact, the two editors shared a great deal: both were ascetic, strongly but independently religious, and immune to public disapproval. Neither was comfortable when channeling his energies into organizations. Both were intellectuals only in a broad sense of the term, and on occasion their single-minded dedication could slide over into an impenetrable self-righteousness. Both were widely regarded by the public as being humorless, intolerant, and fanatical—impressions not shared by their closest associates. Neither Trotter nor Garrison struck people as bland; both were strong, vivid, intense, and easy to worship or to hate. By turns abrasive and insufferable, and then attractive and charismatic, Trotter revered Garrison, adopted some of his tactics (the fulminating language, the protest meetings and resolutions, the financial independence and consequent poverty of his newspaper), and in his

[24] *Guardian*, December 28, 1918, p. 4, William Monroe Trotter Papers; W. M. Trotter to Freeman H. M. Murray, September 23, 1913, Freeman H. M. Murray Papers; *Guardian*, October 26, 1907, p. 4; "Fair Play" [Kelly Miller], "Washington's Policy," *Boston Evening Transcript*, September 18, 1903, p. 8.

admiration for the *Liberator* editor reflected much about himself.

Trotter felt almost a proprietary interest in Garrison's memory. Through the New England Suffrage League he organized an elaborate series of ceremonies to mark the Garrison centenary on December 10, 1905. Concurrently, the Bookerites—following a call sent out from Tuskegee on October 2—planned their own celebrations. Trotter claimed precedence, but the Washingtonians went ahead. Said the Indianapolis *Freeman*, "If the cohorts of the Boston Guardian wish to have a little one-horse Garrison celebration all by themselves no one will say them nay." But all right thinkers will take part in the Washingtonian "monster observance." The *New York Age* declared that the "crazy editor" and his "New England Suffering League" will not "hog" the occasion, but "will have to accept a share of it in common with the rest of us." A few days before the event Samuel Courtney described the situation to Washington.

> Great preparations are being made for the Garrison Celebration. Mr. Trotter tried to include every Colored man woman and child in and about Boston. He has used *every* body's name as serving on some Committee, but the majority of the names he is using without consent. Mr. Forbes was here to-day and it was really amusing to hear him talk about Mr. Trotter making a "Jim Crow" affair out of it. Trotter wrote Forbes to join them but he refused, and took occasion in his letter to remind him that the plan to celebrate was originated by you.

Trotter tried to interest Garrison's descendants, but was rebuffed. Francis Garrison told Washington that the important affairs "will be practically dissociated from the Faneuil Hall and other demonstrations which W.M.T. and his friends are engineering. I have had some plain words

with Mr. T., and there is no misunderstanding on his part
or those with him of my position." [25]

The battle over the centenary was a standoff. Trotter's
celebrants began things on the morning of December 10
by placing a wreath on Garrison's grave in Forest Hills
Cemetery. They moved on to his home in Roxbury. There
Deenie Trotter called on Negroes to make some sacrifices
for their race, just as Garrison "sacrificed himself for us."
Early in the afternoon the Trotterites assembled at the
Garrison statue on the Commonwealth Avenue mall to
hear a short address by Clement Morgan, and then recon-
vened in Faneuil Hall to hear speeches by Moorfield Storey
(once secretary to Charles Sumner and the future president of the NAACP), Albert E. Pillsbury (a nephew of
the abolitionist Parker Pillsbury), Frank Sanborn (one of
the last living abolitionists), and others. Meanwhile,
across town on Beacon Hill the Washingtonians were having their own ceremonies. At a church on Joy Street Francis Garrison spoke to an audience that included his sister
Fanny Garrison Villard and her son Oswald. That evening, in the church where the Boston Riot had taken place,
the same group met again for more oratory by Archibald
Grimké, Fanny Villard, Storey once more, and others. The
Trotterites had the last word a day later when the Niagara
Movement's spokesman, Reverdy Ransom, gave a stirring
address at Faneuil Hall. Charles Alexander followed all
these events and, with his usual perceptiveness, told Washington that "as far as I have been able to observe, absolute
harmony prevailed." [26]

[25] Indianapolis *Freeman*, October 14, 1905, p. 4, and November
11, 1905, p. 2; *New York Age*, November 25, 1905, p. 4; Samuel
E. Courtney to Booker T. Washington, December 8, 1905, Francis
J. Garrison to Washington, November 28, 1905, Washington
Papers.
[26] *The Celebration of the One Hundredth Anniversary of the
Birth of William Lloyd Garrison, By the Colored Citizens of
Greater Boston under the Auspices of the Suffrage League of
Boston and Vicinity* (Boston, 1906); *Boston Evening Transcript*,

IV

The Niagara Movement, despite harassment by Tuskegee, was making some headway. Toward the end of its first year Du Bois sent a progress report to the group's 170 members in 34 states. During that first year Niagara men had distributed over 10,000 "pamphlets, tracts, and circulars." They had worked in cooperation with local protest groups in New York, Georgia, Philadelphia, and the District of Columbia. They had agitated against a segregated exposition in Jamestown, Virginia, and against an amendment to the Hepburn railroad-rate bill which gave implied sanction to Jim Crow passenger seating. (They could not affect the exposition, but did help defeat the amendment.) The Movement's great problem was money. The Tuskegee Machine cut off most potential white sources of capital. Du Bois and others started an unofficial organ for the Movement, the *Moon*, but it expired after a few impoverished months. The *New York Age* observed, without tears, the death of "the dear, illusive Moon" and pointed out that its readers gave it no money but just "a frenzied brand of hot air, warranted to create confusion." Du Bois advised the members that only $300 of the first year's anticipated income of $850 had been received by the treasurer. On balance, though, said Du Bois, "The outlook for vigorous growth and work is excellent." [27]

They met in Harpers Ferry in August for their second annual conference. The inevitable spy for the enemy was there: Washington sent Richard T. Greener with instructions "to get on the inside." Greener, not a member of the Movement, was permitted to give one of the speeches. Du

December 11, 1905, p. 2, and December 12, 1905, p. 14; Charles Alexander to Booker T. Washington, December 11, 1905, Washington Papers.

[27] W. E. B. Du Bois to Niagara Movement members, June 13, 1906, in Box 320, Washington Papers; *New York Age*, August 2, 1906, p. 4.

Bois and Trotter again dominated the proceedings. "In the whole meeting," one of the participants recalled years later, "Du Bois insisted on having his way and had it as usual. Monroe Trotter was there snorting and gnashing." The heritage of John Brown provided the theme; Trotter presented a stick of wood from Brown's house in Springfield, Massachusetts. "We do not believe in violence," the resolutions declared, ". . . but we do believe in John Brown, in that incarnate spirit of justice, that hatred of a lie, that willingness to sacrifice money, reputation, and life itself on the altar of right. And here on the scene of John Brown's martyrdom, we reconsecrate ourselves, our honor, our property to the final emancipation of the race which John Brown died to make free."

Again the message was aimed at white America. This time there was not even a perfunctory listing of the black man's duties. "We claim for ourselves," said the Niagarites, "every single right that belongs to a freeborn American, political, civil, and social; and until we get these rights we will never cease to protest and assail the ears of America." They reelected Du Bois and Jackson to their posts and adjourned for another year. "The Niagara Movement's address is too bitter and lugubrious," the *Age* complained. "Let's have something cheerful." [28]

Tuskegee's opposition and the lack of funds were considerable problems, but as long as Trotter and Du Bois remained in rough harmony the Movement could continue. Du Bois, as general secretary, held the official authority, and Trotter, with the *Guardian*, shared the substantive influence with him. "Trotter is the real guiding power of the 'Niagara Movement,' " Kelly Miller observed, not too accurately, "for he, almost by his single hand, created the growth that made it possible. . . . DuBois ostensibly

[28] Rudwick, *Du Bois*, pp. 102–103; J. B. Watson, "Recalling 1906," *Crisis*, XLI (1934), 100; *Guardian*, August 25, 1906, pp. 1, 4, 5, 7; *Autobiography of Du Bois*, pp. 249–251; *New York Age*, August 23, 1906, p. 4.

manages the new movement, but when he dares to deviate from the inflexible intentions of Trotter, there will be war within, and victory will rest with the intrepid editor." The first sign of a breach came early in 1906 when Du Bois organized a woman's auxiliary of the Movement. It was Du Bois's own undertaking, and he appointed the wife of his old friend Clement Morgan to be the National Secretary for Women. Trotter was opposed to the admission of women (he supported woman suffrage, but one of the ways in which he was *not* a Garrisonian was his skepticism of much of the women's rights movement). In this case, though, Trotter compromised, agreed to let women in the Movement, and even permitted his wife to join. At the Harpers Ferry meeting there was another hint of friction between Trotter's Press Committee and the office of General Secretary, again resolved in Du Bois's favor. The differences were smoothed over, and after the meeting Trotter praised Du Bois in the *Guardian* as a "wise and courageous leader," "a literary genius," and an "able and intrepid race champion." [29]

More serious trouble developed that fall with a feud between Trotter and Morgan. Morgan, after Trotter the most prominent anti-Bookerite in Massachusetts, was state secretary of the Movement's local branch. He had been Trotter's attorney in the Boston Riot trials and the Forbes bankruptcy case and the two men seemed to be on the closest terms. The factions in Boston were constantly in motion, though, and Trotter evidently retained a certain wariness of Morgan. Grimké had held Morgan's respect for some time after Trotter had written him off; and in the

[29] Kelly Miller, *Race Adjustment: Essays on the Negro in America* (New York and Washington, D.C., 1908), pp. 15–16; W. E. B. Du Bois to Anna Jones, January 23, 1906, and to Niagara Movement members, February 28, 1906, Du Bois Papers; "Brief Resume of the Massachusetts Trouble in the Niagara Movement," typescript in Du Bois Papers; minutes of Harpers Ferry meetings, August 18, 1906, Du Bois Papers; *Guardian*, August 25, 1906, pp. 1, 5.

spring of 1905 a social encounter between Morgan and
George Forbes prompted Trotter to report it to Du Bois in
terms of an imminent defection ("Forbes and wife called
on the Morgans this week!!!"). In the political campaign
of 1906 Morgan supported Governor Curtis Guild for
reelection. Trotter opposed Guild because the governor
had been instrumental in persuading the legislature to vote
an appropriation for the segregated exposition at Jamestown. Morgan's support for Guild was bad enough, in
Trotter's view. He was furious when he learned that the
Republican party would nominate Morgan for a seat in the
legislature out of gratitude for his "loyalty." This violated
one of Trotter's main canons: race champions could not
seek or hold political office because their independence
would thus be curtailed. Trotter printed a Morgan speech
in the *Guardian*, setting in boldface type some unfavorable
sections that had not been so emphasized in the speech
itself—much to Morgan's annoyance. Morgan lost his election, but the battle had been joined.[30]

The following spring Du Bois tried to reconcile the two
parties. He urged the Morgans to bury their differences
with the Trotters. Morgan replied that Trotter was trying
to usurp his control of the Massachusetts branch and was
exploiting the Movement in the interests of his own personal pique. Early in June the Morgans put on a play in
Cambridge for the benefit of the Movement. The Trotters
did not attend, contending that Deenie had only been asked
to assist at a late stage, that the Forbeses had been allowed
to take part, and that the patronesses—the wives of the
mayor and the governor, among others—were objectionable. The Morgans responded that the play could not have
succeeded without the assistance of Mrs. Forbes, and that
the Trotters had done their best to thwart the whole affair.

[30] W. M. Trotter to W. E. B. Du Bois, March 26, April 22,
1905, Du Bois Papers; Rudwick, *Du Bois*, p. 111; "Resume of
Massachusetts Trouble."

The situation was becoming intolerable. In mid-June Du Bois and his family came to Boston and stayed at the Trotter home. Du Bois played the peacemaker, and things seemed to be smoothed out; Morgan agreed to put Trotter on the Committee of Arrangements for the Movement's annual meeting in Boston in August. But then the Trotters submitted a 22-page bill of particulars against Morgan and demanded that he be reprimanded. This Du Bois refused to do. Du Bois then left for a two-month trip to Europe, and in his absence Deenie Trotter resigned from the Movement.[31]

Over the summer Trotter resigned from the Committee on Arrangements, reconsidered, offered to return to the committee, and was turned down by Morgan. Du Bois, back from Europe, asked Morgan to reinstate Trotter, Morgan was agreeable, and this time Trotter declined the offer. The quarrel had become a bitter struggle for the control of the Massachusetts branch, one of the most active chapters and one that was crucial to the Movement's future. Du Bois was in an impossible position in the middle, and finally he decided to support Morgan.[32]

The Movement convened in Boston in the last week of August, with the local Bookerites observing the feud with pleasure. "There does not seem to be any enthusiasm," Peter Smith wrote to Washington. "The Trotter faction is standing idly by watching the Morgan faction which of course feels the need of just such support as the Trotter faction would under normal circumstances give it." The Trotterites appeared for the business meetings, but did nothing else for the conference. The Forbeses and Archibald Grimké took some part in the public meetings, no doubt to Trotter's annoyance. On August 29 the executive

[31] "Resume of Massachusetts Trouble." This "Resume," apparently drawn up by Du Bois, is the only source for the maneuverings in the spring of 1907. The Trotters' 22-page statement is not in the Du Bois Papers.

[32] "Resume of Massachusetts Trouble."

committee held a private session with all the principals in attendance. Morgan offered to resign, but Du Bois ruled him out of order. George W. Crawford of New Haven, chairman of the Committee on Membership, suggested that a new man "who, as far as possible, is free from factional entanglements" be named to head the Massachusetts chapter. Du Bois was then reelected general secretary, but refused to accept the post unless he could disregard Crawford's recommendation. He had done his best, said Du Bois, but he was not fit for a job that required a diplomat; he had tried to settle the Massachusetts trouble for five months, but matters had only gotten worse. If he did accept a new term, Du Bois said, his first act would be to reappoint Morgan. Trotter then charged that Forbes and Grimké had been improperly admitted to the Movement through Morgan's scheming. Du Bois, "astounded & angered" at the accusation, took it personally and declared that the admissions had been *bona fide*. In any case, Du Bois had won. He and Morgan held their posts, and Trotter was replaced—perhaps at his own insistence—as head of the Press Committee. Kelly Miller had been partly wrong: Du Bois and Trotter had clashed and Du Bois had won. The crippled movement adjourned in Boston *sine die*, and Washington happily advised an associate that the meeting had been "practically a failure." [33]

Trotter picked up some unlikely support from the Washington *Bee*. A year earlier Calvin Chase had reversed his paper's former editorial line by announcing his support of the Bookerites. And now, with the Niagara Movement falling apart, Chase spoke up for Washington's most bitter

[33] Peter J. Smith to Booker T. Washington, August 28, 1907, Washington Papers; minutes of Boston meetings, August 26, 29, 1907, Du Bois Papers; "Resume of Massachusetts Trouble"; Washington to Ralph Tyler, August 29, 1907, in Jack Abramowitz, "Accommodation and Militancy in Negro Life 1876–1916" (Ph.D. thesis, Columbia University, 1950), p. 222.

enemy. "The attempt of Secretary Du Bois to thrust upon the people of Massachusetts a man they do not want will be suicidal to his cause," said Chase. "The Bee and all honest people will stand by Editor Trotter and it will not be long before Secretary Du Bois is put out of business." Perhaps Chase was merely hoping to make the fight warmer and destroy the radicals' effectiveness. Du Bois, Chase announced, "doesn't understand the colored American and it would be better for the Niagara Movement if he resigned." [34]

Trotter did have an ally of purer motive: Mary White Ovington, a white settlement worker in New York, a socialist, and the descendant of an abolitionist. She was a sensitive and genuine friend of the Negro; the *Guardian* called her a "noble woman and a fascinating speaker." She reported on the Movement's Harpers Ferry meetings for Villard's New York *Evening Post*. During the following winter Du Bois asked her to be the first white member of the Movement. After some hesitation she replied, "If the members really want me, I shall be most glad to be one of your members." Now she watched with sorrow as personal rivalries tore the group apart. "I cared little for Mr. Trotter when you introduced him to me with such eulogy at Harper's Ferry," she wrote Du Bois, "but I have grown increasingly to admire the man. . . ." She added that Morgan, "while very pleasant, has great vanity, and that often blinds a man's judgement. How happy Washington must be over this. I can see him rubbing his hands with glee, and calling on the good work to go on." At the same time, she minimized the gravity of the split to outsiders. "It is serious to men who take part in it," she wrote to Ray Stannard Baker, "but I doubt if it has any important effect upon the Niagara movement. As Dr. Du Bois said to me,

[34] Meier, *Negro Thought*, p. 232; Washington *Bee*, September 14, 1907, p. 4.

such things are bound to come among men of pronounced individuality." [35]

But she knew it was having a lethal effect. The *Age* reported that Du Bois, Morgan, and their supporters had read the Trotterites out of the Movement. With satisfaction the *Age* observed the vindication of its prediction that the group "must eventually disintegrate from the inertia of its own ravings." William Lewis leaped into the dispute by sponsoring a banquet for Du Bois which was attended by Morgan, Forbes, Grimké, William Ferris, and other erstwhile associates of Trotter's. The *Guardian* howled a protest, but the Bookerites and the radicals sat down in friendship; "the pins are all down but one," Lewis exulted to Washington afterward.[36]

Trotter and Ferris were in another open feud. Early in October the *Guardian* charged that Ferris owed the paper $100. When Ferris joined in Lewis's dinner for Du Bois, he made his break from Trotter obvious. "Mr. Trotter wouldn't boom me in his paper no matter what I said," Ferris wrote, rather plaintively, to Deenie Trotter, and so "on the call to arms" I "cast in my lot with those who seemed to be my friends." In mid-November the *Guardian* ran a cryptic reference to "Rolling Stone pay-your-travelling-expenses out of other people's money, Weary Willie Windy, eat and lodge on your friends . . . exposing the private business of the N.M. The thing for Willie to do is to 'give up' the Guardian's stolen money like a little man." A few days earlier Ferris had written a letter to the *Age* which described Trotter as "overbearing and domineer-

[35] *Guardian*, October 26, 1907, p. 4; Mary White Ovington to W. E. B. Du Bois, April 20, 1907, Broderick notes on Du Bois Papers; Ovington to Du Bois, October 8, 1907, in Worthy, "Trotter," p. 89, and in Broderick notes on Du Bois Papers; Ovington to Ray Stannard Baker, October 17, 1907, Ray Stannard Baker Papers.
[36] *New York Age*, October 10, 1907, p. 4, and October 17, 1907, p. 4; William H. Lewis to Booker T. Washington, October 25, 1907, Washington Papers.

ing," with a "child's mind" and "many of the characteristics of an overgrown unsophisticated school boy." According to Ferris, Trotter "became notorious not through his own efforts, but through a newspaper that others had built up and through a riot that he did not plan." "It is impossible for a man with ideas and opinions of his own," said Ferris, "for a man with personality and individuality to get along with Trotter. . . . He is a good locomotive, but not a wise engineer. He is a good fighter, but a poor general." And he writes a prose that is "absolutely devoid of literary dignity." Soon Ferris was ingratiating himself with Washington. We need both conservatives and radicals, he wrote to the Tuskegeean, "the men who bring things to pass & also the men who see a vision & dream of the ideal. We don't need though such a fiery, fire-eating firebrand as Trotter." [37]

During the fall, as plans for another meeting took shape, Trotter proposed that someone other than Du Bois should preside, and further suggested that the head of the

[37] William H. Ferris to *Age*, November 11, 1907, in *New York Age*, November 14, 1907, pp. 1, 2; *Guardian*, November 16, 1907, p. 4, also quoting Ferris to Geraldine Trotter, October 31, 1907; Ferris to Booker T. Washington, December 9, 1907, Washington Papers.

Ferris was an interesting, erratic individual. A graduate of Yale, in 1903 he tried to obtain a position at Howard University through the good offices of Connecticut's Senator Orville Platt. "He is a pushing, rather aggressive colored man," Platt wrote to the president of Howard's board of trustees, "but I think he is well read, and has capability" (Orville H. Platt to Tennis S. Hamlin, February 12, 1904, and Ferris to Platt, March 27, 28, 1903, February 10, 1904, and other materials in Orville H. Platt Papers). Evidently he did not get the job and therefore—if one may take Trotter's testimony literally—spent much of his time freeloading, an embarrassing illustration of the classically educated, unemployed Negro Washington was always denigrating. For an apparent reference to Ferris in these terms, see Washington, *My Larger Education: Being Chapters From My Experience* (New York, 1911), p. 114. In 1913 Ferris published his magnum opus, *The African Abroad*, in two ponderous volumes, a chaotically organized mass of material with some significant details and insights. In the 1920s he was a Garveyite of some prominence.

Massachusetts branch should be elected by the local members instead of being appointed by the general secretary. Both ideas were evidently rejected by Du Bois and Morgan. At midwinter the executive committee of the splintered Movement held a conference in Cleveland. Trotter, Du Bois, and Morgan were not present. In their absence the committee could only decide to send letters to the principals urging them to bury their personal differences in the greater interest of the cause. It was too late in any case. Trotter was through with the Niagara Movement.[38]

V

Just before the New Year Bishop Alexander Walters of the African Methodist Episcopal Zion Church came to Boston to address the Boston Literary. One of the most prominent black clergymen, he had been president of the Afro-American Council for most of the time since 1898. He was a free spirit within the politics of the race, going through endless, perplexing shifts from one camp to another, charged by his own thirst for a leadership role and a whimsical lack of convictions. The Niagarites had taken control of his Council from the Bookerites, but in so doing purged the Council of its effective core of members: thus it was a sterile coup. "Will the Afro-American Council absorb the Niagara Movement," the Indianapolis *Freeman* had wondered, "—or be absorbed by it?" The Movement won the struggle, after a fashion, and left Walters without a mooring. So in Boston Walters conferred with Trotter, also recently bereft of an organization. Joining in the discussions was William H. Scott, an elderly minister and one of Trotter's most reliable supporters, then serving as president of the Boston Suffrage League. The three men sent out a call for a race conference in Philadelphia in

[38] Clement G. Morgan to W. E. B. Du Bois, November 13, 1907, Du Bois Papers; note on meeting of Niagara executive committee, midwinter 1907–1908, Broderick notes on Du Bois Papers; Cleveland *Gazette*, January 4, 1908, p. 1.

April. "We must council together," the *Guardian* urged in
March, "meditate, pray that out of this seeming serfdom,
we shall be able at last to grasp our freedom and liberty.
. . ." But, Trotter cautioned two weeks later, "Race traitors, spies and stool-pigeons are not wanted nor will such
as are known to be of that class be admitted." [39]

Meanwhile Walters, unpredictable as ever, joined the
District of Columbia branch of the Niagara Movement and
invited Du Bois to the Philadelphia conference. Over the
objections of Trotter and Scott, Walters offered to pay Du
Bois's traveling expenses from Atlanta to Philadelphia. Du
Bois was undecided. Early in April Walters advised him
that Trotter was all but impossible to work with (which,
Du Bois must have thought, was hardly news). Du Bois
then decided not to come, pleading his heavy work load in
Atlanta and his fear that his presence would only stir up
trouble with Trotter, who—said Du Bois—could not function well unless he dominated the proceedings. [40]

Which he intended to do as chairman of the two-day
meeting held in a church on April 7–8. Passing on the
credentials of those in attendance, he only reluctantly admitted Archibald Grimké. Others were barred entirely.
Presidential politics hung over the affair. Trotter would
admit no one who did not declare his irreconcilable opposition to President Roosevelt and his apparent successor,
Secretary of War Taft. Calvin Chase, Bookerite that he
was, stayed loyal to the Republican administration and was
turned away; he and five others held a rump meeting in the
church basement and issued a dissenting manifesto. Up-
stairs the anti-Roosevelt radicals launched the Negro-
American Political League. They elected a president, J.

[39] Meier, *Negro Thought*, pp. 218, 180–181; Indianapolis *Free-
man*, August 31, 1907, p. 3; *Guardian:* January 4, 1908, pp. 1, 4;
March 7, 1908, p. 4; March 21, 1908, p. 4.
[40] Rudwick, *Du Bois*, p. 114; Alexander Walters to W. E. B. Du
Bois, March 28, April 4, 1908, and Du Bois to Walters, March 31,
April 7, 1908, Broderick notes on Du Bois Papers.

Milton Waldron, a minister from Washington. (According to the Indianpolis *Freeman*, Walters had expected the presidency and was greatly annoyed at Waldron's election.) Trotter had himself designated the corresponding secretary. From this lowly post he would control the organization.

He took a few initial liberties. The *Guardian* claimed an attendance of 200, while Chase, still angry, said that there were only 40 present and that the meeting was "the greatest farce that has ever been attempted by Negroes." Trotter published a list of associated members, including Du Bois, F. L. McGhee, and James Hayes—all of whom were prominently absent from Philadelphia. But Trotter called it "a complete, an astonishing success" and said that "it was God's work." J. Max Barber of Atlanta, an editor of the *Voice of the Negro* and a prominent member of the Niagara Movement, read an Address to the Country at the final session. It called for the routing out of the national Republicans and ticked off the usual radical program. Its peroration, probably the work of Trotter, was an echo of Garrison's promise in the first issue of the *Liberator:* "We want all that belongs to full-fledged American citizens. We are in earnest. We cannot be bulldozed. We cannot be bought off. And under God, we will be heard!" [41]

"There was just a handful of them, under the leadership of Trotter and Bishop Walters," the *Age* commented, "but from the noise they made one would have suspected that they were many, and that they really did represent something besides ego and wind." [42]

VI

With Trotter's departure Du Bois hoped to pick up the Movement and keep it going. "I am glad you like the

[41] Washington *Bee*, April 11, 1908, pp. 1, 4; Indianapolis *Freeman*, April 18, 1908, p. 1, and June 13, 1908, p. 1; Cleveland *Gazette*, April 18, 1908, p. 1; *Guardian*, April 11, 1908, pp. 1, 4, 5, and August 1, 1908, p. 4.
[42] *New York Age*, April 16, 1908, p. 4.

Niagara men," he wrote a Negro in Cleveland early in
1908, "they are a fine set of fellows if we can only keep
them together and keep them working. I very much want
to start a branch in Cleveland, and shall write you further
about it later." [43] But without Trotter and the *Guardian*
Du Bois could not make it go. The group held two more
annual meetings, neither of much consequence, and it had
practically ceased to exist by 1910, when Du Bois urged
its members to join the fledgling NAACP. The group's
effective life was no longer than three years.

There were several reasons for its quick decline: Washington's spirited opposition, chronic financial difficulties,
the lack of a formal national headquarters or regular paid
staff. The Movement articulated a strident protest viewpoint that, for one reason or another, many blacks and
almost all whites were not ready to embrace. In the South,
where 90 per cent of American Negroes lived, its activities
were essentially limited to Atlanta. Anywhere else in the
South was unrewarding and sometimes dangerous territory for a Niagara member: Byron Gunner, a black minister from Rhode Island and later New York, held a pastorate for a time in South Carolina, but reported to Du Bois
late in 1907 that "I could do but little for our N.M. while
in Columbia. The field for our kind of service was particularly difficult in Columbia." Moreover, the Movement was
distinguished by a rather elitist approach. Du Bois insisted
on the "very best class" of black men, "thoughtful" and
"dignified" Negroes only. A prospective member had to
submit an application to his state's secretary; the state
committee would pass judgment and send the application
to the national executive committee; if final approval was
granted, the applicant could then pay his admission fee and
consider himself a member. This extended procedure was
necessary to keep the group from being riddled with
Washington's spies. But it helped make the Movement, as

[43] W. E. B. Du Bois to E. C. Williams, January 11, 1908, Joel
E. Spingarn Papers.

Ferris observed, "a cult instead of a crusade." [44]

Beyond these logistics was the personal collision of Du Bois and Trotter, which Reverdy Ransom remembered as being "chiefly responsible for the dissolution of the Niagara Movement." It was essentially a matter of personalities, not of programs. As Trotter recalled it in a letter to a friend in 1914:

> You will remember that when I, with reason, considered the Niagara Movement as to it's leadership "mean," "tricky," "petty" & worse, I said but little against it in The Guardian, in fact made no Guardian attack against it. And I did this because . . . Dubois, even though he had sought & was seeking my life, or head, was advocating right principles, and because some of our accepted men were in the N.M., also because I did not want to show up the division of the race men. On the other hand, I worked at the proposition of building up a sincere, honest, race organization.

After he started his "sincere, honest" Negro-American Political League, Trotter wrote off "Du Bois and his crowd" as "self seekers," and the two men never tried to work together again. [45]

[44] Rudwick, "The Niagara Movement," p. 180; Byron Gunner to W. E. B. Du Bois, November 15, 1907, Du Bois Papers (Gunner had earlier been forced to leave a pastorate in New Iberia, Louisiana, under pressure from whites who objected to his militant statements: see Silas Jones to editor, September 28, 1905, in *New York Age*, October 5, 1905, p. 4); *Guardian*, August 10, 1907, p. 4; William H. Ferris, *The African Abroad: or His Evolution in Western Civilization; Tracing His Development Under Caucasian Milieux* (2 vols., New Haven, 1913), II, 912.

[45] Reverdy C. Ransom, *The Pilgrimage of Harriet Ransom's Son* (Nashville, Tenn., n.d.), p. 164; W. M. Trotter to Freeman H. M. Murray, January 6, 1914, Murray Papers; Trotter to William H. Scott, April 23, 1908, William Monroe Trotter folder, Moorland Room, Howard University.

CHAPTER IV

Interracial Organization: The NAACP

T HE NIAGARA MOVEMENT succumbed to
internal bickerings, leaving two legacies not readily
apparent at its demise: its catalytic role in the shift of the
consensus of black thought from the Bookerite orthodoxy
of 1900 to a return to the protest tradition, and its effect on
the handful of white men and women who would launch
the National Association for the Advancement of Colored
People in 1909.

Trotter's relations with the new NAACP were foreshad-
owed by the nature of his prior contacts with whites over
issues of racial leadership. From 1903 on Trotter spent
more time within the race and less time making forays into
white America. Nonetheless he recognized that white sympathy was crucial to his integrationist program, and to
some extent he tried to communicate with whites. Thus in
the spring of 1905 he asked Du Bois for the names of
white people in New York and New England who might be
open to the radical argument. And he made an effort to

keep up his contacts in white Boston. For example, he would attend the meetings of the Twentieth Century Club, an organization of civic-minded progressives which met for lectures and dinners in a clubhouse on Beacon Hill. At one of these affairs he sat beside Edward Clement, editor of the *Boston Evening Transcript*. As Trotter reported the conversation to Du Bois, Clement "said he told Booker I was a first class man and B. agreed with him, said he sympathized with me in my contest but that I was 'all wrong politically.' " Trotter, a little amused, advised Du Bois that "Clement *means* well." [1]

I

Actually many white progressives did, by their own lights, *mean* well when they dealt with what they generally called "the negro problem." Certainly they were not unaware that the country had its racial difficulties. Even Woodrow Wilson, who for the most part represented progressive racial opinion at its worst, could confide to Oswald Garrison Villard in 1913 that "I say it with shame and humiliation, with shame and humiliation, but I have thought about this thing for twenty years and I see no way out." Progressive magazines of the era were littered with earnest, baffled discussions of the issue. By 1910, in fact, one progressive journal had concluded that "Both races and the whole country have become weary of the 'problem.' Unnecessary discussion has gone on a long time and it has buttered no parsnips." [2]

Part of it was simple exhaustion: it seemed that the

[1] W. M. Trotter to W. E. B. Du Bois, April 1, May 15, 1905, W. E. B. Du Bois Papers. On the club, see *The Twentieth Century Club of Boston: The Record of Twenty Years* (Boston, 1914). Trotter was not a formal member.

[2] Oswald Garrison Villard, *Fighting Years: Memoirs of a Liberal Editor* (New York, 1939), p. 240; *World's Work*, XVII (1908–1909), 11421. For a general discussion, see Dewey W. Grantham, Jr., "The Progressive Movement and the Negro," *South Atlantic Quarterly*, LIV (1955), 461–477.

problem had been around for a long time, with little obvious progress in racial harmony or in the Negro's position. Further, white progressives generally agreed that Reconstruction after the Civil War had been botched and that the experiment should not be repeated. "The North has too long regarded the South as missionary ground," said the *Outlook*, an organ of moderate progressivism. "Too many Northerners have gone South as propagandists of Northern ideas." [3] So, the progressive consensus ran, the South should be left alone to work out its peculiar problem, and any other course would only revive sectional animosities and divide the nation.

In any case, it seemed that the black man was not innately equal to the white man. Most anthropologists and sociologists of the day—with significant dissents from Franz Boas and a few others—applied Social Darwinist tests to the question of racial equality and found Negroes wanting. A typical study announced in 1910 that "The Negro reveals himself a mass of physiological reactions and reflexes. His whole being is volatile, without continuous or stable form, easily disturbed, as easily quieted." Practically all whites could agree that the Negro was different and in some sense inferior. "I entirely agree with you," Theodore Roosevelt wrote to the novelist Owen Wister, "that as a race and in the mass they are altogether inferior to the whites." Most other white progressives echoed Roosevelt, often with a more vicious tone. [4]

With the political difficulties and this scientifically approved racism as primary considerations, most progressives reacted to the race problem with a fastidious concern for law and orderly process which prompted them to condemn southern white demagogues and lynch mobs on one

[3] *Outlook*, LXXIII (1903), 609.
[4] Howard W. Odum, *Social and Mental Traits of the Negro* (New York, 1910), p. 239; Theodore Roosevelt to Owen Wister, April 27, 1906, in Elting E. Morison, ed., *The Letters of Theodore Roosevelt* (8 vols., Cambridge, Mass., 1951–54), III, 190.

hand and northern black agitators on the other. Since
progressives generally were themselves racists, they could
hardly recognize racism as the key to the problem. Instead
they pointed to the problem of law enforcement, or the
durability of southern white folkways, or the Negro's laziness and immorality.[5]

For all these reasons the white progressives embraced
Washington's race program: stressing education, work,
and material advancement, it was peaceful, gradual, and
inoffensive to all but the more rabid southern race-baiters.
By 1910 white approval of Washington, as a white observer not friendly to Tuskegee noted, was "nearly universal in the North." And for that reason, along with the
general limitations of their analysis, Trotter could not
tolerate most white progressives when they spoke out on
racial matters. Lyman Abbott, editor of the *Outlook*, was
one of Tuskegee's most influential supporters, and Trotter
called him "a fool, a knave or a deliberate falsifier" and
"one of the most dangerous enemies of the Negro because
of his intellectual rating and his claim to be a friend of the
Negro." He was equally caustic about other progressive
"experts" on the racial situation.[6]

His relations with the Garrison-Villard family of Boston
and New York illustrated his troubles in getting along
with well-intended whites (and, incidentally, his larger
problem of subordinating his ego sufficiently to admit mistakes and remain on good terms with *anyone* whom he did
not control). The Trotters and the Garrisons had known
each other for a long time—since 1863, when James Trot-

[5] For an expression of the characteristic progressive concern for
law enforcement as a solution to the race problem, see Oswald
Garrison Villard to Booker T. Washington, August 25, 1908,
Oswald Garrison Villard Papers; for a remarkable—and solitary—
dissent on the role of white racism, see Quincy Ewing, "The Heart
of the Race Problem," *Atlantic Monthly*, CIII (1909), 389–397.

[6] William English Walling, "Science and Human Brotherhood,"
Independent, LXVI (1909), 1318; *Guardian*, February 27, 1904,
p. 4.

ter came to Boston and was introduced to the abolitionist family. After that the two families, while apparently never very close, had occasional contact with each other. Thus, for instance, James Trotter sought the aid of George and Francis Garrison when he was compiling his book on Negro musicians. His son presided over a temperance society at Harvard which included another Garrison. Oswald Garrison Villard assisted in a history course Trotter took in his senior year. The families were on cordial terms, respecting each other without knowing each other well. Then Trotter embarked on his career with the *Guardian*. The Garrisons and Villard admired Washington, at least until around 1909, and the Tuskegeean was occasionally a house guest at Francis Garrison's home in Lexington. The *Guardian* no doubt cooled relations, and the Boston Riot drove the final wedge between the families. Late in 1904 Francis Garrison told his nephew Villard that he was "disgusted with Trotter's course" and that Tuskegee need not worry about "this little clique of Boston colored men" because "the public at large have taken Trotter at his real value ever since his disgraceful part in trying to break up the Booker Washington meeting last year." Villard quite agreed and—though he was less than a month older than Trotter—advised Du Bois that he considered "young Trotter" to be "a very dangerous, almost irresponsible, young man, whose conduct at the Boston riot should make it impossible for anyone to consider seriously his opinions upon any subject relating to his race." In the dispute over the Garrison centenary in the fall of 1905 the Garrisons refused Trotter's requests for assistance.[7]

Two years later a reconciliation seemed possible when William Lloyd Garrison, Jr., spoke at Faneuil Hall as part

[7] James M. Trotter to Francis and George Garrison, May 28, 1877, Garrison Family Papers; Francis J. Garrison to Oswald Garrison Villard, December 23, 1904, and Villard to W. E. B. Du Bois, April 18, 1905, Villard Papers.

of Trotter's program celebrating the seventieth anniversary of the martyrdom of the abolitionist Elijah Lovejoy.
At the meeting Garrison delivered a vigorous brief for the
importance of voting. Trotter, delighted, printed the statement in the *Guardian* next to one of Washington's
shuffling deprecations of political activity. The Garrisons
were at once annoyed by Trotter's intended implication
that they disagreed with the Tuskegeean on politics. Francis Garrison assured Washington of the family's undiminished respect and added that Trotter was "a yellow journalist of the most unscrupulous sort, and an unmitigated
nuisance." William Garrison sent a "very plainspoken"
letter of protest to the *Guardian* which Trotter, in a mixture of obstinacy and pride, refused to print. A week later
Trotter did announce in the paper that he had not meant to
suggest anything about Garrison's attitude toward Washington, but that "The comparison of their public preach-
ments stands for the perusal and judgment of our readers." With that, William Garrison took his case to the
general public in a letter to the *Boston Evening Transcript*. Without mentioning Trotter or the *Guardian* by
name, Garrison recounted the whole episode and praised
Washington as "the most remarkable living American,
black or white." On the other hand, wrote Garrison, there
were some Negroes, "colored men with academic advantages, secure in the strong-hold of anti-slavery sentiment"
who "affect disdain and indulge in bitter speech." Villard
read this letter "with interest" and wrote his uncle Frank,
"Trotter must be unbalanced. It is a terrible pity that
DuBois lends his name to that crowd." [8]

[8] *Guardian*, November 9, 1907, p. 1; Francis J. Garrison to
Booker T. Washington, December 30, 1907, Booker T. Washington Papers; *Guardian*, January 11, 1908, p. 4; William Lloyd
Garrison, Jr., to the editor, in *Boston Evening Transcript*, January
13, 1908, p. 11; Oswald Garrison Villard to Francis J. Garrison,
January 15, 1908, Villard Papers. On January 21 Trotter sent a
long rebuttal that the *Transcript* in turn declined to print (quoted
in *Guardian*, February 1, 1908, p. 4).

II

In general, whites who took an interest in the Negro in the progressive era were Bookerites, but there were some important exceptions. Trotter could admire an occasional maverick such as Joseph C. Manning of Alabama, an historical oddity, an unreformed Populist egalitarian who wrote and lectured all over the country on the plight of the southern Negro and the need for agitation. By the second decade of the twentieth century, Manning—whom Trotter called the "Garrison of the South"—was practically *sui generis*. Other whites who were amenable to ideas of racial militancy fell into two broad groups. To a remarkable extent, individuals in both groups had abolitionists somewhere in their families or backgrounds.[9]

One group consisted of politically active democratic socialists such as Mary White Ovington, William English Walling, and Charles Edward Russell. All three were involved in the early years of the NAACP. Ovington in particular had been a close student of the Niagara Movement. This group came to racial militancy through the abolitionist heritage and their gently radical economic views, and they saw the race problem at least in part as a class issue and as an aspect of the failings of American capitalism.[10]

The second group, like Joseph Manning something of an historical anachronism, was distinguished by its vigorous Lincoln-style Republicanism and conservative Protes-

[9] On Manning, see *Guardian*, August 10, 1907, p. 1, and Philip J. Allston to Booker T. Washington, May 9, 1911, Washington Papers; on the abolitionist tradition into the twentieth century, see James M. McPherson, "The Antislavery Legacy: From Reconstruction to the NAACP," in Barton J. Bernstein, ed., *Towards a New Past: Dissenting Essays in American History* (New York, 1968), pp. 126–157.

[10] See Mary White Ovington, *The Walls Came Tumbling Down* (New York, 1947); the sketch of Walling in *Dictionary of American Biography: Supplement Two* (New York, 1958), XXII, 689–690; Charles Edward Russell, *Bare Hands and Stone Walls: Some Recollections of a Side-Line Reformer* (New York, 1933).

tant faith. This breed, with its old-style evangelical Christianity, recaptured some of the religious immediatism of the abolitionists. William Hayes Ward of New York, for example, was a Congregational minister and editor of the *Independent*, a progressive journal that published articles by Du Bois, Walling, and other anti-Bookerites. "I was brought up among abolitionists," Ward wrote a Negro acquaintance in 1896, "and the fire still burns; and I regret to see that there are so many who forget that the great work which abolition began to do is yet unfinished." In Boston William D. Brigham, also a Congregationalist and a self-defined "ardent Republican," supported Trotter and the *Guardian* and was apparently the only white man ever to serve as an officer of Trotter's National Equal Rights League. In Congress this breed was represented most prominently by Senator Joseph Benson Foraker of Ohio, a conservative Republican and one of the last Civil War veterans in public life.[11]

The most striking figure in this second group was John E. Milholland of New York, who described himself as a Republican of the "intensive kind." A successful journalist and businessman, he had a vivid personality driven by explosive energies and great enthusiasm—"excitable at all times," Villard remarked, "and sometimes goes off half-cocked." He had the progressive's faith in the inexorable triumph of popular wisdom. "The great heart of the people is sound in the fundamentals of representative government & human rights," he reflected, "but it needs to be aroused; the public conscience must be quickened." Especially on

[11] For general identification of this breed I am indebted to Brian W. Blaesser, "John E. Milholland" (senior honors thesis, Brown University, 1969), especially pp. 12–14, 31, 86, 159–161; and see William Hayes Ward to Francis J. Grimké, March 24, 1896, in Carter G. Woodson, ed., *Works of Francis J. Grimké* (4 vols., Washington, D.C., 1942), IV, 49; W. I. Tyler Brigham, *The History of the Brigham Family* (New York, 1907), p. 465; Joseph Benson Foraker, *Notes of a Busy Life* (2 vols., Cincinnati, 1916), especially II, 326, 378, 392, 404, 512.

the race issue. Drawing on his militant Republicanism, the "crisis-paternalism" of his Presbyterian faith, and contacts with Negro leaders in New York in the 1890s, he developed an extraordinary commitment to working for racial democracy. "I feel that my time has come at last," he scribbled in his diary in 1906, "—to lead . . . this Crusade for the Negro's Political & Civil Rights . . . the Supreme Moral Issue of the Hour in this Republic." [12]

At first his concern had led him to cooperate with Washington. For a few years he supported Tuskegee, but grew increasingly impatient with the Bookerite program. "You will pardon me for saying it," he wrote Washington early in 1905, "the most enlightened sentiment is not reflected in the course that you have marked out. . . ." In the summer of 1905 he and Villard were to give speeches at the annual meeting of Washington's National Negro Business League. Before his speech an aide to Washington drew Milholland aside and asked him not to mention disfranchisement in his talk. He was "indignant" at this interference. That fall he made plans to form an interracial protest group that he had been thinking about for several years. Washington's friends kept him informed on the new heresy. Charles Anderson of New York reported, "The only significant thing about it is, that they have all been dickering with Trotter. . . . These men may be able to give Trotter some money, and thereby keep that old paper alive. This is the only danger I can see." On December 10 Milholland and Washington had a long talk over the suffrage issue and other matters, but "we separated without finding common ground to go forward with the proposed mass meeting. . . ." [13]

[12] Blaesser, "Milholland," pp. 12–14, 20–21, 31; Oswald Garrison Villard to Francis J. Garrison, March 20, 1911, Villard Papers; Diary of John E. Milholland, December 31, 1906, and 1906 volume, n.d., p. 242, in John E. Milholland Papers.

[13] John E. Milholland to Booker T. Washington, January 17, 1905, in Blaesser, "Milholland," p. 45; see also *ibid.*, pp. 42–45,

The meeting was held early in February 1906, as several thousand people filled Cooper Union in New York to witness the official launching of the Constitution League. Trotter and three associates came down from Boston for the occasion; they carried a large banner down the main aisle of the hall and were invited up to the platform. Trotter, Milholland later noted, "showed great enterprise in publishing a full report of the meeting coming all the way from Boston & returning that night to get his paper out nearly a week ahead of his rival 'The Age.'" The speeches, all in the protest vein, came from an impressive variety of race spokesmen: Du Bois, Kelly Miller, Archibald Grimké, Mary Church Terrell of Washington, D.C., William Sinclair of Philadelphia, and others. Milholland thought it was "the greatest event in my life and, I am persuaded, among the most significant in American politics." And "This meeting has shaken my faith in Booker T. Washington to the very foundations" because of his "trying to spread 'Tuskegee' over the entire question. . . ." The Bookerites could not influence the radical platform, however. "Fortune of 'The Age' sulked and other henchmen like Anderson secretly worked against it but the current was too strong for their puny efforts." [14]

The new League cooperated fully with the Niagara Movement; even after the split between Du Bois and Trotter, Milholland stayed on good terms with both factions. The League and the Movement both stressed citizenship rights, especially voting, and were considered to be anti-Bookerite. There were also important differences between the groups: the League was interracial from the start, was actually dominated by Milholland, and did not address itself to economic discriminations and specific indignities

---

47–54; Milholland Diary, August 16, 17, 1905; Charles W. Anderson to Booker T. Washington, September 27, 1905, Washington Papers; Milholland Diary, December 19, 1905.

[14] *New York Age*, February 8, 1906, pp. 1, 2; Milholland Diary, 1906 volume, n.d., pp. 17, 5, 18, 9–10.

as did the Movement. Still, members of the two organizations worked together with remarkable harmony. They spoke at each other's meetings and some individuals belonged to both groups at once. Trotter, in fact, merged a branch of the League with his own local group and presided over the New England Constitution and Suffrage League for several years. Trotter seemed to trust Milholland as much as he could trust any white man. "In all our experience," Trotter wrote of Milholland, "we have found almost no white American as active in and intimate with the Colored people's struggle for equal citizenship in this Republic. . . . He is an incessant fighter for our cause." [15]

Milholland's group shared the Niagara Movement's principles and, unhappily, its problems as well, notably poverty and the opposition of Tuskegee. "I don't think he cares a fig for either the Negro or the suffrage question," Anderson said of Milholland. "He is trying to rescue himself from approaching oblivion." When the Constitution League protested the Roosevelt administration's discharge of the Brownsville soldiers, Washington tried to hurt Milholland financially by advising the Postmaster General that he was "practically all there is to the Constitution League. He uses that name to hide his own personal identity." (Milholland's pneumatic-tube business depended on extensive contracts with the Post Office.) The *New York Age* charged that the League gave a substantial subsidy to the *Guardian*—an intended smear that would hamper the League's appeal to white men. Milholland, beleagured but dogged, kept his group going, pouring his own small fortune into the effort. In March 1909 he took William

[15] Blaesser, "Milholland," pp. 66–70; John E. Milholland to W. E. B. Du Bois, March 21, May 9, 1906, May 9, 1907, Du Bois to Niagara Movement members, February 28, 1906, A. B. Humphrey to Du Bois, April 25, 1907, and Du Bois to Humphrey, May 2, 1907, all in Du Bois Papers; *Guardian:* November 23, 1907, p. 2; January 4, 1908, p. 4; January 11, 1908, pp. 2, 4; February 8, 1908, p. 3; March 25, 1911, p. 4.

English Walling out for an automobile ride and a discussion of the racial situation. "He seems to be the man I want
for Secy of League," Milholland wrote in his diary, ". . .
but we shall see—alas!—what we shall see." [16]

By the spring of 1909 both the Niagara Movement and
the Constitution League were losing momentum. Just at
that point a new group arose, borrowed ideas and person-
nel from the League and the Movement, and forged the
beginnings of a powerful new coalition of black radicals
and white socialists and neo-abolitionists.

III

The sequence of events leading to the new coalition had
begun the previous summer with a race riot in Abraham
Lincoln's home town, Springfield, Illinois. Walling wrote
an angry report of the riot in Ward's *Independent* and
called for a "large and powerful body of citizens" to come
to the black man's aid. Mary White Ovington read the
article and met with Walling and a few others in New
York in the winter of 1909. They roughed out some plans
and asked Villard to send out an appeal to be released on
the centennial of Lincoln's birth. Villard responded with a
call for a conference that reflected his own growing militancy. The call was signed by over fifty whites and seven
blacks, Trotter not among them; since Villard drafted the
call, Trotter presumably was not asked to join in the
appeal. Washington also was not among the signers. At
the last minute Villard invited Washington to the conference itself, but left him the option of a graceful refusal,
which Washington took.[17]

[16] Charles W. Anderson to Booker T. Washington, October 3,
1905, and also Anderson to Washington, March 6, 23, 1906,
Washington Papers; Washington to George S. Cortelyou, January
28, 1907, in Blaesser, "Milholland," p. 93; *New York Age*, April
16, 1908, p. 4; Milholland Diary, March 20, 1909.
[17] William English Walling, "The Race War in the North,"
Independent, LXV (1908), 529–534; Charles Flint Kellogg,
NAACP: A History of the National Association for the Advance-

Whether invited or not, Trotter went to New York for the conference at the end of May. The meeting consisted of an expertly organized series of symposia. On the morning of May 31 there were speeches by five whites, with a keynote address by Ward; in the afternoon came speeches by two more whites and by two Negroes, Du Bois and William Bulkley, a New York high school principal. Afterward comments were invited from the audience, and Trotter seized his chance. "The grossest calamity," he declared, ". . . the grossest outrage, seems to me the attitude of the federal government, which is guilty of standing in the position of giving its authority to color proscription." President Taft's recent statement on black suffrage, said Trotter, "reads to me like a justification of colored disfranchisement" and was "the most insidious and skilful, and therefore the most dangerous attitude ever taken by a President." Trotter also rebutted someone's earlier suggestion that there was too much racial agitation, and then sat down. Charles Edward Russell agreed that there had not been enough agitation. J. Max Barber of the Niagara Movement agreed with Trotter's emphasis on voting. The Chicago radical Ida Wells-Barnett and others gave their responses. The first day's sessions ended. They were informative and good-tempered, and the two races seemed to be willing to listen to each other.[18]

On the second day that interracial good will evaporated. In the evening the floor debates over the conference resolutions were loud and bitter, as Villard and Walling tried to maintain order from the chair. According to Du Bois's later report on those evening sessions, "The black mass moved forward and stretched out their own hands to take charge.

ment of Colored People, Volume I 1909–1920 (Baltimore, 1967), pp. 11–15, 297–299; Oswald Garrison Villard to Booker T. Washington, May 26, 1909, and Washington to Villard, May 28, 1909, Villard Papers.

[18] [William English Walling, ed.], *Proceedings of the National Negro Conference 1909* (New York, 1909), pp. 9–116.

It was their problem. They must name the condition."
Villard, in a letter a few days later to Francis Garrison,
saw things differently:

> All of the speeches from the floor were by colored
> people—how they do love to talk!—and hardly one
> was relevant, while not one contributed anything of
> value. . . . After the Resolutions were introduced we
> had a very hard time and the colored men wrangled
> for an hour over them, the Rev. J. M. Waldron and
> Trotter behaving very badly, speaking incessantly,
> and making the most trivial changes in the language,
> always with a nasty spirit. Trotter was really unbear-
> able and I took great pleasure in telling him so at the
> end of the evening. A good many of the others came
> up and apologized afterwards for the conduct of these
> two men and asked us not to consider them repre-
> sentatives of the race. Their attitude was one of open
> suspicion, ill-concealed hostility, and open charges
> that the whole proceeding was rigged up in advance
> —which naturally it had to be—so that at one time,
> when we seemed to be making no headway whatever,
> I seriously considered with Walling, withdrawing the
> whole scheme of a National Committee and doing it
> ourselves as we saw fit. . . . I suppose we ought
> really not to blame these poor people who have been
> tricked so often by white men, for being suspicious,
> but the exhibition was none the less trying.[19]

Trotter asked that the phrase "segregated by common
carriers" be added to the list of Negro grievances, and in
this case Villard was amenable. The revised statement
read, "Often plundered of their just share of the public
funds, robbed of nearly all part in the government, segregated by common carriers, some murdered with impunity,

[19] W. E. Burghardt Du Bois, "The National Committee on the
Negro," *Survey*, XXII (1909), 408; Oswald Garrison Villard to
Francis J. Garrison, June 4, 1909, Villard Papers.

and all treated with open contempt by officials, they are held in some States in practical slavery to the white community." That was manly. Trotter wanted to add a plea that lynching be made a federal crime. The committee on resolutions replied that lynching was covered by the "murdered with impunity" clause, and Trotter's proposal lost by a floor vote of 53–21. Trotter requested a blanket condemnation of President Taft. The final resolutions equivocated: "We deplore any recognition of, or concession to, prejudice or color by the federal government in any officer or branch thereof, as well as the presidential declaration on the appointment of colored men to office in the South, contradicting as it does the President's just and admirable utterance against the proposed disfranchisement of the colored voters of Maryland." But the core of the resolutions was militant enough: insistence on the Fourteenth Amendment to guarantee the Negro his civil rights, on the Fifteenth Amendment to ensure the right to vote, and for "equal educational opportunities for all and in all the States." These were demanded of Congress and the President.[20]

The conference organizers appointed a Committee of Forty, including about a dozen Negroes, to form a permanent organization. The Committee's membership was crucial. Washington was not on it, but neither was Trotter, Waldron, or Wells-Barnett. "It is impossible," said Walling, "that twelve colored members could thoroughly represent all the ideas, sentiments, standpoints, and organizations which ought to receive a constant hearing inside of our Committee." Eventually Waldron and Wells-Barnett were added, but Trotter was not.[21]

He went back to Boston, piqued at being left off the Committee and less than satisfied with the resolutions. During the next year he at one point urged the Committee

[20] *Proceedings of the National Negro Conference*, pp. 222–225.
[21] Kellogg, *NAACP*, pp. 22, 29–30; William English Walling to W. E. B. Du Bois, June 8, 1909, in *ibid.*, p. 30.

to take action against a series of racist articles appearing in
Pearson's Magazine, but for the most part ignored the new
group. This was fine with Villard. He spoke with Washington "at some length and in good spirit" about the
Committee. "He is obviously not willing to commit himself," Villard noted, "until he is sure that Trotter and
DuBois do not control the whole thing, but I do not think
after this talk that he will be actively hostile." [22]

After a year the Committee met again in New York and
took on an unwieldy new name, the National Association
for the Advancement of Colored People. Trotter stayed at
home, and his absence from the militant conference was
noted. "What in the world has Mr. Trotter done?" asked
the Washington *Bee*. "Is he too radical, or is he too
conservative? Is he moving too fast or too slowly?" Essentially he was merely skeptical of such a white-dominated
group. The new slate of officers consisted of Moorfield
Storey, national president; Walling, chairman of the executive committee; Milholland, treasurer; Villard, disbursing
treasurer; and—the only Negro—Du Bois, director of pub-
lications and research. Villard gave the Association office
space at his *Evening Post*, and Du Bois came up from
Atlanta to start publishing a monthly magazine, the *Crisis*.
Neither Villard nor Du Bois, the two most forceful personalities among the leaders, regretted the absence of the
Guardian editor. Said Villard that summer, "I should not
want to back Trotter in anything." [23]

IV

Other NAACP officers were more kindly disposed toward Trotter and hoped to attract his support for the new

[22] Minutes of Board of Directors Meetings, April 21, 1910,
NAACP Papers; Oswald Garrison Villard to Francis J. Garrison,
November 15, 1909, Villard Papers.
[23] Washington *Bee*, June 11, 1910, p. 4; Kellogg, *NAACP*, pp.
43–44, 50–53; Oswald Garrison Villard to Francis J. Garrison,
July 1910, Villard Papers.

group. Late in 1910 his name appeared on NAACP stationery as one of six Bostonians on the General Committee.[24] That was merely ceremonial. By the end of the year
he had reason for being more receptive to the Association's
overtures, as the NAACP took his side in a factional
struggle in Boston that recalled the trouble over the Garrison centenary in 1905.

The occasion was the celebration of the centennial of
Charles Sumner's birth, just after the New Year. As early
as August 1910 Du Bois had proposed that the Association
sponsor an appropriate meeting in Boston in January. The
New York office agreed, and Clement Morgan hired Faneuil Hall for the NAACP. But Trotter and his New
England Suffrage League had a similar idea. He claimed
precedence because his was the local group and because he
had run similar affairs in the past. On November 18 Trotter met with Storey, Francis Garrison, Archibald Grimké,
and Albert Pillsbury of the Boston NAACP. The real
problem was not Trotter's resentment of the NAACP but
his simmering feud with Morgan and Du Bois, left over
from the Niagara Movement. Morgan, Garrison wrote his
nephew, "like everyone else who has anything to do with
Trotter, is at swords' points with him, and scarcely on
speaking terms. Grimke gave Trotter some good advice to
hold his tongue and not stir up trouble." Trotter offered to
let three NAACP men speak at his celebrations. The Association spokesmen, not so much impressed with this mag-
nanimity as reluctant to make an issue of the matter,
decided to leave the field to Trotter. In New York the
NAACP board of directors voted, on a motion by Villard
and second by Mary White Ovington, not to hold a Sumner celebration in Boston. "But I am frank to say," Villard
warned his uncle, "that I think it establishes a very dangerous precedent and that sooner or later, we shall have to

[24] Frances Blascoer to Mary Church Terrell, November 16,
1910, Mary Church Terrell Papers.

fight him down in his own territory." [25]

Morgan, not willing to back down before Trotter, would not release Faneuil Hall and decided to hold a Sumner meeting himself. He announced an extraordinary list of invited speakers including Du Bois, Storey, Pillsbury, Washington, Boston's Mayor John F. Fitzgerald, and United States Senators Henry Cabot Lodge, Murray Crane, and Joseph Benson Foraker. "What worse treason to race and insult to the sainted dead?" Trotter asked Grimké. "This is the final result of Dubois reaching way over into Boston to reduce the Suffrage League and the Guardian. What a breeder of dissension among the radicals. Now Morgan joins the ranks of the tricksters." Despite pressure from the NAACP Morgan would not yield. Two separate affairs were held in Boston. Storey, once private secretary to Sumner, stayed neutral and appeared at neither. Together they were "a grand success," said Trotter, "the smoothest two day celebration ever managed by Colored people in Boston," and a fitting tribute to Sumner because the affairs were put on "by citizens of Color in whose behalf he used his talents so unselfishly." [26]

The matter was still not at rest. Garrison and Storey agreed that the controversy had left the factions "accentuated and embittered" and that Trotter would be "likely to make trouble" at the NAACP's convention in Boston in April. Then Du Bois made things worse by noting the

[25] Moorfield Storey to W. E. B. Du Bois, September 14, October 13, 20, November 19, 1910, to W. M. Trotter, October 25, December 2, 1910, to Albert E. Pillsbury, December 5, 1910, Moorfield Storey Papers; Francis J. Garrison to Oswald Garrison Villard, November 19, 1910, Villard Papers; Minutes of Board of Directors Meetings, November 29, 1910, NAACP Papers; Villard to Garrison, November 21, 1910, Villard Papers.

[26] W. M. Trotter to Archibald Grimké, December 20, 1910, Archibald Grimké Papers; Moorfield Storey to W. M. Trotter, December 7, 19, 20, 1910, Storey Papers; *Guardian,* January 14, 1911, p. 4; W. M. Trotter, ed., *The Two Days Observance of the One Hundredth Anniversary of the Birth of Charles Sumner . . . January Fifth and Sixth, 1911* (Boston, 1911).

Sumner meetings in the *Crisis*, calling Morgan's "the
main meeting" and Trotter's "a branch meeting." Garrison advised Villard that Storey was "disgusted that Du-
Bois should make this deliberate thrust at Trotter's meetings, which were really much better attended and more
important, if that word can be used, than Morgan's. It was
wholly gratuitous for DuBois to do this, and it illustrates
how easily he can keep open the rawness that exists. Storey
was so disgusted he felt like washing his hands of the
whole business." "That is evidently the danger with Du-
Bois," Villard remarked. Storey gingerly approached Trotter and urged him to try to "work cordially with men with
whom in some respects you differ." [27]

Actually he was ready to try. His quarrel with Du Bois
and Morgan was a personal matter beyond the reach of
rational persuasion. But he could appreciate the fact that
the NAACP's white men had taken his side in the Sumner
matter and its aftermath. In January he called the attention of the Association's New York office to the approaching centennial of Horace Greeley's birth and suggested
that they celebrate it. They had let him have Sumner, the
implication was, and now they could have Greeley. On
March 1 he, Storey, and others testified at a State House
hearing on a new bill to prohibit racial intermarriage in
Massachusetts. The bill was killed, and Trotter congratulated Storey on his particularly effective testimony. Relations seemed to be smoother on the surface. Planning for
the April conference in Boston went forward. Trotter was
asked to take part, but at first did not help with the
preparations. "He did not come to our committee meetings, though invited," Garrison noted, "and even if he

[27] Moorfield Storey to Frances Blascoer, January 14, 1911, Storey Papers; Francis J. Garrison to Oswald Garrison Villard, January 20, 1911, Villard Papers; *Crisis*, I (February 1911), 5;
Garrison to Villard, March 21, 1911, and Villard to Garrison,
March 22, 1911, Villard Papers; Storey to W. M. Trotter, March
16, 1911, Storey Papers.

should take a hostile position, he can do us no real harm."
Then in mid-March Trotter asked that he and his Suffrage
League be given a part in the planning. "He is always
eager for 'recognition' & submission," Garrison grumbled.[28]

The situation took a new turn a few days later when
Washington was assaulted by a white man in New York
under mysterious circumstances. Washington, severely
battered, denied the white man's insistence that he was
defending his wife's honor from the Tuskegeean. The
incident gave Trotter a rare chance to crow over the compromised Washington. Deenie Trotter told Garrison that
they had received many letters and cables congratulating
them on their opportunity. But Trotter's response was
generously restrained. The *Guardian* said, "Our opposition to Mr. Washington because of his propaganda and
methods, even to his method of treating reputable Colored
men who get into trouble, as he has now, is well known,
but we do not desire to take any advantage of his present
troubles. We want to fight men when standing up." "Editor Trotter even admitted that Booker T. Washington had
done no wrong," the Indianapolis *Freeman* observed, not
quite accurately. "That makes it unanimous." There was a
truce of sorts as the radicals backed off from attacking the
convalescent. Garrison was delighted to see that Trotter
"held himself in" and thought that "if Pillsbury & Storey
take him in hand, they may be able to curb & steer him
into this new path, if W. will give public evidence of his
sincerity in not wishing to oppose or obstruct our
movement. . . ."[29]

The Boston conference was starting to look as though it

[28] Minutes of Board of Directors Meetings, January 3, March 7,
1911, NAACP Papers; *Guardian*, March 11, 1911, p. 2; Francis J.
Garrison to Oswald Garrison Villard, February 21, March 15,
1911, Villard Papers.
[29] *Guardian*, March 25, 1911, p. 4; Indianapolis *Freeman*, April
8, 1911, p. 4; Francis J. Garrison to Oswald Garrison Villard,
March 25, 26, 1911, Villard Papers.

would be a celebration of harmony. "Co-operation is very much needed," wrote Trotter as it approached, "co-operation of both races for justice and human brotherhood." He worried about the makeup of the National Committee, which included "some friendly and true, some indifferent, some not friendly and not true." As a racial group under the leadership of white men, it was a new force in the struggle for Negro freedom, and "such a movement has great power, at least in means, brains and influence. It's effectiveness depends on the principles the movement espouses, its consistency and the number of white Americans it can win to its program." [30]

The convention was a smooth success. The speakers, Du Bois, Milholland, Mary Church Terrell, Storey, Pillsbury, and others, represented a careful spectrum of viewpoints. After some debate the committee on resolutions—despite Milholland's objection—recorded its "profound regret" over the attack on Washington. The NAACP was taking a catholic approach, trying to embrace all factions at once. Trotter opposed the Washington statement (it was one thing to refrain from capitalizing on Washington's embarrassment, he reasoned, but quite another to express sympathy for the Tuskegeean), and he fretted over "the wide-open-door policy of membership" but called the resolutions "strong and right," and concluded that "the Association is a great, important and noble movement and we should all wish it success, and take part in making it of great benefit to race and country." This was remarkably close to the *New York Age*'s comment that the NAACP, if it held to the themes of the Boston meeting, would enjoy "the united support of the colored people throughout the country." The race seemed to be more united than it had been at any time since the founding of the *Guardian*.[31]

[30] *Guardian*, March 18, 1911, pp. 1, 4, and March 25, 1911, p. 4.
[31] *Boston Evening Transcript*, March 30, 1911, p. 2, and March 31, 1911, p. 3; Milholland Diary, March 30, 31, 1911; *Guardian*, April 1, 1911, pp. 1, 4, 5; *New York Age*, April 20, 1911, p. 4.

For Trotter the honeymoon with the NAACP lasted for a year or two. In May he attended a local Association meeting in Boston and secured approval for a resolution opposing the establishment of a segregated YMCA clubhouse. He also told the meeting about a light-complexioned Negro nurse at the Boston Floating Hospital who had been fired when her race had been discovered. He asked the NAACP men for advice on how to proceed in the matter, "whether it was best to make a quiet fight, or to make the matter public, or to drop it." Later that year a repetition of the Sumner imbroglio was threatened when both Trotter and the Association decided to honor the centenary of the birth of Wendell Phillips. "It is needless to say," Villard told his uncle, "that we feel this meeting should go ahead even if Trotter wants to prevent it." This time Trotter "cooled off," according to Garrison, and held his own affair while granting equal time to the NAACP's celebrations. He even invited Garrison to speak at the Suffrage League's meeting, and Garrison, surprisingly enough, accepted the offer and sat on the same Faneuil Hall platform with Trotter.[32]

Yet Trotter never committed himself to the NAACP. He stayed on the periphery, giving his support whenever the leaders of the group met his demanding principles. "I was very favorably impressed by your remarks," he wrote Joel Spingarn of the New York office early in 1912, "and should like very much to see you at any time. . . . I am with you in your work." By which he meant that he was with *Spingarn*, not the entire NAACP. For reasons of principle or personality he could not cooperate with other Association men, particularly Du Bois and Villard. He remained in touch; as late as November 1912 he went to

[32] Minutes of Board of Directors Meetings, May 10, 1911, NAACP Papers; Oswald Garrison Villard to Francis J. Garrison, September 11, 1911, and Garrison to Villard, November 5, December 1, 1911, Villard Papers; *Boston Herald*, November 30, 1911, p. 8.

one of the group's meetings in Boston. Gradually, though, he was moving away from the "great, important and noble movement." [33]

<h1 style="text-align:center">V</h1>

Part of the problem was the Boston chapter of the NAACP. In 1912 its top three officers were Francis and George Garrison and Butler Wilson. The executive committee was made up of four whites and two Negroes, one of them being Clement Morgan. For Trotter to establish any rapport with such a group of leaders was out of the question. Wilson, for example, was one of the early anti-Bookerites in Boston but had repudiated Trotter as early as 1904. Trotter considered him a "social politician" who stayed aloof from the Negro masses and worked for genteel causes in the company of upper-class whites. One day Mary White Ovington and Wilson were walking through the South End, arguing about the establishment of a settlement house for black youth. They passed by a group of young Negroes engaged in a desultory crap game. "What's to become of them?" she asked Wilson. He replied, "Let them rot." That, to Trotter, seemed to be the basic attitude of the NAACP in Boston. He told Spingarn, "We need your live, thorough-going, radical, courageous activity in our local branch here." [34]

Furthermore, the Association pursued a curiously am-

[33] W. M. Trotter to Joel E. Spingarn, February 12, 1912, Joel E. Spingarn Papers; Francis J. Garrison to Oswald Garrison Villard, November 10, 1912, Villard Papers.

[34] *Crisis*, III (1912), 203; Francis J. Garrison to Oswald Garrison Villard, December 23, 1904, Villard Papers; Ruth Worthy, "A Negro in Our History: William Monroe Trotter, 1872–1934" (M.A. thesis, Columbia University, 1952), pp. 91–92; Ovington, *Walls Came Tumbling Down*, p. 24; W. M. Trotter to Joel E. Spingarn, February 12, 1912, Spingarn Papers; and see also Charles W. Puttkammer, "William Monroe Trotter: An Evaluation of the Life of a Radical Negro Newspaper Editor, 1901–1934" (senior thesis, Princeton University, 1958), pp. 51–53. Du Bois shared Trotter's distaste for the leadership of the Boston Branch: see W. E. B. Du Bois to Spingarn, January 20, 1916, Spingarn Papers.

bivalent policy in regard to Washington. It was regarded as a protest group, and Tuskegee treated it as a threat to Washington's leadership. "These fellows will be troublesome for a few months," said Washington, "but will soon wear themselves out." The NAACP asked William Lewis to join in 1912. He was agreeable ("It may be that I can be of service by being on the inside") but first asked for Tuskegee's opinion. Emmett Scott advised against it. "Their first movement always seems to be to go about 'annexing' those friends of ours that they can," Scott warned Lewis, "so as to put themselves in position to continue their underhanded, and . . . malicious attacks upon the Doctor and his work, and at the same time, say they have our friends as members of the association, and therefore are not opposing him." In fact, as Scott wrote this letter, the current issue of the *Crisis* carried a discreet piece by Villard which described certain racial spokesmen who found the Association "too radical." [35]

Yet the very discretion of Villard's article would have bothered Trotter. The Association might take strong non-Bookerite positions, but it would not explicitly denounce the pernicious effect of Washington's leadership. In 1914 Trotter told Spingarn that his approach was identical with what the *Guardian*'s had been in 1901, "except that I named my man who was undermining the rights of Colored Americans. Had such men as Mr. Villard and Mr. Garrison and others taken the same position then, instead of upholding Booker Washington and denouncing me for opposing Washington, the Colored race would not be where you said they are." The leaders of the NAACP did criticize Washington on a private, individual basis. "Your optimism is leading you astray," Villard wrote the Tuske-

[35] Booker T. Washington to Charles W. Anderson, January 10, 1911, in Kellogg, *NAACP*, p. 57; May Childs Nerney to William H. Lewis, June 17, 1912, Lewis to Booker T. Washington, June 19, 1912, Emmett J. Scott to Lewis, June 22, 1912, Washington Papers; *Crisis*, IV (1912), 81–82.

geean after he had been making cheerful speeches during a trip to Europe, ". . . from my point of view, your philosophy is wrong . . . you are keeping silent about evils in regard to which you should speak out, and . . . you are not helping the race by portraying all the conditions as favorable." [36]

But when Du Bois, Trotter, and twenty-one other Negroes published a statement denouncing Washington for his European statements, Villard disclaimed any NAACP responsibility in the matter. And the Association decided not to go through with a planned merger with the more outspoken Constitution League. Villard advised Washington that the groups would not combine, "so that you may not in any way hold us liable for actions taken by the Constitutional League." It was an attempt at consensus, aiming to pull in the Trotterites on the left and sympathetic Bookerites on the right. "So far as making our organization include everybody," Storey wrote Du Bois, "I am entirely in harmony with you. I think it is a great mistake to shut anybody out who shares our view, and the more people we can get, the stronger we shall be." True enough, and the success with which the NAACP enlisted the aid of such moderates as Mary Church Terrell and Kelly Miller, and such old Bookerites as S. Laing Williams of Chicago and John Q. Adams of St. Paul, proved the wisdom of the consensus approach—at least in broadening the group's influence. But to Trotter this was not open-mindedness, but mushiness, the regrettable consequence of "the wide-open-door policy of membership." [37]

[36] W. M. Trotter to Joel E. Spingarn, January 28, 1914, Spingarn Papers; Oswald Garrison Villard to Booker T. Washington, December 13, 1910, Villard Papers.

[37] Herbert Aptheker, ed., *A Documentary History of the Negro People in the United States* (New York, 1951), pp. 884–886; Kellogg, *NAACP*, pp. 77–78; Oswald Garrison Villard to Booker T. Washington, January 19, 1911, Villard Papers; Moorfield Storey to W. E. B. Du Bois, May 10, 1911, Storey Papers; August Meier, *Negro Thought in America, 1880–1915: Racial Ideologies*

Both the nature of the Boston chapter and the muddled treatment of Washington were tied in with the real source of Trotter's wariness: the presence of white money and white leadership in the NAACP. In contrast, Trotter's group, the Negro-American Political League, was virtually all black. It could not match the Association's budget, membership, or influence. It went through reorganizations and name changes—the National Independent Political League, the National Independent Political Rights League, the National Independent Equal Rights League, and finally the National Equal Rights League. The main source of continuity through all this was Trotter's stubborn presence as the corresponding secretary. Through him the NERL could trace its lineage, however tenuously, back to the Philadelphia convention of April 1908. And his group was always, as he described it in 1920, "an organization of the colored people and for the colored people and led by the colored people." [38]

A complex of motives lay behind his insistence that *his* group, at least, must be black-led. On a tactical level, he knew that whites in any racial group would have a moderating function, and he did not want to waste his time arguing for radical approaches with men from the other side of the color line. On a philosophical level, he thought it only proper that blacks should lead and finance a movement for their own freedom. And finally, there was the problem of his own ego and insistence on utter independence. In the NAACP he would have been competing with other strong and even brilliant personalities for the positions of leadership. Trotter was not able to attract such people to his own group. In the NERL he was the generally acknowledged spokesman for lesser men; after himself

---

in the Age of Booker T. Washington (Ann Arbor, Mich., 1963), pp. 183–184.

[38] Puttkammer, "Trotter," p. 56 *n; Antilynching Hearings before the Committee on the Judiciary . . . on H. R. 259, 4123, and 11873 . . . January 29, 1920* (Washington, D.C., 1920), p. 27.

there was no one to compare with Du Bois, Villard, Milholland, Storey, and Mary White Ovington. Whereas these and other NAACP leaders had to thrash out the Association's decisions, often with some debate, Trotter as corresponding secretary would simply issue a statement in the NERL's name, and that would stand as the group's position. The NERL was his personal fief.

Inevitably the two groups collided. They worked in the same cause, appealed to the same people, and were always suspicious of each other. Du Bois, Trotter's nemesis, edited the *Crisis* with freewheeling independence. In Trotter's opinion the *Crisis*, supposedly published in the general interest of the race, did not give fair coverage of the activities of the NERL. Early in 1913 Trotter declined Spingarn's invitation to an NAACP meeting, and added that he thought the NAACP should have two paramount functions: "It should oppose non-legal segregation, at least in the north, and promote mixing in semi-public institutions." And, he added pointedly, "It should also be free from decrying or slighting equal rights organizations whose members & officers are Colored. . . . Colored organizations commend the N.A.A.C.P. at their annual meetings but there is no evidence of reciprocation." [39] Over the next few years the feud between the "white" NAACP and the "Colored" NERL smoldered, occasionally bursting into a spate of private mutual recriminations.

Trotter cut down the extent of his influence over the race by refusing to join forces with the NAACP, but he also thereby avoided the persistent—and unpublicized—intramural racial friction within the Association. Du Bois was the only Negro in the top group of leaders that ran the Association from the New York office, and his personal quarrels with other members of the staff often seemed to derive in part from racial tensions. Villard resigned as

[39] W. M. Trotter to Joel E. Spingarn, January 2, 1913, Spingarn Papers.

chairman late in 1913 after a long conflict with Du Bois, and Ovington sadly called the resignation "a confession to the world that we cannot work with colored people unless they are our subordinates. . . . It puts us back five years." Du Bois contributed to the problem with his own prickly, difficult personality.[40]

His white associates—those well-intentioned whites who *meant* so well, and of whom Trotter was so wary—had their own limitations, which came out at odd moments of frustration and discouragement. Villard was a trustee of a Negro industrial school, and in that capacity spent much of his time, he said, "struggling with the colored people and their easily hurt feelings. . . . truly they are a child race still!" Storey confided to Villard, "The difficulty which you call 'temperamental' in the case of DuBois sometimes seems to me almost racial." (But when Villard, of all people, objected, Storey replied, "I have no doubt you are right, and the weakness of which you speak is common to human nature and not the property of any particular race.") Ovington noted after a report by the New York office's May Childs Nerney, "She seemed to believe the colored people had made a mess of pretty much all their branches, and she spoke of them with quite brutal frankness." Albert Pillsbury of Boston admitted to Archibald Grimké that "the best of us are infected and are in a hypocritical attitude."

> Would Villard himself invite negroes, though gentle-
> men and scholars, to his house or his clubs, or invoke
> general association with them exactly as though they
> were white men? No, he would not. He could not. I
> am obliged to confess that the same is true of myself.
> If we attempted any such thing we should be in
> trouble with our friends, our wives and even our

[40] Mary White Ovington to Oswald Garrison Villard, November 21, 25, 1913, in Kellogg, *NAACP*, p. 96; and on this point generally see *ibid.*, pp. 92–97, 101–104, 107–115.

cooks and it would not be long before we too should
be socially ostracised.

"Increasingly we are learning that the Negroes want to do
things undirected," Ovington wrote in 1917. "They, naturally, want all the glory. When a Branch produces a Negro
capable of the secretaryship I hope we shall engage him—
but they haven't produced one yet." [41]

In the fall of 1914 the problem reached a crisis. Du
Bois told Spingarn, his closest white friend, that "when we
confer I continually feel that you are not meeting me
frankly & openly as soul to soul. . . ." Spingarn, taking
the opportunity to broach a matter that had evidently been
on his mind, told Du Bois with equal candor that "Surrounding you always, I may say frankly, I have found an
atmosphere of antagonism." Spingarn urged Du Bois to
submerge his talents and sensitivities for the sake of the
NAACP's survival. "If you are not willing to espouse our
cause whole-heartedly as your own," Spingarn wrote, "I
am afraid that the Association is doomed." In reply Du
Bois conceded that "I do not doubt in the least but that my
temperament is a difficult one to endure." But, Du Bois
insisted, racial distinctions lay at the heart of his trials
with his white associates:

> No organization like ours ever succeeded in America;
> either it became a group of white philanthropists
> 'helping' the Negro like the Anti-Slavery societies; or
> it became a group of colored folk freezing out their
> white co-workers by insolence and distrust. Every-
> thing tends to this break along the color line. . . .
> You say the experiment has failed. Has it? Is it

[41] Oswald Garrison Villard to Francis J. Garrison, March 14,
1913, Villard Papers; Moorfield Storey to Villard, October 17, 19,
1911, Storey Papers; Mary White Ovington to Joel E. Spingarn,
December 13, [1915?], Spingarn Papers; Albert E. Pillsbury to
Archibald Grimké, November 26, 1913, Grimké Papers; Ovington
to Spingarn, October 29, 1917, Spingarn Papers.

necessary that it should fail? . . . How can this be changed? By changing it. By trusting black men with power.[42]

Du Bois chose to stay in the Association, seeing it as a kind of laboratory testing racial democracy in microcosm. Trotter, not interested in such an experiment, kept to his own group, and as the NAACP's influence grew he was increasingly isolated on the left wing of the race's leadership.

[42] W. E. B. Du Bois to Joel E. Spingarn, October 23, 28, 1914, and Spingarn to Du Bois, October 24, 1914, James Weldon Johnson Memorial Collection; and see also May Childs Nerney to Archibald Grimké [October, 1914], Grimké Papers.

CHAPTER V

Three Presidents

T H E   R I S E of the NAACP marked the culmination
of the anti-Washington movement. The weight of
Negro thought was moving back toward the protest-inte-
grationist tradition, and Trotter was ready to concede that
even Washington himself was less offensive than formerly.
"There would be little or no criticism of Mr. Washington
by Colored men to-day," he wrote in January 1908, "if he
confined himself to his school work and kept out of politics." Trotter proposed a peace settlement: if Washington's white friends persuaded him to keep to Tuskegee and
leave politics alone, then the black anti-Bookerites would
stop attacking him; "I am sure his Colored critics will keep
their part of the understanding." [1] That proposal, which
was perhaps a little fanciful in any case, was never acted
upon. Even without it, Trotter's great campaign against
Tuskegee leadership—the main cause for which he had
started the *Guardian* and plunged into race work—was

[1] W. M. Trotter to *Boston Evening Transcript*, January 21,
1908, in *Guardian*, February 1, 1908, p. 4.

essentially over. By 1910 he had made the bulk of his historical contribution to the black liberation movement.

Of secondary importance, but also significant, were his efforts in the realm of national politics. In his political endeavors he generally attracted neither the support nor the notoriety that came his way when he was bearding Washington. But in taking his predictably strong and idiosyncratic positions he managed to have some influence on the race's political action, especially during the presidencies of Theodore Roosevelt, William Howard Taft, and Woodrow Wilson.

I

Though his father had been a Democratic officeholder, Trotter did not admire most Negro politicians. They had the right to seek office, he admitted, "especially if they have nothing else to do." But "these political gamesters very carefully avoid the dangers of a fight with powerful and influential interests. They will encourage a man to go ahead to do everything that makes for unpopularity but when personal interests are at stake they will dare publically to repudiate the man and the methods which they privately endorsed." Most black politicians in the age of Washington were dependable Bookerites, since it was unlikely that any political career could succeed without Tuskegee's approval. Thus Trotter cautioned that such men as Charles Anderson (collector of internal revenue in New York), W. T. Vernon (register of the Treasury), R. W. Tyler (auditor for the Navy), Robert Terrell (a magistrate in the District of Columbia), and J. C. Dancy (who held James Trotter's old post as register of deeds from 1901 to 1910) should not be taken at face value, because they "say things for the Republicans and against the Democrats in order to retain their jobs. The Colored people understand they are talking for pay and not for truth, and so pay little heed to their orations." [2]

Besides, they were merely federal appointees: bureaucrats without any substantive, practical power to be used in the interest of the race. No Negro served in Congress from 1901 to 1929. White men also controlled the important state and municipal offices. Still Trotter stressed the importance of political power—not from officeholders, but at the ballot box. If Negroes voted in an independent bloc, Trotter argued, they could swing close elections in their favor and then make demands on the men they elected. "The Negro holds the balance of power in several of the northern states," the *Guardian* would announce; or, again, "according to a well calculated estimate, the colored race can decide the congressional election this fall. . . . We can yet save ourselves by a judicious placing of our ballot." For this to happen the race would have to be liberated from its traditional allegiance to the Republican party. Black Republicanism was a stubborn tradition, rendered even more tenacious by the obvious reluctance of southern white Democrats to seek black converts. In the elections of 1906, the *New York Age* observed, the Democratic cause was taken up by the southern Negrophobes James K. Vardaman, Hoke Smith, and Pitchfork Ben Tillman, and by Monroe Trotter.[3]

Strange bedfellows, indeed, but to Trotter it seemed that the racial policies of Theodore Roosevelt left him no other choice. From the early days of his first administration, Washington was the President's arbiter on Negro appointments and general adviser on all aspects of the race problem. "How does he know anything about the fitness of people for office?" the *Guardian* demanded. "It is simply

[2] *Guardian*, November 2, 1907, p. 4, and August 22, 1908, p. 4; August Meier, *Negro Thought in America, 1880–1915: Racial Ideologies in the Age of Booker T. Washington* (Ann Arbor, Mich., 1963), pp. 254, 251, 239, 252.

[3] *Guardian*, January 10, 1903, p. 4, and September 6, 1902, p. 4; *New York Age*, November 15, 1906, p. 4.

an insult to every Negro to have such a trimmer made a
boss by President Roosevelt." There was an obvious contradiction between Washington's private ties to the White
House and his public denigration of political activity. Trotter thought he saw a plot between Tuskegee and the GOP
to remove the last vestiges of the Negro's political power.
"The Guardian calmly asks the colored people of America
do they not see that a conspiracy is on to take away their
rights to ballot and equal opportunity with others? It is
being engineered by the Republican party leaders of the
country. . . . It is the party, the Republican party leaders,
who have deserted the Negro." In the fall of 1902 the
Negro press carried a report that, contrary to previous
stories, Roosevelt was not intent upon a lily-white appointment policy in the South. This encouraging news came
from an anonymous Negro spokesman for Roosevelt.
"This high authority is of course Gen. Booker T. Washington," said the *Guardian*, "who, as usual is trying to
lead from an ambuscade! He is afraid to have his name
known, yet is trying to lead!" [4]

Washington could speak with authority about the President's intentions, though, for shortly thereafter Roosevelt
named a black man to be collector for the port of Charleston, South Carolina. Outraged howls came from the white
South, but Roosevelt sent a firm letter to the mayor of
Charleston: "It seems to me that it is a good thing from
every standpoint to let the colored man know that if he
shows in marked degree the qualities of good citizenship
—the qualities which in a white man we feel are entitled to
reward—then he will not be cut off from all hope of similar
reward." It was a "magnificent" letter, said Trotter, "and
will prove a veritable balm of Gilead on that subject in
these troubled times. Now let him drop the black boss and

[4] *Guardian* quoted in Washington *Bee*, June 28, 1902, p. 1;
Guardian, September 27, 1902, p. 4, and October 18, 1902, p.
4.

all will be forgiven." [5]

He would not drop the black boss, but for a while the *Guardian* approved the "very strong-handed and fair-minded" President. He retained a Negro woman to be postmistress of Indianola, Mississippi, and when the white townspeople would not accept her he closed the local post office temporarily. "One of the bravest acts of the president's administration," Trotter called it. Then Roosevelt changed his mind and named a white man to the job, and Trotter had to retract his praise. "Whatever excuses may be given he has surrendered to the enemy," the *Guardian* mourned. "The southerners will certainly get very arrogant now. They perceive that all they have got to do is to make a firm enough stand to keep out all Negroes from office. We fear the consequences." [6]

Obviously the Republican party of 1904 had little in common with the party of Lincoln. It was controlled, in Trotter's view, by men "who have no conception of the meaning of the rights of man, and absolutely none of the spirit which made the name of that party honored and respected the world over. . . ." After the party conventions that summer, though, Trotter decided that Negroes could do no better than to vote for Roosevelt in November. The Republican platform promised to reduce the representation of any Congressional delegation chosen by a partly disfranchised electorate. That was vaguely encouraging. "The most critical issue in this campaign," Trotter declared, "is the real intention of the Republicans, whether they intend to be fair with the Negro voters and especially whether they will reduce southern representation." Late in September he went to New York for a conference with GOP chieftains and was given assurances and, perhaps, some campaign money. A few weeks later the *Guardian*

[5] *Guardian*, November 29, 1902, pp. 1, 4, and December 6, 1902, p. 4.
[6] *Guardian:* January 10, 1903, p. 4; January 23, 1904, p. 4; January 30, 1904, p. 4.

announced its choice: Roosevelt was no race champion, yet "under his administration the terrible condition of peonage has been unearthed and a start made to abolish it. Besides he has stood his ground in most cases against the assault of southern color prejudice, even when practically deserted by his own party." Therefore, choosing between the tickets, "the Republican candidates seem to us clearly to be the safer for Colored Americans." [7]

Roosevelt swept to victory and proceeded to give no evidence of deserving even Trotter's measured endorsement. "Laziness and shiftlessness," the President declared three months after the election, "these, and above all, vice and criminality of every kind, are evils more potent for harm to the black race than all acts of oppression of white men put together." The GOP's promise to act on black disfranchisement—merely an affirmation of a provision of the Fourteenth Amendment—came to nothing. Roosevelt made fewer Negro appointments than during his first term. His alliance with Tuskegee seemed even more conspiratorial. And in the face of all this the mass of Negroes stayed loyally Republican. "Thank God," said Trotter in the summer of 1906, "that at last in the Niagara Movement we have a national organization that is not afraid to speak to the Republican party like any element of the party would when similarly treated." [8]

Even as he spoke, the worst Republican outrage was unfolding. It had started a few weeks before in the Mexican border town of Brownsville, Texas. At midnight on August 13 ten or a dozen armed men ran through the

[7] *Guardian:* June 18, 1904, p. 4; July 16, 1904, p. 4; August 13, 1904, p. 4; Booker T. Washington to Charles Anderson, September 7, 1904, Anderson to Washington, September 22, 23, 1904, Booker T. Washington Papers; *Guardian*, October 15, 1904, p. 4.

[8] *The Works of Theodore Roosevelt* (Memorial edition, 24 vols., New York, 1923–26), XVIII, 465; Meier, *Negro Thought*, p. 164; George E. Mowry, *The Era of Theodore Roosevelt* (New York, 1958), pp. 165–166; *Guardian*, August 25, 1906, p. 4.

streets of Brownsville, firing their guns, killing one man, wounding two others. Then the marauders disappeared into the night. The next day a committee of Brownsville citizens charged that the culprits were soldiers from the all-Negro Twenty-fifth Infantry regiment stationed just outside town. Several townspeople who had seen the raiders were sure they were black men, and some spent Army shells had been picked up in the street. A few weeks later Major Augustus Blocksom, a white man of southern background, completed an "official" inquiry and agreed that some of the soldiers were guilty, though he could not say which ones. Unable to crack what he called the soldiers' "conspiracy of silence," he recommended that if no confessions were forthcoming the entire battalion should be discharged. Roosevelt had his Inspector General, Ernest A. Garlington, review the case and take new testimony. Garlington agreed with Blocksom's conclusions. Accordingly, just after the fall elections Secretary of War Taft, acting on Roosevelt's orders, discharged the whole battalion without honor and declared the soldiers to be ineligible for pensions or for civilian employment by the government. There was no trial and no chance for appeal.[9]

"I never dreamed," Villard mused, "that it would give the President the worst set-back in his history, or that the press would be so unanimous in its protest." It was not quite unanimous; the *Outlook*, for example, sustained the administration. But black men were uniformly horrified— and furious. "The Constitution of the United States has been violated," said one of the more conservative Negro newspapers, "and Congress must act or go out of business." Even Washington, in private, vowed that "I am not going to give up. . . . There is no law, human or divine, which justifies the punishment of an innocent man." Having tried to dissuade Roosevelt from ordering the dis-

[9] James A. Tinsley, "Roosevelt, Foraker, and the Brownsville Affray," *Journal of Negro History*, XLI (1956), 43–46.

charge, Washington then kept silent, and even defended the administration and discouraged anti-Roosevelt protest: "One thing the American people will not stand for any length of time, and that is abuse by any group of people of the President of the United States, and if our people in the North make the mistake of going too far there will be a reaction. . . ." [10]

It was an act of "meanness, injustice, and unwarranted cruelty," wrote Trotter in the *Guardian*, and a "monstrous breach of equity." Any guilty individuals should be punished. "But the charge is simply that the soldiers refused to inform on their comrades. We can not find anywhere in civil or military law or practise that this constitutes a crime or an offense punishable as such." Where is the right to a trial, or the presumption of innocence until guilt is proven? "This notion that law-abiding colored private citizens are under obligation to play detective and police officer is improper. . . . Everywhere it endangers the personal safety of innocent colored persons." At a protest meeting in Faneuil Hall in mid-November, Trotter, Archibald Grimké, Reverdy Ransom, and others signed a statement that deplored the discharge's "unmerited severity, unprecedented injustice and wanton abuse of executive power." The raid itself was "an act of sheer lawlessness" and the criminals should answer for it. But why the whole battalion? [11]

In fact, why *any* members of the battalion? The Constitution League sent its own investigators to Brownsville

[10] Oswald Garrison Villard to Francis J. Garrison, November 26, 1906, Oswald Garrison Villard Papers; *Outlook*, LXXXIV (1906), 810–812; Washington *Bee*, November 17, 1906, p. 4; Booker T. Washington to Villard, November 10, 1906, Villard Papers; Washington to Ralph Tyler, December 5, 1906, in Emma Lou Thornbrough, "The Brownsville Episode and the Negro Vote," *Mississippi Valley Historical Review*, XLIV (1957–1958), 476.
[11] *Guardian* quoted in *Literary Digest*, XXXIII (1906), 832–833; Faneuil Hall Brownsville protest, November 16, 1906, in Allen Washington folder, Archibald Grimké Papers.

and turned up evidence that none of the soldiers was
involved: roll calls were taken while the firing was still
going on and all men were accounted for; Army clips and
shells could have been picked up at the firing range and
scattered in the streets; there had been trouble between the
town and the fort, and the raid might have been planned to
make scapegoats of the soldiers. The League's report was
taken up in Congress by Senator Joseph Benson Foraker of
Ohio. Foraker, who had some hopes for the Republican
presidential nomination in 1908, decided to press for an
investigation of the case in the Senate. On Christmas Eve
in New York he conferred with Milholland and other leaders of the Constitution League. "Cordial cooperation
agreed upon all around," Milholland noted in his diary.
"The Senator is full of fight. Seemed deeply in earnest."
The soldiers had found their champion.[12]

It was rough going in the Senate. Foraker had to contend with Republicans loyal to Roosevelt and southern
Democrats loyal to white supremacy. Stephen Mallory of
Florida waved Trotter's Faneuil Hall protest and declared,
"Mr. President, if there were wanted any better evidence
than we already have as to the incompetency of the average
colored man in this country to grapple with great questions, we could get no better testimony than that which is
presented in this protest." "Here, in the great city of
Boston," said Edward Carmack of Tennessee, ". . .
where negroes have been educated and elevated and illumi-
nated for forty years, we have this barefaced justification
of a criminal assault by armed soldiers upon peaceful

[12] "Preliminary Report of Commission of the Constitution
League of the United States on Affray at Brownsville, Tex.,
August 13 and 14, 1906," *Senate Documents*, 59 Cong., 2 Sess.,
Vol. 3; Diary of John E. Milholland, December 24, 1906, in John
E. Milholland Papers (see also Andrew B. Humphrey to Joseph B.
Foraker, March 28, April 5, May 11, 1907, telegram from "S. &
M." to Humphrey, June 10, 1907, and memorandum by Hum-
phrey, June 11, 1907, all in Joseph B. Foraker Papers, and
Milholland Diary, June 17, 1908).

citizens. . . ." After considerable debate the Senate authorized its Committee on Military Affairs to review the entire case. Over the next year the Committee heard some 160 witnesses and accumulated nearly 6,000 pages of testimony. Trotter followed the matter closely and predicted in the *Guardian*, "the truth is coming out. The Brownsville conspiracy of shotguns and silence is going to break down pretty soon." [13]

In March 1908 a majority of the Committee released a report that essentially endorsed Roosevelt's conduct of the case. Foraker dissented from the majority report and urged that Congress pass legislation to clear the record and allow the men to reenlist. Eventually Foraker had to accept a compromise measure that set up a Court of Inquiry consisting of five white Army officers. Of the 167 men who had been discharged, the Court took testimony from 82 and then announced that no further cases could be heard. Of the 82, 14 were found eligible for reinstatement. Of the 14, 11 actually reenlisted. [14]

II

"We do not need to argue," said the *Guardian*, "to convince our readers that the gravest crisis since Reconstruction has been forced on Colored Americans by the course of President Roosevelt since his cruel Brownsville discharge, especially by his attempt to make as his successor a man who in his acts and speeches has been as dangerous to the rights of Colored Americans and as anxious to toady to the Bourbon South as President Roosevelt himself. . . ." William Howard Taft carried out Roosevelt's orders, "outdid Roosevelt in his denunciation of the Negro soldiers," and, according to Trotter, "stands for the national policy of laissez-faire with reference to all the

[13] *Congressional Record*, 59 Cong., 2 Sess., 1074–1075, 1199–2000; *Guardian*, August 10, 1907, p. 4.
[14] *Congressional Record*, 60 Cong., 1 Sess., 3122–3124, 4709–4723; Tinsley, "Brownsville Affray," p. 61.

abominable oppressions under which our people suffer in the Southland." Any black man who supports Taft thereby assents to Republican mistreatment and "puts himself in eternal disgrace. He is branded with the mark of Cain." The Niagara Movement, meeting in Boston in the summer of 1907, set the theme for the coming presidential election: "We call on the 500,000 free black voters of the North: Use your ballots to defeat Theodore Roosevelt, William Taft, or any man named by the present dictatorship. Better vote for avowed enemies than for false friends." [15]

Mostly as a gesture of gratitude, Trotter supported Foraker's quixotic hopes for the Republican nomination. Late in 1907 the *Guardian* endorsed "the great advocate for constitutional rights and liberty for all," "the best and most powerful friend of equal rights among Republicans in elective office." "The Guardian will go with Foraker to the last ditch," and this "despite the fact that he does not seem to have a chance to win." The last ditch was the Republican convention to be held in Chicago in June. Trotter and other anti-administration black leaders decided to meet there, challenge the credentials of the pro-Taft delegates, and generally make Taft's nomination as difficult as possible. Trotter held one of his Faneuil Hall gatherings in order, he announced in the *Guardian*, "to secure from the audience several hundred dollars to send accredited delegates to Chicago to fight against Taft on the ground at Chicago." [16]

At the convention the credentials challenge got nowhere, so the black dissidents had to confine their activities

[15] *Guardian:* January 25, 1908, p. 4; November 2, 1907, p. 4; March 21, 1908, p. 4; Herbert Aptheker, ed., *A Documentary History of the Negro People in the United States* (New York, 1951), p. 914.
[16] *Guardian*, November 23, 1907, p. 4, and February 15, 1908, p. 4; Cleveland *Journal* quoted in *New York Age*, June 18, 1908. p. 4.

to nightly protest meetings at a Negro church and a black
Odd Fellows hall. Among the speakers at these affairs
were J. Milton Waldron and Alexander Walters of Trotter's Negro-American Political League, Gilchrist Stewart
and William Sinclair of the Constitution League, and
Oliver Randolph of Washington, D.C., representing an *ad
hoc* group called the National Foraker League. Others in
prominence were Trotter's old friend William H. Scott
from Woburn, Massachusetts; Trotter's fellow prisoner
from the Boston Riot, Granville Martin, since moved to
New York; and Joseph C. Manning, the egalitarian white
Populist from Alabama. These men and others kept up the
spirit of indignation night after night. "Foraker by prefer-
ence," Trotter cried on June 9, "and if we can't vote for
Foraker, anybody but Taft."

> The president has insulted, injured, and degraded the
> Negro. He has maltreated him in a way that I can
> find no words to describe. He has made an open
> alliance with the Bourbon democracy of the south.
> . . . He is using every means in his power to bribe,
> coerce, and intimidate not only a National committee,
> but a National convention in order to place his man
> Friday in nomination. The situation is worse than
> that. We are threatened by the possible election of a
> man who owes everything to this Bourbon Republi-
> can president—a man who must obey Roosevelt or be
> destroyed. If you don't resent this insult you are not
> worthy of the name of men.

"I may be down on the ground," said Waldron at another
meeting, "but they won't tie me. I'll bite, and kick, and
scratch until I die. Blood may flow, but I'll not permit
them to rob me of my rights." [17]

Inevitably there was friction with local pro-Taft blacks,

[17] *Boston Post*, June 7, 1908, p. 4; Chicago *Broad Ax*, June 13,
1908, p. 1, and June 20, 1908, p. 2.

who found the loud protest an embarrassment in their own back yard. "For the most part these meetings were largely attended," the Chicago Bookerite Fannie Barrier Williams conceded in the *New York Age*, "partly because they had in them a good deal of the circus element." And, she added, "by their incendiary speeches they cultivated a spirit of lawlessness which had in it the real Southern Democratic brand." On June 15 the regulars put on a pro-Taft rally and brought in three black Republican politicians—Charles Anderson, R. W. Tyler, and W. T. Vernon—to address the gathering. But anti-Taft men packed the church, took over the meeting, and passed resolutions condemning the administration. Vernon spoke and asked, rhetorically, if anyone in the church would vote for the Democratic ticket. "Yes! Yes!" came the answer from all over the hall. "It was," wrote Mrs. Williams, "the most fantastic, unseemly and meanly Democratic trick ever played in a house of worship." [18]

Trotter and the other dissidents carried the day in the local community, but in the convention it was all Taft. On the first ballot Taft won 702 votes and the nomination; Foraker managed 16 votes, 11 of them from Negroes. Trotter was not reconciled, and he still argued that "A vote for Taft is one for Roosevelt." As his father had done in 1884, Trotter left the Republican national ticket in 1908. [19]

He toyed with the idea of supporting the socialist ticket but decided that such a course would only dilute the anti-Taft vote. So he gingerly turned to the Democrats. The NAPL's secretary, William T. Ferguson, went to the Democratic convention in Denver and told the Resolutions Committee that his group represented 600,000 black vot-

[18] *New York Age*, June 25, 1908, p. 1; Chicago *Broad Ax*, June 20, 1908, p. 2.

[19] Everett Walters, *Joseph Benson Foraker: An Uncompromising Republican* (Columbus, O., 1948), p. 268; *Guardian*, August 8, 1908, p. 4.

ers ready to support Bryan. But, he said, "We must know
that at any rate you will not treat us any worse than the
Republicans do." It was a modest request, and Ferguson
was assured that "under Democratic rule Negroes would
be treated like all other citizens." Still, Bryan was something less than a race hero, and Trotter had a difficult time
finding positive reasons to boom his candidacy. Bryan had
given money to Tuskegee, Trotter pointed out, though
such a donation did not usually earn the *Guardian*'s praise.
Actually the main goal was "to purge the Republican
party" of the Roosevelt-Taft leadership and thereby "to
make the Republican party respect the colored Republicans." Trotter urged the Negro to vote Democratic as a
tactical aberration, not to make himself a permanent home
in Democracy.[20]

The anti-Taft black men lopped off some of the GOP's
traditional Negro vote, but not enough to elect Bryan in
November. The results in Massachusetts were especially
embarrassing: Taft carried the state by over 100,000
votes. Trotter had put enormous emphasis on the election
("To the Negro as a race the coming political battle is
more important, and means more to him than any election
since he has had the rights of citizenship"), and its out-
come was a debacle for him and for the overextended
finances of his newspaper, the most telling blow yet to his
prestige and to his racial leadership. The Boston Bookerites Samuel Courtney and William Lewis, said the *New
York Age* just after the election, "are sharpening their
knives in unholy glee! Take your time, boys. Have a little
pity; we plead for them. They know not what they do."

---

[20] *Guardian:* October 24, 1908, p. 4; July 11, 1908, pp. 1, 4;
August 1, 1908, p. 4; July 25, 1908, p. 4; August 29, 1908, p. 4.
Bryan was a typical white progressive on the race question: he
temporized on social equality, admired Washington's work at Tus-
kegee, and hoped for gradual, peaceful progress; see Willard H.
Smith, "William Jennings Bryan and Racism," *Journal of Negro
History*, LIV (1969), 127–147, especially 136–146.

Charles Alexander informed Tuskegee that he could "put this Boston Bull dog to the bad" because he had learned from Trotter's associate Edgar Benjamin "that Trotter had used up all the campaign money he was able to get his hands on." With a contribution from Tuskegee, Alexander promised, "if I went after him now he would have to give up the paper and take the poor debter's oath." Washington saw the opening and wrote to Lewis:

> Now is the time, in my opinion, for you to begin and get yourself into such intimate and close relations with the masses of the colored people in Boston and Massachusetts that you can become their real leader and guide. . . . You have this advantage: The people see now the folly of those who have been trying to lead them and deceive them. . . . The people are tired of foolishness and are ready for sensible leadership. Now is your time. . . . Do not let the other fellows get you on the defensive any more. You have them on the run now, and be sure that you keep them in that position. Work from the bottom up, not from the top down.

A clubhouse would help, Lewis replied, and suggested to Washington that "five or ten thousand dollars" from "your great and good friend Mr. Carnegie" would do the trick. He added, though, that he had no taste for mass leadership: "I would much rather serve in the cause than lead." [21]

To be precise, he wanted a political appointment. Lewis was a good Republican politician and had not joined in the race's outcry over the Brownsville incident. ("He appointed me assistant United States attorney in Massachu-

---

[21] *Guardian*, March 21, 1908, p. 4; *New York Age*, November 5, 1908, p. 4; Charles Alexander to Booker T. Washington, November 6, 1908, Alexander to Emmett J. Scott, November 13, 1908, Washington to William H. Lewis, November 9, 1908, Lewis to Washington, November 24, 1908, Washington Papers.

setts," Lewis said of Roosevelt in 1912, "and in return I defended the discharge of the Brownsville soldiers, a thing which no other colored Federal office-holder did.") Such expediency brought him the *Guardian*'s scorn—he has "repeatedly and flagrantly sold his honor and sold out his race in order to get a political position with a salary which he has seemed unable to earn at the law," the paper charged in the fall of 1907—but left him in favor at Tuskegee. "Of course I can speak frankly with you," Lewis wrote Washington in the spring of 1908, "I want the place of Assistant Attorney General." It took Washington several years, but he finally managed, in 1911, to deliver the job Lewis wanted, an Assistant Attorney Generalship, the highest federal office any Negro had held. Since Lewis was the recipient, Trotter found no cause for satisfaction. In fact, he tried to stop the appointment, carrying on a campaign in the *Guardian* and even—according to Lewis—bringing an anti-Lewis petition of two hundred names to Congress. But Trotter could not match the resources of the Tuskegee Machine. As Lewis remarked to Emmett Scott, "Yours and Dr's Underground Rail Road work was very effective."[22]

The Lewis appointment was the practical extent of the Taft administration's efforts in behalf of the Negro. Early in the term the *Guardian* said of Taft, "He has done more to foster and encourage race prejudice and race antagonism than any man in the history of the country." Later Trotter found no reason to moderate that indictment. Taft announced that he would not offend any southern whites

[22] Lewis speech, *Boston Evening Transcript*, September 25, 1912, in Leslie H. Fishel, Jr., and Benjamin Quarles, eds., *The Negro American: A Documentary History* (New York, 1967), p. 389; *Guardian*, October 26, 1907, p. 4; William H. Lewis to Booker T. Washington, May 24, 1908 (1909?), April 9, July 1, 1909, April 27, 1911, Lewis to Emmett J. Scott, June 16, 1911, and other materials, especially in Box 428, in Washington Papers; *Guardian*: October 29, 1910, p. 4; March 11, 1911, p. 2; March 18, 1911, p. 7; March 25, 1911, p. 7; April 1, 1911, p. 7.

by appointing objectionable Negroes to office in the South. The Dixie branch of the GOP was built up on a lily-white basis. And to cap it, Trotter noted, Taft named two former Confederates to the Supreme Court and elevated a third, Edward White, to be Chief Justice.[23]

III

To counter Taft's inadequacies and to prepare for the election of 1912, Trotter labored to build up a Negro-led protest group of national scope. It was a difficult undertaking, hampered both by the direct opposition of Tuskegee and by competition from the new NAACP, with its access to white money and influence. To Trotter, though, it was vital for black men to have a group of their own. "Our race is better provided with newspapers, even radical ones, than it is with political rights organizations," he wrote an associate a few years later. "Unless we solve the problem of such organization all the newspapers together will not save us, & the struggle of the Guardian would not be worth while. It would be a mere sound which is not adequate to meet foes in human form. We must meet men by men & only organizations are men." To the same correspondent, Freeman Murray of Virginia, Trotter outlined his technique of behind-the-scene group leadership:

> Be the secretary rather than president or chairman & put some one else . . . as head and give him (or them) pointers & suggestions, help them out & preside or speak yourself whem emergency requires it. Don't ponder whether you have the qualities of a leader or not *but keep the boys together & give them something to do*. Scheme & plan *what to do* as each thing comes up of a hostile nature. . . . We are open to all men or women who are not tied to party

[23] Meier, *Negro Thought*, pp. 113, 165; *Guardian:* July 3, 1909, p. 4; February 26, 1910, p. 4; October 29, 1910, p. 5; December 31, 1910, p. 2.

above race, all who put equal rights above party or personal selfishness. I think you are right to open the door to membership in accord with our constitution, also have an executive committee, & let the hard & important work be done by it & "others like-minded."

As corresponding secretary, Trotter held his group in a loose union. Through the *Guardian* he took charge of publicity and, sometimes without the approval of his officers of greater titular authority, sent out declarations, statements, and directives in the group's name. His power in the organization was personal, not constitutional, and that arrangement left his authority vulnerable to internecine challenges.[24]

Taft's election in 1908 had left the Negro-American Political League with a tarnished reputation, and when the group met in Columbus, Ohio, the following spring it still showed the effects of that debacle. The handful of members in attendance chose Alexander Walters to succeed J. M. Waldron as president and passed some anti-Taft resolutions. To stress its freedom from any commitment to the Democratic party—and perhaps to efface its connection with the group that had futilely campaigned for Bryan—the organization adopted a new name, the National Independent Political League, and adjourned. Nothing was decided about future meetings. The affair, according to the *New York Age*, was "a decided frost," and "in every respect a fizzle." Even Harry Smith, who was generally friendly toward Trotter's projects, had to admit that "The attendance was *very* small and there was a woeful lack of harmony." Trotter, having presided over what seemed to be a funeral, went back to Boston, stopping in New York for the founding conference of the NAACP. The proceedings there were less than satisfactory, so he

[24] W. M. Trotter to Freeman H. M. Murray, September 23, November 17, 1913, Freeman H. M. Murray Papers.

remained committed to the NIPL, however moribund it might seem.[25]

A year later he sent out a call for an NIPL convention in Atlantic City. The call struck a note of deepening crisis in which the "most harmful and portentous" aspect was seen to be the casual inaction of the Taft administration. To prevent the spread of southern racial mores to the North, the call argued, we must take quick and concerted action. The meeting in Atlantic City in the first week of August was a moderate success. Du Bois, perhaps at the behest of Walters or Waldron, was persuaded to give one of the speeches. According to one report, "It was reputed to be one of the most interesting and intellectual sessions ever held by free Negroes of this country." Afterward Trotter exulted, "The citizens of Boston responded splendidly" and joined Negroes from all over the country at Atlantic City. "Let us hope the radical sentiments expressed at the meetings will bear fruit in the fall elections." Prospects were better for the NIPL.[26]

Its stock went up further that fall as Democratic victories in the mid-term elections amounted to a virtual national landslide. In several normally Republican states— among them, Massachusetts—Democrats took over the governorships. The new House of Representatives had a Democratic majority for the first time since 1892. Among the victorious insurgents endorsed by the NIPL was the gubernatorial candidate of New Jersey's Democratic machine, Woodrow Wilson. On October 6 in Washington the NIPL formally urged Wilson's election, and he responded with a declaration that as governor he would treat all citizens alike. "We trust," Trotter wrote Wilson after his victory, "that no word or action of yours on the great

[25] *New York Age*, June 3, 1909, p. 1; Cleveland *Gazette*, May 22, 1909, p. 1, and June 5, 1909, p. 1.
[26] NIPL call in Aptheker, *Documentary History*, pp. 859–861; Washington *Bee*, July 2, 1910, p. 1, and August 13, 1910, p. 4; *Guardian*, August 6, 1910, p. 4.

question of equal rights will ever cause us to regret our stand." [27]

The League held its fourth annual meeting in Boston late in August 1911. "Trotter's Independence Political League brought a few people to the city," Butler Wilson advised Archibald Grimké, and none of them was "sane." Wilson was an NAACP stalwart and no admirer of Trotter; he underestimated the NIPL's sanity and its importance as well. But as the group started preparing for the presidential election year, it was not quite the national organization it aimed to be. Not one of its fourteen principal officers lived in the states of the old Confederacy. Waldron, the national organizer, was originally from the South and had held a pastorate in the District of Columbia since 1907. He was articulate—"the whitest colored man I ever saw," Villard said of him, "beside[s] being remarkably eloquent"—but Trotter did not quite trust him. The national president was J. R. Clifford, editor of the Martinsburg, West Virginia, *Pioneer Press*. Trotter pulled strings from his lowly post of corresponding secretary. Of the other officers, five were from the District of Columbia, two from New York, and one each from Ohio, Maryland, Rhode Island, and Massachusetts. The NIPL was not truly national. Nor, according to black Republicans, was it independent either.[28]

Insofar as Trotter's national political attitude could be described in a phrase, it was anti-Rooseveltism. His overriding goal in the election year of 1912 was to keep T.R. out of the White House. So in the Republican primary in

[27] Arthur S. Link, *Woodrow Wilson and the Progressive Era, 1910–1917* (New York, 1954), p. 7; W. M. Trotter to Woodrow Wilson, November 15, 1910, Woodrow Wilson Papers.
[28] Butler R. Wilson to Archibald Grimké, September 5, 1911, Grimké Papers; *Guardian*, August 19, 1911, p. 5; and these items on Waldron: W. N. Hartshorn, ed., *An Era of Progress and Promise, 1863–1910* (Boston, 1910), p. 457; Oswald Garrison Villard to Francis J. Garrison, June 5, 1908, Villard Papers; W. M. Trotter to William H. Scott, April 23, 1908, William Monroe Trotter folder, Moorland Room, Howard University; Trotter to Freeman H. M. Murray, September 7, 1913, Murray Papers.

Massachusetts that spring he swallowed his considerable animosity and supported Taft. "It is not a question of putting Taft in," Trotter explained, "but of keeping Roosevelt out. . . . The Guardian is not for Taft, is against Taft, but Roosevelt is the dominant issue. The issue for all race-loyal is to oppose the third term nomination of the lyncher of our Colored soldiers." At one time, said Trotter, Roosevelt may have seemed to be friendly to the race. "But this was in his *first* administration. In his second administration he went over to the South. He did absolutely nothing for us, and everything against us, including Brownsville." Roosevelt won the primary, 86,089 votes to Taft's 81,854. Trotter found some satisfaction in the fact that Taft carried Boston's predominantly Negro Ward 18.[29]

Roosevelt won the primaries, but Taft controlled the party machinery, and he won the party nomination late in June. A few weeks later, amid rumors that Roosevelt would launch a third-party movement, the NIPL held a strategy meeting in Philadelphia. The executive committee recommended that the conference declare its unalterable opposition to both Taft and Roosevelt and announce its support for any candidate likely to defeat them. Clifford balked at the blanket statement and helped organize its defeat by a floor vote of the conferees. Clifford was then reelected president. Unwilling to accept this challenge, Trotter and Waldron led a walkout by the anti-Roosevelt men. They held a rump conference and chose a different slate of officers, returning Trotter and Waldron to their old posts and electing a different president, Byron Gunner, a minister from New York and an associate of Trotter's since the earliest days of the *Guardian*. With that the two groups girded for the campaign, each claiming to be the true NIPL.[30]

[29] *Guardian*, April 27, 1912, p. 4, and May 4, 1912, pp. 1, 4, William Monroe Trotter Papers.

[30] *Crisis*, IV (1912), 165–166; "Trotter Kicks Over Traces," *New York Age*, July 11, 1912, p. 1; Cleveland *Gazette*, July 13, 1912, p. 2.

Clifford reflected the hopes of a considerable number of race spokesmen who had not despaired of Roosevelt. With the approach of the Bull Moose convention Du Bois drafted a statement for the Progressive platform: "The Progressive party recognizes that distinctions of race or class in political life have no place in a democracy. . . . The party, therefore, demands for the American of Negro descent the repeal of unfair discriminatory laws and the right to vote on the same terms on which other citizens vote." Joel Spingarn and Jane Addams presented the statement to the platform committee in Chicago, but it was brushed aside. Black delegates from the South asked to be admitted, but lily-white delegations from Dixie were seated instead. Jane Addams, rebuffed by the platform committee and a frustrated advocate of seating the southern Negroes, still consented to second Roosevelt's nomination. Trotter fired off a telegram pleading with her not to do it: "WOMEN SUFFRAGE WILL BE STAINED WITH NEGRO BLOOD UNLESS WOMEN REFUSE ALLIANCE WITH ROOSEVELT." She went ahead. Roosevelt, nominated by acclamation, explained his racial program in the *Outlook* —"to try for the gradual re-enfranchisement of the worthy colored man of the South by frankly giving the leadership of our movement to the wisest and justest white men of the South." "What staggers me," Francis Garrison exclaimed, "is Jane Addams's going into the convention after her stalwart attitude on the negro question, and her having anything whatsoever to do with Roosevelt. Is she so blind & stupid as to take any stock whatsoever in him?" [31]

Once again Trotter turned to the Democrats in desperation. Almost any Democrat would do. The *Guardian* de-

[31] *The Autobiography of W. E. B. Du Bois* (New York, 1968), pp. 263–264; W. M. Trotter to Jane Addams, August 6/7, 1912, Jane Addams Papers; Theodore Roosevelt, "The Progressives and the Colored Man," *Outlook*, CI (1912), 911; Francis J. Garrison to Oswald Garrison Villard, August 6, 1912, Villard Papers.

clared its support for the pre-convention favorite, Champ
Clark of Missouri. But Woodrow Wilson, a man of ominous southern connections and antecedents, won the Democratic nomination. On July 16 Trotter and Waldron spoke
with him for twenty minutes. He gave the NIPL men some
bland assurances and deplored the existence of racial prejudice. Somewhat encouraged, two days later Trotter wrote
to Wilson and thanked him for the "considerate hearing."
He urged the nominee to declare his approval of the Fourteenth and Fifteenth Amendments—by an explicit public
statement, not through some intermediary. "When you say
you accept the Amendments as the settlement of the issues
arising out of the Civil war," Trotter promised, "thousands will flock to your standard to rebuke the recreant
Republicanism and begin the era of friendship with traditional foes." Wilson made no such affirmation, but in
August Villard had a long conversation with him and was
"delighted with his attitude" on the race problem. The
candidate promised to speak out against lynching ("every
honest man must do so") and assured Villard, "The only
place where you and I will differ is as to where the opening
wedge should be driven." [32]

When Wilson read Waldron's account of the July interview in the September issue of the *Crisis*, though, he told
Villard that he had not, as Waldron claimed, promised to
veto anti-Negro legislation. Nor had he said anything
about Negro appointments or about the crucial importance
of the black vote in the election. Later he refused to sign a
racial statement that Du Bois had written for him. There
were other warning signs, such as his close relationships
with certain Negrophobic southern politicians. Josephus
Daniels, for instance, wrote in his North Carolina newspa-

[32] *Guardian*, May 4, 1912, p. 1, Trotter Papers; *Guardian*,
October 11, 1913, p. 2, in Box 7, Moorfield Storey Papers, LC; W.
M. Trotter to Woodrow Wilson, July 18, 1912, Wilson Papers;
Oswald Garrison Villard to Francis J. Garrison, August 14, 1912,
Villard Papers.

per on October 1 that "the subjection of the negro, politically, and the separation of the negro, socially, are paramount to all other considerations in the South short of the preservation of the Republic itself." [33]

It was a matter of choosing the least of three evils. Alexander Walters, going his usual independent way, had organized his own National Colored Democratic League to push the Wilson ticket. In an open letter to Walters, the Democratic candidate expressed his "earnest wish" that Negroes receive "not mere grudging justice, but justice executed with liberality and cordial good feeling." Black men "may count upon me for absolute fair dealing and for everything by which I could assist in advancing the interests of their race in the United States." Thus encouraged, Trotter's NIPL worked hard for Wilson, turning out propaganda and proselytizing Negro voters. The Democratic National Committee recognized the League as one of its spokesmen. Du Bois and the *Crisis* also urged Wilson's election. The choice was by no means a consensus among the radicals: Harry Smith and Ida Wells-Barnett both supported Taft in their newspapers. Yet the actual voting produced the first considerable black defection from the GOP. And most important, to Trotter, was Wilson's clear victory.[34]

IV

The meaning of that victory for Negroes was evident within a year. In February Trotter sent his congratulations to the President-elect. "But as your inauguration ap-

[33] Arthur S. Link, *Wilson: The Road to the White House* (Princeton, 1947), pp. 501–505.

[34] *Crisis*, IV (1912), 166; Woodrow Wilson to Alexander Walters, 1912, in Walters, *My Life and Work* (New York, 1917), p. 195; Walters, *Reasons Why the Negro Should Vote the Democratic Ticket in This Campaign* (New York, 1912); Washington *Bee*, November 2, 1912, p. 4; Meier, *Negro Thought*, pp. 187–188.

proaches," Trotter wrote, "the clouds are lowering and a feeling of foreboding is creeping over the Colored people." There had been a sudden flurry of lynching and political race-baiting. And recently the House had passed a bill to make racial intermarriage a felony in the District of Columbia—"the most extreme piece of legislation along the Color line, if not the only Color line legislation, acted upon favorably by either branch of Congress since slavery was abolished." The Democratic party was responsible. "You are the national leader of that party," Trotter wrote to Wilson, and "You have the power to exercise sufficient influence to stop this color-line crusade. . . ." No word from Wilson. Two weeks later Trotter wrote again, asking him not to appoint Albert Burleson, a Texan, to be Postmaster General. The Post Office was the federal department that traditionally employed considerable numbers of Negroes, and Trotter feared that would be jeopardized under a white southerner. "You will doubtless remember my unqualified and active support of your candidacy," Trotter added, "and will believe me to desire nothing to chill the enthusiasm and hope of the Colored people in you as the inaugurator of a new era of equal rights for Colored Americans." Burleson was appointed, along with four other new Cabinet members from southern backgrounds. Clearly it was a new era for the southern white man.[35]

Trotter had no inclination to be part of the administration itself. A political appointment would only shackle his editorial independence, and when an admirer included his name on a list of prospective Negro officeholders, Trotter took himself out of consideration. He did, though, hope to play a direct part in the formulation of the administration's racial policy. A few days after the inauguration he again reminded Wilson of his campaign support and of his father's service as recorder of deeds under Cleveland. There-

[35] W. M. Trotter to Woodrow Wilson, February 12, 26, 1913, Wilson Papers.

fore, Trotter proposed, "From my responsible position in this cause as editor and leader I greatly desire to have your confidence, and to know and be granted the privilege of consultation on your general policy where we are concerned. . . . I am here in Boston, but I would come at any time at your command. We believe we can be of assistance as far as the Colored voters are concerned if we are consulted." [36]

Wilson would have no black adviser, and he began a steady retreat from the "absolute fair dealing" promised during the campaign. In Cabinet on April 11 Burleson proposed to segregate the Negro clerks in his department's Washington offices. Nobody in the room objected, and Wilson gave his approval. Concurrently, black Republican officeholders—among them William Lewis—were removed from office and replaced by white men. Burleson and two other southern Cabinet officers, William McAdoo and Josephus Daniels, went ahead with the segregation of the employees in their respective departments. McAdoo, with Wilson's consent, decided to make the Registry Division of his Treasury Department an all-Negro enclave, and toward that end Wilson appointed a black man to head the division. It was the administration's first Negro appointment. "I am heartsick," the Negrophobe author Thomas Dixon wrote Wilson, "over the announcement that you have appointed a negro to boss white girls as Register of the Treasury. Please let me as one of your best friends utter my passionate protest." Defending the action, Wilson assured Dixon that it was part of "a plan of concentration" —that is, segregation. But the Senate refused to confirm the Registry appointment, and the nominee, under pressure, withdrew his name from further consideration. Shortly thereafter the President named a white man to the

[36] R. S. Hudspeth to Joseph P. Tumulty, May 6, 21, 1913, and W. M. Trotter to Woodrow Wilson, March 11, 1913, Wilson Papers.

ordinarily Negro post of minister to Haiti.[37]

In May, Villard outlined a proposal for a National Race Commission to the President. Consisting of fifteen diverse individuals, it would undertake "a non-partisan scientific study of the status of the Negro in the life of the nation." Wilson seemed "wholly sympathetic" to the idea, but did nothing to implement it. When Villard questioned him on the spreading segregation in the federal departments, Wilson replied that its only purpose was to reduce "the friction, or rather the discontent and uneasiness, which has prevailed in many of the departments" and that "It is as far as possible from being a movement *against* the negroes. I sincerely believe it to be in their interest." Later Wilson told Villard that the Race Commission plan would have to be dropped for reasons of political sensitivity.[38]

For Trotter, Wilson's performance was profoundly humiliating. The NIPL's candidate was dealing the black man one blow after another. In public, at least, Trotter had no regrets. "We can stand criticism," he declared, "but want it understood that we believe we did the right thing. . . . The Democrats were going in anyway and by helping we put the race in a stronger position to oppose hostile treatment than if the Colored voters had solidly opposed the Democratic ticket." The NIPL met in Boston in mid-September and endorsed a plea that Trotter sent on to the President. It recalled Wilson's campaign letter to Walters and demanded, appealing to the President's good faith and "his own personal honor" as well, that he intervene in the

[37] Arthur S. Link, *Wilson: The New Freedom* (Princeton, 1956), pp. 246–248; William H. Lewis to Emmett J. Scott, March 12, 1913, Washington Papers; Thomas Dixon to Woodrow Wilson, June 27, 1913, and Wilson to Dixon, June 29, 1913, in Kathleen Long Wolgemuth, "Woodrow Wilson's Appointment Policy and the Negro," *Journal of Southern History*, XXIV (1958), 462–464.

[38] Oswald Garrison Villard, *Fighting Years: Memoirs of a Liberal Editor* (New York, 1939), pp. 239–240; Link, *New Freedom*, pp. 244–245; Woodrow Wilson to Villard, July 23, 1913, in *ibid.*, p. 251.

segregation matter. "We know the President has been absorbed over the schedules of his tariff bill. But we think it not impertinent to remind him that free wool, etc., is vastly less important than the interests of free men." With all possible patience, we wait for Wilson "to square his actions with his words." [39]

Trotter's voice was part of a chorus of protest from the entire range of Negro opinion and from concerned whites such as Horace Bumstead and the philanthropists Jacob Schiff and Julius Rosenwald. Black criticism of the Brownsville affair had been limited by the conspicuous silence of several Negro spokesmen, from Washington down, who were under obligation to the Roosevelt administration. Given Wilson's inattention to Negro matters, few black men felt beholden to him, and the race could show impressive unity in denouncing the new outrages in Washington, especially the federal segregation. The few black leaders who did court Wilson's favor were roasted for their treachery. Alexander Walters, the most conspicuous example, hoped for an appointment and—according to Wilson and McAdoo—privately told the administration that he was not disturbed by the segregation in the departments. Wilson and McAdoo relayed the information to Villard, and the story leaked out. "Daily," Walters complained to Wilson's aide Joseph Tumulty, "I am being taken to task for not seeing the President and branded as a traitor because I have not presented to the President the colored man's side of the question." Adversity seemed to be giving the race an uncommon degree of unity.[40]

[39] *Guardian*, October 11, 1913, p. 4., in Box 7, Storey Papers, LC; W. M. Trotter to Woodrow Wilson, September 22, 1913, enclosing NIPL statement, Wilson Papers.

[40] W. M. Trotter to William G. McAdoo, July 29, August 21, 1913, and Trotter to Charles S. Hamlin, October 21, 1913, William G. McAdoo Papers; and many letters in the Wilson Papers, such as those of W. Calvin Chase, August 2, Clifford H. Plummer, August 14, Horace Bumstead, August 16, Moorfield Storey, W. E. B. Du Bois, and Oswald Garrison Villard, August 15, Jacob H. Schiff, August 20, Francis J. Garrison, August 21, W. M. Trotter,

Yet the old jealousies and personal divisions remained. The Washington correspondent of the *New York Age* charged in July that Trotter had made no strong objection to the segregation, indeed had dismissed as exaggerated the reports of its spread through the federal offices. Trotter responded that he had been opposing the segregation in the *Guardian* since June, and further cited a protest letter to Burleson dated May 23. The *Age*, not convinced, announced that he had begun to speak out only after learning that he would not be given his father's old job of recorder of deeds. Trotter's "deep interest in the race," according to the *Age*, consisted of "being able to get some important Federal position." Trotter retorted, with justice, that the *Age*'s report was "a baseless, willfull falsehood." [41]

That exchange was left over from the days of the anti-Washington crusade. A more pressing concern for Trotter was to get along with the NAACP. The Association, the NIPL, and the major race newspapers were all working along roughly parallel lines, yet each hoped to scoop the others in uncovering and publicizing the Wilson administration's latest offenses. From Boston, Trotter had to rely on the ferreting operations of two NIPL men in the District of Columbia, Freeman Murray and Maurice Spencer. "I don't know what conditions are there," Trotter wrote to Murray, "but I am sorry you and Spencer cannot find out better the specific facts. I asked Spencer to send me copy of the Jim-Crow orders. I had to copy it out of the Amsterdam News. . . . The New York Age was first to bring out toilets & the wording over them. . . ." The

August 25, William D. Brigham, September 1, Julius Rosenwald, September 4, Francis J. Grimké, September 6, William Pickens, September 24, Archibald Grimké, October 30, and Leslie Pinckney Hill, December 9, 1913.

On the Walters matter, see *Guardian*, November 15, 1913, p. 4; Villard to Archibald Grimké, November 11, 1913, and copy of letter from Villard to Alexander Walters, November 11, 1913, in Grimké Papers; Walters to Joseph Tumulty, January 30, 1914, Wilson Papers.

[41] *New York Age:* July 24, 1913, p. 1; August 21, 1913, p. 4; September 25, 1913, p. 4; October 9, 1913, p. 4.

NAACP issued a circular that described the segregation in detail and blamed it all on the Wilson administration. Murray, as Washington press correspondent for the NIPL, attacked the Association's circular on the ground that much of the segregation was not new, that it was in part a carry-over from Taft and Roosevelt. Murray's correction was accurate enough, but, Trotter pointed out, much too severe and dangerously divisive. "The circular is a great help to the cause of the race," Trotter told Murray. "The Jim-Crow moves now are new in *style*, officially marked & ordered Jim-Crow toilets are new."
Moreover—

> Your trouble is in looking too much at our Colored factional side. . . . We must answer them & point out the truth & fire back, but it is not wise to do so to the extent of a severe attack on a well-meant public appeal by white men which is certainly honestly intended for the good of our race, and which would be palpably weakened by any "ifs" and "ands" and "heretofores." It seems to me a case where you and I must pocket unselfishly any partisan advantages . . . and admit the good done by Villard and Dubois despite the meannesses of both. . . . It may mean adding to the prestige of ingrates or would-be dictators, but the dangers are so great we *must* show a more or less united front by fighters on our side.

NAACP President Moorfield Storey pleaded with Trotter to make a show of unity: "Personal ambitions, personal hostilities, differences of opinion on minor points should all be sunk for the sake of the race as a whole." [42]

[42] W. M. Trotter to Freeman H. M. Murray, September 7, 1913, Murray Papers; Moorfield Storey to Oswald Garrison Villard, September 25, 1913, and Storey to Trotter, September 16, 1913, Moorfield Storey Papers. On the history of segregation in the federal departments, see August Meier and Elliott Rudwick, "The Rise of Segregation in the Federal Bureaucracy, 1900–1930," *Phylon*, XXVIII (1967), 178–184.

To dramatize Wilson's perifidy—and to match the NAACP's efforts—Trotter decided to bring a petition and protest directly to the President. During the fall of 1913 the NIPL collected 20,000 signatures in 36 states. Trotter carefully drafted a precise statement on the nature of the new segregation. He sent a copy to McAdoo: "I have good ground for believing the assertions in regard to your Department to be true, but submit it to you beforehand that you may have the opportunity to pass upon it's accuracy as to facts should you so desire." McAdoo made no answer. Trotter sponsored a dance in Boston to raise the money for the trip to Washington, and on November 6 came to the White House accompanied by Ida Wells-Barnett, William Sinclair, Byron Gunner, and Murray, Spencer, and Thomas Walker of the NIPL's local branch. Trotter and Wells-Barnett spoke for the group, read the statement and presented the petition. After a polite reply from Wilson the delegation left. Deenie Trotter congratulated Murray: "From all the publicity your delegation has received I think you men should feel very proud. You have certainly done your duty." [43]

Trotter felt encouraged. "The President listened attentively to Colored citizens," he wrote in the *Guardian*, "responded courteously and gave them thirty-five minutes of his time. He admitted proofs offered, he promised to investigate and to try to find a satisfactory solution." Six days afterward Trotter sent the President another letter and set of documents. He asked, "May I have the honor of a personal acknowledgement of the perusal of this letter and receipt of enclosures, in view of my position as head of the delegation of our League." No word from the White House. On December 5 he tried again, sending a summary

[43] W. M. Trotter to William G. McAdoo, November 3, 1913, McAdoo Papers; Francis J. Garrison to Oswald Garrison Villard, October 11, 1913, Villard Papers; *Guardian*, November 22, 1913, pp. 1, 2, 3, 4, in Box 7, Storey Papers, LC; Geraldine L. Trotter to Freeman H. M. Murray, November 14, 1913, Murray Papers.

of the interview and reminding Wilson of his pledge to check into the matter. "May we have your response," Trotter inquired, "and how soon?" Again silence.[44]

He tried to keep up the charade of harmonious cooperation with the NAACP. He gave *Guardian* space to an anti-segregation meeting held by the Association in Washington in late October. And three weeks later the *Guardian* declared, "The National Association is still working hard on the matter. Its report of the actual segregation is a valuable help to the protest." Then Du Bois neglected to mention the NIPL's White House interview in the December and January issues of the *Crisis*. "There are individual sharpshooters fighting their own effective guerilla warfare," wrote Du Bois in January. "We greet them and give them all credit. There are a few organizations here and there with some activity. We would not detract a moment from the value of their work." But the NAACP alone is "the battle line."

> The flat fact remains: There is in the United States but one organization with permanent headquarters, paid officials, active nation-wide membership, live local branches, a national organ, law officers and traveling organizers, all organized and prepared to make a front forward fight on racial prejudice in this land. . . . Join us and fight, then. Join or die!

Du Bois's insistence that *everyone* should join the NAACP recalled the authoritarian manner of the Tuskegee Machine, and on this occasion Trotter was provoked into making a public objection. "I shall go after Dubois, you bet!" Trotter promised Murray. "I have him now. But my heaviest guns would be trained on his claim that the N.A.A.C.P. is *the battle-line*. . . . I urge real organization

[44] *Guardian*, November 15, 1913, pp. 1, 4; W. M. Trotter to Woodrow Wilson, November 12, December 5, 1913, Wilson Papers.

and conference there to keep Dubois from having evidence that N.A.A.C.P. is *only* real organization of national character." [45]

"I cannot help feeling that Trotter's criticism is just," Storey confided to Villard, "and if you have any influence with Mr. DuBois I wish that you would urge him to notice it so that we may have a rather more general recognition of what Trotter and his associates are doing." Once again Storey asked Trotter to bury "little personal jealousies." The *Guardian* ran a mildly worded complaint about Du Bois's treatment of the NIPL. Murray favored a more outspoken approach, but Trotter again urged a course of moderation. When the Niagara Movement was foundering, Trotter recalled for Murray, the *Guardian* discreetly made no assault on Du Bois. "Now," Trotter said to Murray, "since it is the same DuBois who is the arch devil in the N.A.A.C.P. am I not pursuing my usual methods & care in attack? And are not dangers greater now and is not the N.A.A.C.P. with its large white element & management an even more critical case than the N.M.?" [46]

Villard took Storey's request to Du Bois but got nowhere. Storey was told of Du Bois's intransigence and, exasperated, asked Villard, "Is Mr. DuBois impervious to argument and suggestion?" Sometimes he was, but other NAACP officers, Joel Spingarn and May Childs Nerney among them, also urged him to give *Crisis* space to race leaders not in the NAACP. Under pressure, Du Bois printed a grudging note in the February issue. "The explanation is simple," said Du Bois. The interview was too late in November to make the deadline for the December

[45] *Guardian*, November 1, 1913, p. 4, in File 152-A, Wilson Papers; *Guardian*, November 22, 1913, p. 4, in Box 7, Storey Papers, LC; *Crisis*, VII (1913–14), 133–134; W. M. Trotter to Freeman H. M. Murray, December 26, 1913, Murray Papers.

[46] Moorfield Storey to Oswald Garrison Villard, January 8, 1914, and Storey to W. M. Trotter, January 8, 1914, Storey Papers; Trotter to Freeman H. M. Murray, January 6, 1914, Murray Papers.

issue, and it was no longer news by January. "There was not the slightest intention on the part of THE CRISIS to belittle or ignore this important event, but monthly newspapers have very distinct limitations." The correction, Trotter told Spingarn, "is better than nothing, but very inadequate—and far from convincing. The point was that the organ of the N.A.A.C.P. had never even mentioned the fact that the N.I.P.L. even was opposed to federal segregation. It has not done so yet. To mention what I did does not meet the case at all, and simply makes it appear that I was piqued out of personal vanity." [47]

His vanity was certainly involved, though. There was no avoiding the fact that the NAACP was much the more substantial and influential group. In 1914 it had some 6,000 members in 50 branches all over the country. It had an annual budget of over $15,000. The *Crisis*, under Du Bois's independent and brilliant editorship, boasted a circulation of over 30,000 and was a robust commercial success. A full-time, paid office staff manned the national headquarters in New York. In contrast, the NIPL had no headquarters, no staff, and no budget worth mentioning. Trotter snatched what time he could from the newspaper and held the group together through the mail and through the *Guardian*. Its leadership was dwindling steadily. William Scott had died in 1910. Alexander Walters gave no assistance after 1912. The schism that year split the

[47] Moorfield Storey to Oswald Garrison Villard, January 13, 1914, Storey Papers; W. E. B. Du Bois to Joel Spingarn, January 22, 1914, James Weldon Johnson Memorial Collection; May Childs Nerney to Archibald Grimké [January 1914], Grimké Papers; *Crisis*, VII (1913–14), 171; W. M. Trotter to Spingarn, January 28, 1914, Joel E. Spingarn Papers.

The *Guardian* quoted in *New York Age*, January 22, 1914, p. 4: "There is surely a marked difference in the treatment of the N.I.P.L. by the organ of the N.A.A.C.P. from the treatment of the N.A.A.C.P. by the chief organ of the N.I.P.L." The *Age* suggested, "We advise each group to discover or invent a few more letters and add them to the list, and in this way we think the difference will be speedily composed."

League in half. J. M. Waldron resigned in the summer of 1913—"a piece of meekness & cowardice," Trotter called it. If Trotter was oversensitive at being slighted by the NAACP, it was because he could only look on in frustration and resentment as the Association succeeded Washington as the dominant force in racial leadership. After the trouble over Trotter's Wilson interview, Du Bois was careful to be somewhat more generous to his old rival in Boston. "Outside the *Guardian* and the Cleveland *Gazette*," Du Bois proclaimed in March, "there have not been more than one or two colored papers from whom the Negro people could expect year in and year out strong, staunch advocacy of the fundamental principles of freedom and justice." That was fine praise. It may have been some consolation as the NIPL—renamed the National Equal Rights League later that year—fell further and further behind the NAACP.[48]

V

Lacking a strong organization, Trotter still managed to bring the protest over federal segregation to a climax. His petition and interview at the White House produced no visible changes. So after a year he decided to try again. In November 1914 he was informed that he could see the President on the twelfth of the month.

Wilson, it must be said, was under ferocious pressures just then. To the ordinary burdens of the Presidency had been added the delicate task of plotting the nation's response to the great war in Europe. His wife had died that summer too, and through the fall Wilson could not shake the sorrow of his bereavement. His confidant Edward M.

[48] Meier, *Negro Thought*, p. 183; *Crisis*, IX (1914–15), 298; J. Milton Waldron to Francis J. Grimké, July 22, 1913, in Carter G. Woodson, ed., *Works of Francis J. Grimké* (4 vols., Washington, D.C., 1942), IV, 131; W. M. Trotter to Freeman H. M. Murray, September 3, 1913, Murray Papers; *Crisis*, VII (1913–14), 240.

House observed on November 6, "He said he was broken in spirit by Mrs. Wilson's death, and was not fit to be President because he did not think straight any longer, and had no heart in the things he was doing." "My instinct," Wilson wrote a friend on November 9, "is to seek some occupation that will take my thoughts far afield where there is nothing that can concern me. . . . In short I want to run away, to escape something." [49]

Three days later Trotter brought his delegation to the White House. We come, he said to Wilson, "to renew the protest and appeal" we presented a year ago. The President replied that his Cabinet officers had investigated and reported that "the segregation was caused by friction between colored and white clerks." He wanted the colored people to make progress, but there was a great prejudice against them among white people. And the race problem had no place in politics. "Segregation is not humiliating but a benefit," said Wilson, "and ought to be so regarded by you gentlemen. If your organization goes out and tells the colored people of the country that it is a humiliation, they will so regard it." Trotter listened and then astonished the President by arguing with him: "For fifty years white and colored clerks have been working together in peace and harmony and friendliness, doing so even through two Democratic administrations. Soon after your inauguration began, segregation was drastically introduced." Wilson interrupted, declaring that "If this organization is ever to have another hearing before me it must have another spokesman. Your manner offends me."

"In what way?"

"Your tone, with its background of passion."

"But I have no passion in me, Mr. President, you are

[49] Diary of Edward M. House, November 6, 1914, in Edward M. House Papers; Woodrow Wilson to Nancy Toy, November 9, 1914, in Ray Stannard Baker, *Woodrow Wilson: Life and Letters* (8 vols., Garden City, N.Y., 1927–39), V, 141.

entirely mistaken; you misinterpret my earnestness for passion."

Trotter went on, saying that he could not control the minds of the Negroes, and on the segregation question would not do so even if he could. Again Wilson broke in. Trotter was not through: "Two years ago you were regarded as a second Abraham Lincoln." Wilson demanded that there be no personal references. You will see my intent, said Trotter. I am the one to do the interrupting, not you, said Wilson. "Now," Trotter shot back, "we colored leaders are denounced in the colored churches as traitors to our race." "What do you mean by traitors?" "Because we supported the Democratic ticket in 1912." Bringing in the political issue was a form of blackmail, Wilson insisted. He would act as he saw fit. After all, he was no office seeker. In fact, anyone who pursued the Presidency was "a fool for his pains." His burdens were intolerable. Some of his tasks were "more than the human spirit could carry." And the segregation issue must be treated factually, not emotionally. For forty-five minutes the two stubborn men fired back and forth. Then Wilson declared the interview at an end. Trotter said he was sorry if the President had felt offended. "Oh, we'll call it all right," said Wilson, and Trotter thought he saw him smile.

Trotter was still angry, though. Stopping in Joseph Tumulty's office, he told reporters what had been said, and added that Wilson's explanation "was entirely disappointing. His statement that segregation was intended to prevent racial friction is not supported by facts. For fifty years Negro and white employees have worked together in the Government departments in Washington. It was not until the present Administration came in that segregation was drastically introduced. . . ." The reporters left. Trotter started to go, but Tumulty called him back: "Mr. Trotter, you have violated every courtesy of the White House by quoting the President to the press." [50]

The next morning it was on the front page of the *New York Times* and other papers across the country. Beyond the drama of a private citizen—a Negro, in fact—arguing toe to toe with the President was the fact that Wilson, for the first time, had let it be known that he both knew of the segregation and approved of it. "Daniels," Wilson said to his Secretary of the Navy, "whenever a man loses his temper he loses his judgment. When the Negro delegate threatened me, I was damn fool enough to lose my temper and to point them to the door. . . . I raised that incident into an issue that will be hard to down." Tumulty, hoping to minimize the political consequences, told Villard that Trotter's presentation was "one of the most eloquent" he had heard, and that the segregation issue "is having our most earnest attention and we are trying to settle it in a satisfactory way." "There is but one satisfactory way," Villard replied, "and that is to do simple justice to these people and not to discriminate against them." [51]

Southern whites were of course horrified by the incident. "The Tucker darkey who tried to 'sass' the President is not a Booker T. Washington type of colored man," fumed a Texas newspaper. "He is merely a nigger." A Georgian congratulated Wilson for the way he handled "this negro, the hot blood of his savage fore-bears coursing

[50] "Mr. Trotter and Mr. Wilson," *Crisis*, IX (1914–15), 119–120; *New York Times*, November 13, 1914, p. 1; reminiscence by Thomas H. R. Clarke in *Guardian*, July 8, 1939, p. 4; unidentified clipping in W. M. Trotter folder, *Boston Herald Traveler* Library.

[51] Wilson's statement to Daniels is drawn from the latter's two recollections in the 1930s: Josephus Daniels to Frank P. Graham, November 5, 1936, in Joseph L. Morrison, *Josephus Daniels: The Small-d Democrat* (Chapel Hill, N.C., 1966), p. 66, and Daniels to Franklin D. Roosevelt, June 10, 1933, in Martin Duberman, *In White America* (Signet Book edition, New York, 1965), p. 85. On the Tumulty-Villard exchange, see Joseph P. Tumulty to Oswald Garrison Villard, November 18, 1914, Villard to Tumulty, November 23, 1914, and Villard to Francis J. Garrison, December 11, 1914, Villard Papers.

madly through his own being as he demanded that which might become a stepping-stone." Nor was this kind of sputtering restricted to Dixie.[52]

In the North the white press impartially chided Trotter for his "insolence" and Wilson for his approval of the segregation. The patrician *Boston Evening Transcript* observed, "The wonder is that such a poor representative of his race as the impudent mischief-maker from Boston was permitted the privilege of an interview with the President, and his exclusion for the future is well deserved." At the same time, "The segregation of the negro clerks is not only political, but it is sectional and partisan, and as unnecessary as it is unconstitutional." Trotter "offends many of his own color by his superabundant untactful belligerency," the *Independent* noted, but the delegation "had the right on their side, and the President gave them no satisfaction." "The President used fair words in 1912 in his appeal to the negroes for votes," said the *New Republic*. "We know now that those words meant nothing." Perhaps the most telling comment came from Frank Cobb's New York *World*, an influential supporter of most of the Wilson policies. "The bad manners of the Chairman of the delegation, however deplorable, are no justification of the policy of Jim-Crow government," Cobb wrote. It is, despite Wilson's denial, a political question, "a small, mean, petty discrimination," and "a reproach to his Administration and to the great political principles which he represents." [53]

Some of Wilson's mail was more comforting. "Undoubtedly," Julius Rosenwald wrote to the President, "Mr. Trotter is a notoriety seeker, whose methods are

[52] Beaumont, Texas, *Enterprise*, and other press quotations in *Crisis*, IX (1914–15), 121–125; J. Crampton Waters to Woodrow Wilson, November 12, 1914, Wilson Papers.

[53] *Boston Evening Transcript*, November 13, 1914, p. 10; *Independent*, LXXX (1914), 269; *New Republic*, I (1914–15), 5; New York *World*, November 13, 1914, p. 10.

dismaying to the conservative members of his race." "Mr.
Trotter does not represent the negroes of the United
States," a black minister in North Carolina assured Wilson. "We believe that he should not have approached you
with a minor domestic protest when you are filled with
graver responsibilities. . . . You are our President." Robert Moton—who in a few years would succeed Washington
as head of Tuskegee—informed Wilson of Trotter's jail
sentence in 1903 and added, "I want to say that the
Negroes, generally, do not in any way approve of Mr.
Trotter's conduct at the White House." Wilson thanked
Moton for the "admirable spirit" and "good judgment" of
his letter: "It is particularly delightful to me that my real
temper and disposition in matters of this sort should be
understood by those who themselves have the interests of
the negro people most at their heart. . . ." Charles Anderson proudly reported that he had brought about the cancel-
lation of a Trotter meeting in New York, and expressed
the hope that he would not be dismissed from his job as
collector of internal revenue in New York. (He was removed anyway.) [54]

"It was not what Trotter said to him, that angered
him," Harry Smith perceived, "half as much as the fact
that a 'Negro' had said it." But Smith wondered about the
ultimate effect of Trotter's "righteous resentment" of Wilson's "untruthful and almost insulting, patronizing statements." James Weldon Johnson in the *New York Age*
condemned Wilson's attitude, yet had no praise for Trotter. "It was an excellent place from which to get our cause
before the country," said the Indianapolis *Freeman*. "It
was a poor place to fight." [55]

[54] Julius Rosenwald to Woodrow Wilson, November 13, 1914,
E. D. W. Jones to Wilson, November 13, 1914, Robert R. Moton
to Wilson, November 16, 1914, Wilson to Moton, November 18,
1914, Charles Anderson to Joseph P. Tumulty, December 22,
1914, Wilson Papers.
[55] Cleveland *Gazette*, November 21, 1914, p. 2; *New York Age*,
November 19, 1914, p. 4; Indianapolis *Freeman*, November 21,
1914, pp. 1, 4.

Trotter "is a brave man," Du Bois wrote in the *Crisis*. (Though this second Wilson-Trotter meeting took place six days later in November than the first one, Du Bois managed to include it in the December issue this time.) "Of his fearlessness and his unselfish devotion to the higher interests of the Negro race there can be no doubt." Francis Garrison thought that Wilson was "right to resent Trotter's stupid threat of voting against him & the Democrats, but otherwise Trotter was sound & the President insulting & condescending." Villard reflected that perhaps "one has to be rude to get into the press and do good with a just cause!" John Milholland fired off a letter to Trotter praising his "display of moral courage, unswerving loyalty and genuine Americanism." In January Du Bois gave eleven pages of the *Crisis* to the "curious incident," and Joel Spingarn sent an official statement to Wilson: "The Association does not for a moment excuse any rudeness or lack of courtesy . . . but wishes to place itself on record as agreeing with Mr. Trotter that the slightest discrimination against colored people in the federal service is a grave injustice." [56]

Beneath this measured approval by the NAACP was the old undercurrent of jealousy. Albert Pillsbury of the Boston branch wrote to Archibald Grimké, then president of the District of Columbia branch:

I presume you agree with me that Trotter, by accident, has achieved the greatest feat of his life and accomplished more by insulting the President (if he did insult him, which I think possible) than all the polite words ever uttered on segregation could or will accomplish—and added greatly to his personal reputation and prestige, without altering the view which

[56] *Crisis*, IX (1914–15), 82; Francis J. Garrison to Oswald Garrison Villard, November 13, 1914, Villard to Garrison, November 18, 1914, Villard Papers; John E. Milholland to W. M. Trotter, November 13, 1914, in *Guardian*, November 21, 1914, p. 4, in Box 7, Storey Papers, LC; *Crisis*, IX (1914–15), 119–129.

we and others who know him well have been compelled and must continue to take of him.

Pillsbury spoke from an implacable personal dislike of
Trotter. Nonetheless he saw the point, that the incident
was both a score on Wilson and a major personal triumph
for Trotter. It came at a fortunate time, for Trotter's
career had been in disarray. His presidential candidate of
1912 had turned out to be a disaster for the black man.
His protest group, in its third major incarnation as the
National Equal Rights League, was losing the unequal
battle with the NAACP. Then he recovered some of his
losses in one burst: the second Wilson interview, with all
its attendant publicity, restored him to his former prominence. For months he was in demand as a speaker, traveling all over the North to give his version of the incident
and recruit members for the NERL. In mid-November, for
instance, he spoke for 90 minutes before a crowd of 2,000
in Washington, D.C. "I emphatically deny," he cried,
"that in language, manner, tone, in any respect or to the
slightest degree I was impudent, insolent, or insulting to
the President," and the crowd roared its approval.[57]

"I am a bit anxious," the NAACP's May Childs Nerney
fretted, "as to what Mr. Trotter's next coup may be. He
mustn't make us appear to the country as having done
nothing on the segregation issue, which is what he would
like to do." Charles Edward Russell was also upset, and
wondered whether the Washington branch had been working hard enough on the issue. Early in January Trotter
stumped through the Midwest for the NERL and, at a
meeting in Columbus, Ohio, gave the impression that he

[57] Albert E. Pillsbury to Archibald Grimké, December 21, 1914,
Grimké Papers; Washington *Bee*, November 21, 1914, p. 1. Pillsbury's animus toward Trotter was apparently not wholly Trotter's
fault. "He is very much in earnest," Storey said of Pillsbury, "but
his manner and attitude are such that most of us here find it
impossible to work with him" (Moorfield Storey to Oswald Garrison Villard, September 11, 1913, Storey Papers).

was also speaking for the NAACP. This disturbed Nerney, and then on January 12 Trotter wired instructions to the Association's New York office to send an agent to Washington to fight a new anti-intermarriage bill in Congress ("all of which is very interesting and informative," a flabbergasted Nerney wrote to Grimké). In February she worried that at the next annual meeting one of the group's Negro vice-presidents might dramatically refuse to serve and nominate Trotter in his place—and Trotter might be elected "by the rank & file." [58]

She needn't have worried. Trotter was ready to use the NAACP for his own purposes, but he had no intention of giving it any tangible assistance, and would probably have not become an active officer even if a post had been offered to him. He remained the splendid individualist, wonderfully principled and wary of any organization that he did not control. Consequently, the race would remain divided among the old Bookerites, the growing NAACP membership, and—a much smaller group—the Trotter loyalists. "Wouldn't it be a glorious thing," the *Chicago Defender* asked early in 1915, "if the Booker T. Washington faction, the Du Bois faction, and the Monroe Trotter faction would get together on a common ground and fight unitedly for the things that they are now fighting singly for?" [59]

[58] May Childs Nerney to Archibald Grimké, December 7, 1914, [November 1914], January 13, 1915, [February 1915], Grimké Papers.

[59] *Chicago Defender*, January 9, 1915, p. 7, in Paul Worthman, "The Negroes' Political Realignment" (history honors thesis, Williams College, 1962), p. 21.

Back to Boston: Consolidation at Home and National Decline

T H E "Monroe Trotter faction" on the national race scene enjoyed a temporary vogue for a few months after the second Wilson interview, but the publicity from that spectacular incident could not compete with the NAACP's money and organizing efforts for very long. Trotter's career was moving toward a long anticlimax. Two episodes seemed to epitomize the nature of his leadership after 1914. In the spring of 1915 Trotter led Boston's Negroes against a viciously racist motion picture. Then, a year later, Trotter stayed home while most other important Negro leaders met at Amenia, New York, in an extraordinary summit conference of racial spokesmen.

I

In February 1915 Thomas Dixon arranged a private White House showing for a new motion picture, *The Birth of a Nation,* based on one of his novels. President Wilson saw it and was fascinated. "It is like writing history with lightning," he is supposed to have exclaimed. "Of course," Dixon confided to Joe Tumulty, "I didn't dare allow the President to know the *real big purpose back of my film— which was to revolutionize Northern sentiments by a presentation of history that would transform every man in my audience into a good Democrat!* . . . Every man who comes out of one of our theatres is a Southern partisan for life—except the members of Villard's Inter-Marriage Society who go there to knock." The film was indeed violently controversial, and Tumulty, presumably acting from political considerations, urged Wilson to withdraw his endorsement. "I would like to do this," Wilson replied, "if there were some way in which I could do it without seeming to be trying to meet the agitation . . . stirred up by that unspeakable fellow Tucker." [1]

No writer before Margaret Mitchell was more successful than Dixon in popularizing a magnolia version of southern history. "Slippery Tom," the *Guardian* once called him, "the ranting, wandering divine," the "unasylumed maniac" whose madness is expressed in "terms of sound and fury only." His melodramatic novels were overdrawn but essentially consistent with the professionally respected William A. Dunning school of Reconstruction historiography. One Dixon novel, *The Clansman,* was turned into a successful drama that Trotter on two occasions helped

[1] Everett Carter, "Cultural History Written with Lightning: The Significance of *The Birth of a Nation,*" *American Quarterly,* XII (1960), 347; Thomas Dixon to Joseph P. Tumulty, May 1, 1915, Woodrow Wilson to Tumulty, c. April 25, 1915, in Arthur S. Link, *Wilson: The New Freedom* (Princeton, 1956), p. 253 *n.* Wilson evidently relented, because Tumulty wrote a Massachusetts congressman that Wilson "was entirely unaware of the character of the play before it was presented and has at no time expressed his approbation of it" (Tumulty to Thomas C. Thacher, April 28, 1915, in "Fighting a Vicious Film: Protest Against 'The Birth of A Nation,' " p. 30, pamphlet in Moorfield Storey Papers, LC).

force from the Boston stage.[2]

The film pioneer D. W. Griffith recognized a good vehicle and used *The Clansman* as the basis for a brilliant new movie in 1915. Given the combination of Dixon's exciting story and Griffith's creative genius, *The Birth of a Nation* was an artistic masterpiece, longer, more ambitious, and more enthralling than any film had ever been. Set in the Reconstruction era, it showed Negroes leaving the fields to sing and dance, forcing their attentions on white women, sitting in southern legislatures with their hats on and shoes off, whooping through a bill to permit racial intermarriage—in short, making a travesty of Reconstruction until the white man returned to power after the withdrawal of the last federal troops. One character, "Stoneman," was a loutish caricature of Thaddeus Stevens. There was a stirring chase scene: a suitably depraved-looking black man (actually a white actor in blackface) pursued a white girl across the countryside until, to avoid the fate worse than death, the fair maiden threw herself off a cliff. The freedmen were the villains; the law-abiding riders of the Ku Klux Klan were the heroes. It was, as Albert Pillsbury observed, "history upside down, a complete inversion of historical truth." [3]

But few whites recognized it as such. In New York the National Board of Censorship of Motion Pictures listened to protests from the *New York Age* and the NAACP, requested a few excisions, and endorsed the film. The critical response was ecstatic, with only a rare dissent. "It is spiritual assassination," Francis Hackett insisted in the *New Republic*. "It degrades the censors that passed it and

[2] *Guardian*, November 29, 1902, p. 4, William Monroe Trotter Papers; John Daniels, *In Freedom's Birthplace: A Study of the Boston Negroes* (Boston and New York, 1914), p. 125; Francis J. Garrison to Oswald Garrison Villard, July 24, 1910, Oswald Garrison Villard Papers.

[3] Carter, "Cultural History Written with Lightning," pp. 353–355; Albert E. Pillsbury to editor, May 3, 1915, in *Boston Herald*, May 5, 1915.

the white race that endures it." The New York crowds trooped to two performances each day, paying the unheard-of price of two dollars a head.[4]

Early in April the news came to Boston that the film would start a run there on the tenth. Trotter was out of town, delivering his lecture on the Wilson interview. In his absence members of the Boston Literary and the local branch of the NAACP set up a hearing before Mayor James Michael Curley. Trotter cut short his tour and hurried back to Boston. He sent a letter of protest to Curley and then showed up for the hearing. Mary White Ovington—up from New York for the occasion—and two other NAACP officers, Moorfield Storey and Butler Wilson, spoke effectively against the film. Following them, Trotter tried to apply the kind of pressure that Curley would understand: Negroes had supported Curley in the past, but their future votes depended on his handling of *The Birth of a Nation*. D. W. Griffith testified in behalf of his film and, turning to Storey, announced that he would contribute $10,000 to charity if Storey could point out any incident that was not historically true. Was it true, Storey asked, that a black lieutenant governor of South Carolina had locked a white girl in his room and demanded that she marry him? The hearing ended with the protesters scoring most of the points. Afterward Griffith walked up to Storey, expressed his pleasure at meeting him, and stuck out his hand. "No sir," said Storey, and he drew back.[5]

Curley decided that the film could be shown if a few

[4] Thomas R. Cripps, "The Reaction of the Negro to the Motion Picture Birth of a Nation," *Historian*, XXV (1962–63), 350–351; Francis Hackett, "Brotherly Love," *New Republic*, II (1915), 185; *New York Times*, March 4, 1915, p. 9, and March 31, 1915, p. 9.

[5] *Guardian*, April 17, 1915, p. 2, in Box 7, Storey Papers, LC; Mary White Ovington, *The Walls Came Tumbling Down* (New York, 1947), pp. 128–129; Elizabeth C. Putnam to Archibald Grimké [April 1915], Archibald Grimké Papers; *Crisis*, X (1915), 87.

parts were cut out: the opening statement ("The bringing of the African to America in the seventeenth century planted the first seed of disunion"), the forced marriage, part of the chase scene, an incident between Stoneman and his Negro mistress, and some shenanigans in the South Carolina legislature. The Tremont Theatre made the changes and launched the film on schedule on Saturday, April 10. During the next week Trotter, William Lewis, and others made further appeals to Curley and Governor David Walsh, both of whom insisted that they could do nothing. It was good publicity for the film, though. The Tremont Theatre's newspaper advertisements proclaimed TICKETS SELLING FOUR WEEKS AHEAD, and there seemed to be no recourse for the frustrated black community.[6]

The situation exploded on Saturday night. The Tremont's management, acting on rumors of a Negro plot to pack the house and seize and destroy the film, put scores of plainclothesmen on duty inside the theater. More policemen milled around outside. At about seven-thirty Trotter led a group of Negroes into the lobby and tried to buy tickets. Abruptly the ticket windows slammed shut. The performance was sold out, the management explained. Not true, said Trotter, pointing to a white man who had just bought three tickets. Again he demanded to be sold a ticket; the management was adamant. The Negroes were ordered out of the lobby. They refused to leave. Trotter, furious by then, shouted a charge of discrimination. Then the police moved in. One white plainclothesman struck Trotter. The lobby was finally cleared with billy clubs, and Trotter and ten others were arrested. But some black men had already managed to be admitted to the performance.

[6] Cripps, "Reaction to Birth of a Nation," pp. 354–355; *Boston Sunday Post*, April 11, 1915, p. 6; *Boston Post:* April 11, 1915, p. 6; April 15, 1915, pp. 1, 15; April 16, 1915, p. 22; April 17, 1915, p. 9.

The film was run, punctuated by occasional jeers from the audience. At the point when the fair maiden was about to leap to her death a Negro in the audience stood up and, according to a newspaper account, "spattered a very ancient egg by a well-directed shot over the exact middle of the white screen." Plainclothesmen took the egg-thrower out and booked him for malicious mischief. Mysterious parties set off stink bombs a few moments later. At eleven o'clock the show ended and the audience spilled out into the street, to more arguments and more arrests. A few blocks away a fist fight between whites and blacks sent four men to the hospital. "It is a rebel play," cried Trotter, out on bail, and "an incentive to great racial hatred here in Boston. It will make white women afraid of Negroes and will have white men all stirred up on their account. If there is any lynching here in Boston, Mayor Curley will be responsible." [7]

It was the most ominous racial incident in Boston in anyone's memory, probably the most ominous since the Civil War era. There was an echo from that era on Sunday afternoon when the Wendell Phillips Memorial Association, under the old abolitionist Frank Sanborn, sponsored an overflow meeting at Faneuil Hall. The crowd, mostly black, cheered speeches by several white men, but held its greatest approval for Trotter. "Where is the valiant Jim Curley of old," Trotter demanded, "—the friend of the people—lovable Jim Curley, whom we colored people supported for the mayoralty against the advice of some of our white friends?" When he ran for mayor, said Trotter, "I overlooked his record as a jailbird. Now he admits that this film is a disgrace, but says his hands are tied." And yet, Trotter told an overflow group outside the hall, "Mayor Curley has stopped other plays. If this was an attack on the

[7] *Boston Post*, April 18, 1915, p. 2; *New York Times*, April 18, 1915, Sec. II, p. 15; *Boston Daily Globe*, April 18, 1915, pp. 1, 3; *Boston Post*, May 4, 1915, p. 7, and May 5, 1915, p. 1. Trotter was fined $20 but appealed his case, apparently successfully.

Irish race he would find a way pretty quick to stop it." The
meeting adjourned with a resolve to bring the matter to
Governor Walsh.[8]

Early next morning Negroes marched up Beacon Street,
singing "Nearer, My God, to Thee," gathering to confront
Walsh at the State House. Trotter appeared at nine-thirty
and, standing by the door, called out sixty names. He and
his delegation were admitted to the columned hall inside,
and the crowd settled down to wait. Numbering perhaps
1,500 or 2,000 people, it overflowed the broad steps down
to Beacon Street and the Common. The crowd was orderly
but grim; someone started singing "America" and was
hissed to silence. This mass support was responsive to
Trotter and awaited news from him. Inside the State
House, though, more moderate black spokesmen had
Walsh's ear. William Lewis, Butler Wilson, and two
others saw the governor first and worked out a solution
with him. Following them, William Brigham—one of the
few white men in Trotter's NERL—and a white group
talked with Walsh, and finally Trotter's band of sixty saw
him. Trotter asked him to speak to the crowd outside. He
refused, but designated Trotter his spokesman. So Trotter
stood on a balcony overlooking the front steps and announced that Walsh, through his Attorney General, would
prosecute the management of the Tremont Theatre under
a 1910 censorship law that prohibited any performance
judged to be "lewd, obscene, indecent, immoral or impure,
or suggestive of lewdness, obscenity, indecency, immorality or impurity." And if that did not work, said Trotter,
Walsh would try to obtain a new censorship law. These
developments seemed so promising that a planned demon-
stration at the theater was called off, and that evening
Trotter declared at a meeting of the Boston Literary that

[8] *Boston Daily Globe*, April 19, 1915, pp. 1, 3; *Boston Post*,
April 19, 1915, p. 9; *Boston Herald*, April 19, 1915, clipping in
David I. Walsh Scrapbook, David I. Walsh Papers.

the battle "was won in spite of colored traitors." [9]

The traitors he had in mind were Alexander Cox and Philip Allston, two officers in the Boston branch of the National Negro Business League. On Saturday they had been quoted in the Boston press as having said that the film "was historical and would have a good effect." The quotation was somewhat suspect, since it came secondhand from one of the film's ardent defenders. Nonetheless it provoked a fierce reaction against Cox and Allston in the Negro community. "Since Saturday night," Samuel Courtney wrote to Tuskegee, "it has been considered dangerous for them to show themselves in the street." Otherwise, Courtney noted, "The Negroes are a unit in their determination to drive it out of Boston." Under the popular pressure Allston wrote a letter to the *Boston Post* saying that he did in fact object to the film, and he even went so far as to compliment Trotter: "his attitude should speak for itself as one seeking justice." To a remarkable degree the old factions were pulling together against the film, submerging the old animosities, at least for a while. As J. H. Harris, another Bookerite, remarked early in May, "the best thing of all to my mind is that for the first time during my 27 years in Boston the entire Negro population is a unit." [10]

Two days after the march on the State House a municipal judge, Thomas H. Dowd, ruled that the chase scene was the only part of the film that violated the censorship law. If that was eliminated, he would not issue a summons

[9] Interview with Walter J. Stevens, August 23, 1965; *Boston Evening Transcript*, April 19, 1915, and *Boston Herald*, April 20, 1915, clippings in Walsh Scrapbook; *Boston Evening Globe*, April 19, 1915, p. 12; Minutes of Boston Literary and Historical Association, April 19, 1915, Trotter Papers.

[10] Henry MacMahon to editor in *Boston Post*, April 17, 1915, p. 12; Samuel E. Courtney to Booker T. Washington, April 19, 1915, Booker T. Washington Papers; Philip J. Allston to editor, April 23, 1915, in *Boston Post*, April 24, 1915, p. 6; J. H. Harris to Washington, May 3, 1915, Washington Papers.

to the theater. Trotter was not satisfied. Cutting the chase sequence was helpful, he said, but the worst scene—the black politician forcing a white girl into marriage—was still intact. Moreover, Lewis checked the revised version of the chase and reported that the audience could still see the leering pursuer and his victim's poignant death, leaving the audience to make the obvious conclusion. But the incomplete change was allowed to stand, and the theater continued its sellout business.[11]

That left one course: to seek a new censorship law and then have the film banned under it. On April 30 the legislature's judiciary committee approved a bill to establish a censorship board in Boston consisting of the mayor, the police commissioner, and the chief justice of the municipal court. The board's members would be empowered to revoke a theater's license for any reason "satisfactory to them." During the next three weeks, as the bill progressed through the legislature, the enemies of *The Birth of a Nation* kept up their agitation through meetings, resolutions, and letter-writing campaigns. Trotter was especially busy, noted the *Boston Post*, and his "activities to have the photo play run out of the city have been unceasing. . . ." "The movement," Albert Pillsbury grumbled, "has suffered severely from too much Trotter." [12]

On May 21 Walsh signed the censorship bill into law. That evening Trotter held a meeting in the *Guardian* office and formed a delegation to call at City Hall and demand that Curley and his new board act at once. "Every performance heaps new undeserved ignominy on the Negro race," Trotter told reporters, "and we think it should be stopped at once. We hope to let not a day elapse before we request the censors to act." The next day, Saturday, the local branch of the NAACP petitioned the board for a hear-

[11] *Boston Post*, April 22, 1915, p. 1, and April 23, 1915, p. 9.
[12] *Boston Post*, May 1, 1915, p. 16, and May 25, 1915, p. 5; Albert E. Pillsbury to Archibald Grimké, May 17, 1915, Grimké Papers.

ing. Curley was in no hurry. The film was a volatile issue that he would have preferred to ignore, but he called a hearing for the following Wednesday. The hearing was a restricted affair. The NAACP's three petitioners, Wilson, Lewis, and one white man, J. Mott Hallowell, were admitted; Trotter and his followers were not. Afterward the board's three members said that they would view the film individually and reconvene in a week to give their decision.[13]

By this time the film had been kept out of Chicago, St. Louis, all of Ohio, and elsewhere, including Massachusetts outside of Boston. When the new censorship board met again on June 2 it had ample precedents for banning the film in Boston. That day the board held another hearing, received a pro-censorship petition of 6,000 signatures, and then announced its decision: the film was not objectionable, the Tremont Theatre's license would not be revoked, and thus the film could continue its run.[14]

After that, nothing else could be done. There were a few more protests and demonstrations. One in front of the theater on June 7 resulted in eight arrests. But *The Birth of a Nation* was impregnable. It played on and on, changed theaters in September, and finally left town in late October, after six and one half months and 360 triumphant performances.[15]

II

The battle was lost, yet Trotter could count a few gains. For the first time since the Civil War a significant number of white Bostonians had directly taken up the Negro's

[13] *Boston Post:* May 22, 1915, p. 3; May 23, 1915, p. 13; May 27, 1915, p. 6.

[14] Cripps, "Reaction to Birth of a Nation," p. 359; *Survey,* XXXIV (1915), 210; Mary Childs Nerney to Charles Edward Russell, June 9, 1915, Charles Edward Russell Papers; *Boston Post,* June 3, 1915, pp. 1, 16.

[15] *Boston Post,* June 8, 1915, p. 1; *Boston Evening Globe,* October 30, 1915, p. 12.

cause in a public controversy. A Unitarian minister called
one meeting, he said, to prove that "the old Boston spirit of
friendliness and good will toward the colored people is still
strong." At least it was not dead. The city's Negro population, moreover, had responded to the crisis with unity and
purpose. Trotter, more than anyone else, spoke for that
community and directed its efforts to oppose the film. That
July he was one of five speakers (and the token Negro) at
the dedication of a statue of Wendell Phillips on the Common. Curley's representative, hoping to rebuild City Hall's
bridges to the black community, said that Negroes should
have a "spokesman" at the dedication of a monument to
Phillips, and that "there could be no more fit representative than William Monroe Trotter, whom every Bostonian
who is half alive knows." "Phillips believed with us,"
Trotter declared, "that there can be no freedom without
equality and no equality without the ballot." Black men
must complete the work that Phillips started, "using his
methods of agitation, organization and courage. . . ." At
the same time, Trotter, conscious that he was speaking for
his entire community, made no barbed references to Curley, or Woodrow Wilson, or Booker T. Washington.[16]

Trotter's campaign against Tuskegee had been dormant
for several years, and without its acrimony Boston's Negroes could start to move together. The nature of Washington's race leadership had changed drastically since the
bitter days of 1903. His political power eroded under
Taft's Presidency, and stopped altogether in 1913. Freed
of the necessity to honor his political debts, and in response
to the resurgence of militant ideas among Negroes, during
the last years of his life Washington began to speak out
with more frankness and directness. He told a white group
in 1914, "You cannot shut the Negro away from the white

[16] *Boston Post*, April 26, 1915, p. 1; *Exercises at the Dedication
of the Statue of Wendell Phillips July 5, 1915* (Boston, 1916), pp.
36–42.

man." And to a black audience that same year, "Segregation is not only unnecessary, but, in most cases, it is unjust." He dealt in the same spirit with lynching, school discrimination, and other issues. As his power dwindled, his candor grew.[17]

He never became "manly" enough for Trotter, but gradually the *Guardian* confined its opposition to sporadic sniping. In a speech in 1913 Trotter recalled the Boston Riot and, according to Philip Allston, "he apologized for his fiendish actions ten years ago!" To which Emmett Scott replied, "I am very glad to hear that the sinner is at the mourners' bench. Of course there is nothing of genuineness in any protestations that he may make." Two years later it was apparent that Scott had been too cynical about Trotter's sincerity. Washington, overworked as usual, died in November 1915 in his sixtieth year. Du Bois's obituary was self-consciously generous, yet still concluded that "in stern justice, we must lay on the soul of this man, a heavy responsibility for the consummation of Negro disfranchisement, the decline of the Negro college and public school and the firmer establishment of color caste in this land." Trotter, in contrast, summarized Washington's achievements, quickly noted the anti-Washington campaign, and ended on a note of astonishing compassion: "Nor is this hour of grief for his family and admirers appropriate time for adverse criticism. The controversy may well subside on both sides. This is the time for the race to unite in defense of its rights and liberties. 'De Mortuis nil nisi Bonum.' "[18]

[17] August Meier, *Negro Thought in America, 1880–1915: Racial Ideologies in the Age of Booker T. Washington* (Ann Arbor, Mich., 1963), p. 115; E. Davidson Washington, ed., *Selected Speeches of Booker T. Washington* (New York, 1932), pp. 229, 248; Samuel R. Spencer, Jr., *Booker T. Washington and the Negro's Place in American Life* (Boston, 1955), pp. 190–192.

[18] Philip J. Allston to Emmett J. Scott, November 10, 1913, and Scott to Allston, November 21, 1913, Washington Papers; *Crisis*, XI (1915–16), 82; *Guardian*, November 20, 1915, p. 4,

In Boston he made his peace with some of the old
Bookerites, notably William Lewis. The two former enemies had worked along parallel lines, without apparent
friction, in fighting *The Birth of a Nation*. Lewis, no
longer seeking a federal office, could lend his talents to the
struggle with a fervor that must have impressed Trotter.
At a hearing on the new censorship bill Lewis stirred the
audience with his rebuttal of one of the bill's opponents:
"He said that he is glad that we are being forced to face
the Negro problem. I am not. Why should I be a problem
to any man? I am a problem only to the man who seeks to
take away my rights as a human being. . . ." That fall
Lewis and Trotter supported Walsh in his campaign for
reelection as governor. Trotter published a circular reminding black voters of Walsh's help against the film.
Butler Wilson, campaigning for Walsh's Republican opponent, wrote a letter to a Boston newspaper arguing that
any Negro who voted for Walsh would thereby implicitly
endorse the national Democratic administration's racial
policies. That was precarious logic, and Trotter spent an
issue of the *Guardian* refuting the argument. Nonetheless
Walsh lost a close election, with most Negroes probably
voting against him, and Wilson was greatly amused.
"Lewis & Trotter are classed together," he told Archibald
Grimké, "& both are in for very severe criticism. It's really
absurdly laughable." [19]

Wilson and his Boston branch of the NAACP were the
main obstacle as Trotter tried to forge genuine black unity
in the city. The branch's prodigious efforts against *The
Birth of a Nation* brought it publicity and many new
members. The branch spent nearly $1,000, and Du Bois
proclaimed in the *Crisis* that the center of the national

Trotter Papers. The contrast between the final judgments
of Du Bois and Trotter was noticed at the time (Charles H. Moore
to editor, in *New York Age*, January 27, 1916, p. 4).

[19] *Boston Post*, April 28, 1915, p. 6; Butler Wilson to Archibald
Grimké, November 12, 1915, Grimké Papers.

campaign against the film was in Boston. At the end of the year Wilson could justifiably boast to Joel Spingarn, "The fight against 'The Birth of a Nation' won state-wide recognition of our Boston Branch as a fighting machine with resources and intelligent methods." Trotter, of course, would not join the branch, so his feud with the NAACP remained tenacious and unpleasant.[20]

Otherwise Boston's Negroes were moving toward a detente among themselves. In November 1916 the *Guardian* was tendered a fifteenth-birthday party in ceremonies at the site of the Boston Riot. White men such as Moorfield Storey and William Brigham joined Negro leaders such as Lewis and Emery Morris (but not Wilson, Samuel Courtney, or Clement Morgan) in praising Trotter and his newspaper for their fifteen years of labor. Lewis provided the dramatic high point. "I claim to be a sort of Godfather to the Guardian," Lewis said, "but the infant grew too lusty for me, kicked, squirmed, and cried out on every occasion. I abandoned the child; and I think the Guardian abandoned me." But finally they were ready to work together again. As Trotter put it in the *Guardian*, a little extravagantly:

> Here in this celebration the big chiefs buried the hatchet and smoked together the pipe of Peace and now the spirit of good fellowship once more reigns supreme, and with a united front and unbroken ranks they once more turn to renew the warfare against race discrimination, segregation and lynching. This fact is prophetic of a brightening future. This is the spring-time of the race's hopes in America and the Guardian must plant the seeds of hope.[21]

[20] Charles Flint Kellogg, *NAACP: A History of the National Association for the Advancement of Colored People, Volume I 1909–20* (Baltimore, 1967), p. 121; *Crisis*, X (1915), 87; Butler R. Wilson to Joel Spingarn, December 28, 1915, Joel E. Spingarn Papers.

[21] *Guardian*, December 2, 1916, pp. 1, 4, 5, Trotter Papers.

"The spring-time of the race's hopes in America."
Washington's death left national black leadership in a fluid
state. Without pressure from Tuskegee, the factions might
be able to come together into some kind of more militant
consensus. Toward that end, in the summer of 1916 Joel
Spingarn invited every important black leader to a unity
conference at his estate in Amenia, New York. It was
organized by NAACP men but designed to include every
spokesman and point of view of any consequence within
the race. "I appreciate much your invitation to the conference of Colored men," Trotter told Spingarn. It was impossible, he added, for him "to agree far ahead to be at any
meeting away from Boston." He said that he hoped to be
there, for "I want to help your work in the N.A.A.C.P."
But—and here was the crucial point—the Association
should "do it's good without doing harm" and therefore "encourage and not discourage national self-organization and
self-leadership for freedom of this proscribed group. . . ."
Spingarn added Trotter's name to the printed program for
the conference, but at the last moment Trotter wrote him,
"It finally turns out that I cannot be present. . . ." He
sent his greetings to the conferees and endorsed the purpose of the meeting: "These are indeed times to consider
a unity of feeling, spirit and purpose within the racial
group." And, from his "15 years of constant thought and
work," he implored the leaders at Amenia to recognize
the "urgent, fundamental need" for "racially autonomous
organizations" as well as "friend-helping cooperative organizations." In other words, the NAACP must concede
a role for the NERL.[22]

So he stayed in Boston while over fifty diverse individuals met at Amenia in an atmosphere of remarkable harmony. There were a few whites, but essentially it was a
candid summit conference of American Negroes. From the

[22] James C. Daniel, "Negro Leadership Minus Booker T. Wash-
ington: Depolarization and Consensus in 1916" (seminar paper,
University of Maryland, 1968); Kellogg, NAACP, p. 87; W. M.
Trotter to Joel Spingarn, August 16, 23, 1916, Spingarn Papers.

Tuskegee camp were Emmett Scott, Fred Moore of the *New York Age*, William Lewis, and James Weldon Johnson. From the old Niagara Movement were Du Bois, Atlanta's John Hope, and others. Somewhere between the two poles were Kelly Miller, Eugene Kinckle Jones of the Urban League, Mary Church Terrell, and Charles Chesnutt. It was, in Terrell's recollection, "the first time that so many colored people who differed so widely . . . had come together since the Emancipation Proclamation had been signed." The discussions, on a great diversity of subjects, were free and open, limited only by Spingarn's insistence that no time be wasted when it was clear that agreement was impossible. The principal parties knew each other well through black America's underground, and anyone who stood up to pontificate was hooted down. They unanimously adopted some generally worded resolutions, agreeing on the need for "complete political freedom," recognizing the "peculiar difficulties which surround this problem in the South," and calling for the elimination of "antiquated subjects of controversy, ancient suspicions and factional alignments." Then they departed in a euphoric cloud of racial unity. Said Moore in the *Age*, "It marks the birth of a new spirit of united purpose and effort that will have far-reaching results." That was a trifle excessive, for no minds were swayed, no permanent organization came out of it, and in a little while the factions had returned to the old feuding. And yet it was a significant and revealing occasion, if only because all those disparate personalities had been able to talk to each other for three days. "Probably," Du Bois concluded a few years later, "on account of our meeting the Negro race was more united and more ready to meet the problems of the world than it could possibly have been without these beautiful days of understanding." [23]

[23] *Crisis*, XII (1916), 276–277; Mary Church Terrell, *A Colored Woman in a White World* (Washington, D.C., 1940), p. 195; Eugene Kinckle Jones to Joel Spingarn, September 12, 1916, Spingarn Papers; *New York Age*, September 14, 1916, p. 4;

And Trotter was not there. There is no reason to doubt his sincerity in telling Spingarn that he would have liked to come. He also genuinely granted the NAACP an important function in the black man's freedom struggle. His primary concern, though, was to carve out a niche of at least equal importance for the NERL. He reasoned that attending an event sponsored by the NAACP would do little for the recognition of his own group. Consequently he made no special effort to go to Amenia. Instead he aimed to pick off likely Negroes of militant inclinations who were not committed to the NAACP.

A week before the Amenia Conference, for instance, he wrote a letter to James Weldon Johnson, then writing editorials for the *Age* in New York. In the past Johnson's quiet support of the Bookerites—his song, "Lift Every Voice and Sing," long considered the national anthem of black America, was dedicated to Washington—had won him consular appointments in Latin America. Trotter was wary of him, and it was mutual: early in 1916 Johnson drew up a list of the twenty-five foremost American Negroes which omitted Trotter's name. Since his return to New York the NAACP had been wooing him. "We are glad indeed that the Association has caught you at last," May Childs Nerney wrote him. "Are you going to be in New York permanently? If so, we are going to be presumptuous and ask you to serve on some of our committees." Still, he had not cast his lot with any specific group during the reshufflings after Washington's death, and in August 1916 Trotter sought his editorial support for an NERL project. "I have been looking for one of your good editorials," Trotter explained, "ever since you wrote me of

---

W. E. B. Du Bois, *The Amenia Conference: An Historic Negro Gathering* (Amenia, N.Y., 1925), p. 17. Elliott Rudwick, in his *W. E. B. Du Bois: A Study in Minority Group Leadership* (Philadelphia, 1960), pp. 185–190, has argued that the significance of the Amenia Conference has been generally "overrated," for some of the reasons which I present above.

your endorsement of the idea and my publication of your support." The NERL venture, said Trotter, was "a great race movement. You are in a position of power & that means responsibility. . . . You are of the new school and present generation. Let us all pull together." [24]

Johnson gave no support to the project, and a few months later he joined the NAACP staff as national organizer, thus becoming only the second Negro to assume an important office in the Association. It was painfully apparent, and Trotter must have seen it, that the focus of racial leadership was drifting toward the NAACP. Johnson was an urbane gentleman of superb intellectual and literary gifts and proved to be a valuable addition to the Association staff. After nearly a year of working with him, Mary White Ovington felt the need for "someone to keep Mr. Johnson stirred up a little more," she confided to Spingarn. "But he's a fine worker and in his quiet way accomplishes a great deal. I am glad you overruled my judgment in the matter of his coming to us." [25]

The pattern of Trotter's later career was set during his effective leadership against *The Birth of a Nation* in Boston and in his conspicuous absence from the Amenia Conference a year later. It was a pattern of declining national influence and of consolidation in his home city.

III

At home he faced a crisis almost every week as he tried to scrape together enough money to keep his newspaper going. "The lack of practical business is the one feature of Trotter that I cannot understand," wrote an admirer in

[24] Meier, *Negro Thought*, p. 255; Emmett J. Scott to James Weldon Johnson, March 27, 1916, Johnson to E. B. Reuter, February 20, 1916, May Childs Nerney to Johnson, March 9, 1915, W. M. Trotter to Johnson, August 16, 1916, all in James Weldon Johnson Memorial Collection.

[25] Meier, *Negro Thought*, p. 255; Mary White Ovington to Joel Spingarn, September 26, 1917, Spingarn Papers.

1911. "I can understand how he believes as he does, but I cannot see how he expects to make bricks without straw. If he permits his zeal to run off with his good sense, he ought to see that his own failure will be the very proof which white people will use of the unfitness of the Negro race for twentieth century civilization." [26]

The *Guardian*, unlike some Negro newspapers, was not designed to show a profit. Essentially, Trotter pointed out, it was "not a mere money-making business venture but a public work for equal rights and freedom." Its local constituency was tiny: in 1910 the Negro population of Boston was only 13,564, and in all of New England there were only some 66,000 black people. Such urban centers as New York and Washington, on the other hand, had concentrated Negro market areas of 90,000 people and more. The *Guardian*'s insistent political independence cut off the regular party subsidies that some other papers enjoyed. Many of Trotter's rival editors had outside sources of income—Harry Smith of the Cleveland *Gazette* was a composer and band leader, Calvin Chase of the Washington *Bee* was a lawyer, T. T. Fortune of the *New York Age* was a free-lance journalist, George Knox of the Indianapolis *Freeman* was a barber. Trotter's real-estate business had gradually been forgotten, and he also ran his own protest group, an exhausting side activity that no other editor tried to carry on. [27]

The paper's well-known militancy no doubt scared off significant black and white sources of advertising revenue. And, true to the oath of total abstention he had taken as a Harvard undergraduate, Trotter would accept no advertisements for liquor and tobacco. Indeed, he proudly noted,

[26] [C.A.?] Franklin to John E. Bruce [1911?], John E. Bruce Papers.
[27] *Guardian*, December 19, 1914, p. 1, in Box 7, Storey Papers, LC; Emma Lou Thornbrough, "American Negro Newspapers, 1880–1914," *Business History Review*, XL (1966), 472 *n*, 478–482, 485.

"We have never during our existence ever advertised but one place where liquor was sold and we voluntarily discontinued that when we felt that the place was not conducted as we thought it should be." As a matter of racial pride, he also refused the lucrative notices for skin lighteners and hair straighteners that other papers ran. Wary of losing his editorial independence, he was reluctant to delegate authority to the volunteer workers who came into his office, and for the same reason would not sell shares in the *Guardian* or incorporate it as a business enterprise. "Leave me . . . and the Guardian untrammelled," he would tell friends who proposed incorporation; "no syndicate can be formed to finance the Guardian." Moreover, he simply was not ruthless enough in collecting his bills. He let unpaid subscriptions run on interminably and trudged around Boston seeing his many creditors personally. Thus he would show up at a meeting of the Boston Literary with a bill of $3.25 for advertising. Someone asked that the bill be reduced to $2.75, Trotter agreed, and then it was paid. "Of course we have many delinquent subscribers," he admitted, ". . . more than we ought to have, but that is the fate of every Colored paper." [28]

Since he wanted his paper to be primarily an instrument of protest, it was neither as racy nor as entertaining as some of its competitors. The *Guardian* was earnest and full of news. After the departure of George Forbes in 1903, though, it lacked literary polish and journalistic distinction. Kelly Miller remarked that Trotter edited his news-

[28] Ruth Worthy, "A Negro in Our History: William Monroe Trotter, 1872–1934" (M.A. thesis, Columbia University, 1952), pp. 35–36; *Guardian*, February 26, 1910, p. 4; Charles W. Puttkammer, "William Monroe Trotter: An Evaluation of the Life of a Radical Negro Newspaper Editor, 1901–1934" (senior thesis, Princeton University, 1958), pp. 18–19; *Guardian*, April 19, 1941, p. 4; Minutes of Boston Literary and Historical Association, December 15, 1913, Trotter Papers; *Guardian*, January 11, 1908, p. 4. For an early statement of Trotter's views on liquor and tobacco, see W. M. Trotter to John A. Fairlie, June 15, 1902, John Archibald Fairlie Papers.

paper "with as little regard to literary form and style as if he were a backwoodsman." "I rarely ever see it," Francis Garrison said of the *Guardian*, "& its typography gives me the jim jams!" [29]

In 1901 he had owned and held by inheritance pieces of property all over Boston. The *Guardian* devoured them one by one. The *New York Age* crowed: "When a man has all of his property mortgaged to the limit and his miserable soul mortgaged to the devil, he may smile as a guaranty of good faith, but he deceives no one. Watch the sheriff, Mr. Trotter, and when your collapse overwhelms you, remember that he laughs best who laughs last." In 1908 he put a second mortgage on his home in Dorchester. A year later he had sold his last two houses. As editor, businessman, and racial organizer, he drove himself mercilessly, working incredibly long hours, taking no vacations, granting himself no respite from his labors.[30]

From time to time he would insert a reminder in the *Guardian*. "It is not right to take a Colored paper and not pay for it," he would say, or "We have been going over our books this week. Our subscribers owe us hundreds of dollars. We should very much appreciate it if we might have this coming week a testimonial of money due by delinquent subscribers and agents." He showered Freeman Murray in the District of Columbia with pleas and entreaties: "Would it increase the sales in D. of C. if Guardians reached there on Saturday? Have they ever reached the agents on Saturday? . . . My trouble has been to get agents to pay. How do you find that part of it? Would Guardian placards help?" "Most of all I need money— There is real question whether I can survive another week

[29] Kelly Miller, *Race Adjustment: Essays on the Negro in America* (New York and Washington, D.C., 1908), p. 14; Francis J. Garrison to Oswald Garrison Villard, July 24, 1910, Villard Papers.

[30] *New York Age*, January 25, 1906, p. 2; *Guardian*, December 28, 1918, p. 4, Trotter Papers.

or 2 weeks—" "Now, Murray, I am about bankrupt. It is base ingratitude for Waldron to withhold the $3.00 for the 100 papers I mailed him. . . . I wish you would telephone him how hard up I am & frankly ask him if he will not mail me that money." "My financial condition is so desperate. . . . If there is any money collectable on Guardians or subscriptions there do your best & quickest for me." "Why is it that . . . in view of my repeated statement that the Guardian is almost gone—you don't collect the unsold or get your little boy to collect old papers & money & send it to me. . . ." [31]

Then when Murray turned around and criticized him for running his newspaper by the "pass-the-hat method," Trotter sat down at six o'clock one morning—having allowed himself no sleep all night—and scribbled out a long and bitter reply. "One answer to you is that the 'pass-the-hat method' was Garrison's & by it he brought about the abolition of human slavery. Garrison's paper never paid, never supported his family. But for financial lifts by those who devoted their time to money-making it would have gone under." Furthermore, "I feel as Garrison felt that I must promote oral agitation & organization in order to do the cause & the race any good." As for the *Guardian*, "You are right." It "is precarious. That has been it's condition for several years." Why? "*Principle* robs it of much money," and it is better for people to sneer at its poverty "than get money against my principles. Nor do I care how much they carp about money. The Guardian is run solely for the Colored people." Don't blame the *Guardian;* blame its readers instead.

The Colored race will be weak just as long as they remain too selfish, or unintelligent to donate to such a

[31] *Guardian*, January 4, 1908, p. 4 and July 15, 1911, p. 4; W. M. Trotter to Freeman H. M. Murray, January 20, 1914, two undated letters, March 27, 1914, [November 1, 1913], Freeman H. M. Murray Papers.

paper as the Guardian as an instrument for their
welfare. . . . I believe that if I can educate them to
cooperate with their means to promote their rights I
will do them a fundamental good. They do not begin
to regard me for soliciting with the contempt & pity I
have for those who have money & criticize me for
asking for it. The Colored people are inferior to all
other people in refusing to contribute to definite agitation. . . . I solicit *because* people should pay for
what is done solely for their good. I would solicit
even if I had money. The fight means nothing if one
man pays all the bills.[32]

That was written at an hour of exhaustion and discouragement, and in explaining his own predicament he was
unwontedly severe ("contempt & pity") on his people.
The *Guardian* was a black enterprise, more so than the
Crisis, more so than the *New York Age*. Occasionally a
white man would lend Trotter some assistance. Moorfield
Storey sent him a check for five dollars now and then. At
the Harvard commencement of 1914 he ran into John
Milholland, had a long talk with him, and the white man
agreed to subscribe $100 if Albert Pillsbury would do the
same. Pillsbury, of course, would scarcely have made such
a commitment to a man he detested. By his editorial policy,
indeed by his insistence, Trotter's newspaper had to rely
on black support.[33]

His work load put a heavy strain on his health, and in
the spring of 1916 it broke down. An attack of the grippe
and an extracted tooth led to cervical adenitis. He had an
operation to drain the abscess on his neck, stayed in the
hospital for two weeks, and then spent several more weeks

[32] W. M. Trotter to Freeman H. M. Murray, September 23,
1913, Murray Papers.

[33] Moorfield Storey to W. M. Trotter, August 9, September 22,
1913, December 6, 1916, Moorfield Storey Papers; Diary of John
E. Milholland, June 15, 1914, John E. Milholland Papers.

recuperating at home. Nearly a month after his discharge from the hospital Deenie Trotter wrote Harry Smith that "He works some now but we wish he would not as it does him no good." Smith and J. R. Clifford started a Trotter Press Testimonial Fund. It ran for two months, and when it was over Trotter, without irony, thanked Smith for the ten dollars that had been raised. Joel Spingarn sent an independent contribution, and Trotter, surprised, wrote him that "the burden & the brunt of the fight must fall to a few colored men & women & a few of their friends. I shall keep up the fight as long as I can." [34]

Through some mysterious alchemy the *Guardian* still appeared every Friday evening. Trotter doggedly kept the subscription price at the original rate of $1.50 a year until 1920, when he reluctantly announced in an editorial that it would have to be raised to $2. During his lifetime the paper missed only two issues—in 1919 when he was in Europe and in 1932 when he was bedridden with an infected leg. And some observers were fooled into thinking that it was all done easily. In 1914 a white social worker making a study of Boston's Negroes congratulated Trotter "for having made his paper a business success." He must have had a wry laugh over that.[35]

IV

Fortunately, Deenie Trotter's commitment matched her husband's. First drawn into helping the *Guardian* after the Boston Riot, she adjusted to the harsh life of racial agitation and left behind her life as a genteel young wife in Dorchester. At the Garrison centenary in 1905 she spoke

[34] File on Wm. Monroe Trotter, Case No. 85984, Massachusetts Memorial Hospital; Washington *Bee*, June 3, 1916, p. 4; Cleveland *Gazette:* June 24, 1916, p. 4; August 5, 1916, p. 2; September 2, 1916, p. 2; Geraldine L. Trotter to Harry Smith, July 6, 1916, in Cleveland *Gazette*, July 15, 1916, p. 1; W. M. Trotter to Joel Spingarn, June 9, 1916, Spingarn Papers.

[35] *Guardian*, January 10, 1920, p. 4, and November 10, 1934, p. 4, Trotter Papers; Daniels, *In Freedom's Birthplace*, p. 369.

on the need for sacrificing oneself, a subject she knew about firsthand. "That is the great lesson we Colored people should learn," she said, "those of us who have had the advantages of education, who have seen life in its broadest light, to be willing to sacrifice and . . . to do for our own down-trodden people all in our power . . . to make their cause our cause, their sufferings our suffering. . . ." [36]

They had no children. She always told friends that they had not wanted any. In a real sense, the *Guardian* was their child. On it they lavished the time, the care, even the affection they might otherwise have given to children. She was the office half of the partnership, doing the bookkeeping, handling bills and subscriptions, editing the society columns, and performing other chores while her husband made his calls in Boston or traveled in behalf of his rights group. In addition she had her own projects—raising money for the St. Monica's Home for elderly black women, making life more bearable for the Negro soldiers at Fort Devens during World War I, petitioning (successfully) for the release of William Hill, a veteran of James Trotter's Fifty-fifth Regiment who had served forty years of a life sentence for murder. [37]

She had a strong Episcopal faith—once she advised a socialist speaker at the Boston Literary "not to scoff at the Bible"—and that along with the depth of her immersion in the cause of the *Guardian* sustained her through what was, for the most part, a drab existence. Within eighteen

[36] *The Celebration of the One Hundredth Anniversary of the Birth of William Lloyd Garrison, By the Colored Citizens of Greater Boston under the Auspices of the Suffrage League of Boston and Vicinity* (Boston, 1906), p. 14.

[37] Worthy, "Trotter," pp. 16–18; *Guardian*, April 23, 1904, p. 5; Washington *Bee*, December 2, 1905, p. 1; *New York Age*, October 19, 1918, p. 2; Washington *Bee*, October 19, 1918, p. 1, reprinting *Boston Post* obituary of Geraldine Trotter; *Guardian*, August 6, 1910, p. 4; Francis J. Garrison to Oswald Garrison Villard, February 10, 21, 1911, Villard Papers.

months in 1913–14 she lost four close relatives, including a beloved brother. "I do not believe," she wrote Freeman Murray at this time, "I shall ever feel light hearted again." [38]

She fell ill during the influenza epidemic that ravaged the nation in the fall of 1918. She seemed to rally, then relapsed, and died on October 8, five days past her forty-sixth birthday. "She never hesitated or wavered," said Du Bois, who had known her since the early 1890s, "and she yielded every little temptation of home and dress and company and leisure for the narrow office and late hours and public life; yet through it all she shone clear and fine, and died as one whom death cannot conquer."

". . . God took her first," Trotter wrote on Christmas Day. "It was a crushing blow, but we must bow to His will. . . . to so live as to meet her in Heaven, this is the resolve of her sorrowing husband. . . . God help me to fight on for her memory's sake." For years afterward the *Guardian*'s editorial page carried her picture and an anguished dedication.

> To My Fallen Comrade, Geraldine L. Trotter, My Loyal Wife, who is no more. To honoring her memory, who helped me so loyally, faithfully, conscientiously, unselfishly, I shall devote my remaining days; and to perpetuating the Guardian and the Equal Rights cause and work for which she made such noble, and total sacrifice, I dedicate the best that is in me till I die. . . . [39]

[38] *Guardian*, March 18, 1911, p. 4; Geraldine L. Trotter to Freeman H. M. Murray, July 13, 1914, Murray Papers.

[39] *Crisis*, XVII (1918–19), 75; *Guardian*, December 28, 1918, p. 4, and February 15, 1919, p. 4, Trotter Papers.

CHAPTER VII

To Make the World Safe
for Negroes

T HE ERA of World War I was a period of upheaval for the American racial situation. "At no
time since the days following the Civil War," James Weldon Johnson later recalled, "had the Negro been in a
position where he stood to make greater gain or sustain
greater loss in status. The great war in Europe, its recoil
on America, the ferment in the United States, all conspired
to break up the stereotyped conception of the Negro's place
. . . and to allow of new formations." The combination of
agricultural failures in the South and the lure of industrial
jobs in the North produced an enormous migration of the
black population from its traditional home in Dixie. It was
a volatile situation, with people and their racial attitudes in
motion. Late in 1916 the white journalist Ray Stannard
Baker investigated the racial situation and was profoundly
disturbed. Lynching, after subsiding for a time, was back
in vogue. Generally there seemed to be more interracial
friction. The government was more oblivious than ever.
The NAACP's new militancy had taken the place of Tus-

kegee's less demanding leadership. Negroes, better educated and more sensitive to continuing mistreatment, were
growing restless. "It is a condition full of danger," Baker
concluded, "not only to the Negro and the South, but to
the whole country: and its most menacing aspect is the
contemptuous indifference of a large part of white America
to what is going on in the depths of the volcano just
below." [1]

I

"As a nation," Trotter wrote once, "we have always
made professions in respect to human rights and liberties,
which in practice we have flatly contradicted." In the
spring of 1917 Woodrow Wilson took the country into a
war that would be fought, he said, "for democracy, for the
right of those who submit to authority to have a voice in
their own government," and for "a universal dominion of
right." Almost immediately the War Department heard
rumors of disloyalty among parts of the Negro population.
(In fact, as early as 1903 Trotter had warned that if the
United States, "doing battle with some great powers,
should be sorely taxed, it is clear that a fatal element of
weakness would be found in the discontent of our Colored
citizens.") Wartime patriotism was a mass ritual, easily
moved to the edge of hysteria, and Trotter intended to
quash the stories predicting black treachery. It is true, the
Boston branch of the NERL conceded in May, that many
Negroes are bitter over discrimination. "But we have no
thought of taking up arms against our country. Ours it has
been to save the government from rebellion. This work of
our fathers we shall not destroy." But Negroes would fight
harder in war if they could expect better treatment in
peace. "As this nation goes forth to fight 'the natural foe of

[1] *Along This Way: The Autobiography of James Weldon Johnson* (New York, 1933), p. 308; Ray Stannard Baker, "Gathering
Clouds Along the Color Line," *World's Work*, XXXII (1916),
pp. 232–236.

liberty,' let Americans highly resolve that all shall have
liberty within her borders." [2]

Previously, international matters had been of peripheral
concern to Trotter. Early in the century he opposed American imperialism in Latin America and the Far East. With
these adventures abroad, the *Guardian* said in 1902, Negroes must demand whether they have been "cast overboard from the Republican ship, as a barrel to amuse the
Southern whale, while the imperialistic craft proceeds on
her journey?" Trotter deplored "the subjugation of the
brown people of the Philippines" and protested American
intervention in the Caribbean. "Hayti has the same right to
revolution as any other nation," he insisted, "and the
Monroe doctrine which is made to shield Venezuela must
be made to extend even over the black republic!" And after
a revolt in Cuba in 1906, "It looks like from the Cuban
revolution that lilywhitism is not as tamely submitted to by
Colored Cubans as by Colored Americans." Occasionally
he would draw a domestic lesson from international politics: "As the American Jews and Irish have, and must
save their own people in Europe, so must the northern
Negro save himself by fighting the battles of the southern
Negro." But these were just infrequent sallies, a diversion
from the main battle in the United States.[3]

As the nation joined the world war, however, a broader
meaning was thrust on the American dilemma. American
wars have usually been explained to the public in terms of
saving or promoting democracy. In response, black spokes-

[2] *Guardian*, February 6, 1904, p. 4, and April 18, 1903, p. 4;
NERL statement, May 21, 1917, in *Guardian*, September 29,
1917, p. 2, Box 7, Moorfield Storey Papers, LC. Though he did
support, with skepticism, America's entry into World War I,
Trotter evidently respected the pacifist position against the war.
"He was the one individual in Boston," A. Philip Randolph writes,
"who had the courage to preside at an anti-war meeting planned by
Chandler Owen and myself" (letter to author, June 19, 1969).
[3] *Guardian:* September 13, 1902, p. 1; April 16, 1904, p. 4;
September 13, 1902, p. 4; August 25, 1906, p. 4; May 23, 1903,
p. 4.

men in wartime have customarily said: Yes, white America, we shall fight for you, for our country, and for democracy—but will you not grant us some of that democracy at home? Trotter's response to World War I was a variation on this recurrent theme. He was immensely proud of the military record made by his father and hundreds of thousands of other Negro soldiers in previous American wars. Some of his fury at Roosevelt over the Brownsville discharge came from the incident's besmirching of what had been a remarkable tradition of military valor. To redeem that honor, and to provide further proof of the Negro's claims to full citizenship, Trotter seized the chance offered by the world war. In a circular letter announcing the tenth annual convention of the NERL he declared that "war is the time all proscribed classes get relief, and therefore a real national convention representing the colored race itself is a necessity, is a paramount duty. . . ." The convention, held in New York in September 1917, attracted 100 delegates. "Despite progress," the resolutions announced, "we are still surrounded by an adverse sentiment which makes our lives a living hell." That "killing which is called war always requires justification," and American entry "into the most terrible war in history and one in the other hemisphere, can be justified only by vouchsafing freedom and equality of rights to all citizens of the United States regardless of the incidents of race or color over which they have no control." Again, the pledge of loyalty—"We believe in democracy"—yet "We hold that this nation should enter the lists with clean hands. . . ."[4]

There were four Negro regiments in the regular Army but practically no black officers. Joel Spingarn and James Weldon Johnson of the NAACP asked Secretary of War Newton Baker to admit Negro candidates to the regular

[4] NERL circular letter, August 22, 1917, in Washington *Bee*, September 8, 1917, p. 1; *New York Age*, September 20, 1917, p. 1; *Guardian*, September 29, 1917, p. 1, Box 7, Storey Papers, LC.

officer training camps. Such an arrangement, Baker replied, "simply *could not be made*." That was final. So
Spingarn, acting as an individual and without the sanction
of the NAACP, persuaded General Leonard Wood to establish a separate training camp if 200 prospective black
officers of adequate educational background would come
forward. Spingarn published an appeal and had his 200
names within a few weeks. Wood increased his minimum
number to 250 candidates. In a short while Spingarn had
350 volunteers.[5]

Most of the Negro press, including the *Guardian*, protested against the establishment of the Negro camp. The
issue, for the time being, came down to choosing between
Negro officers trained at a segregated camp or no Negro
officers at all. As far as Trotter was concerned, to consent
to the camp was to capitulate to the Wilson administration's racism and to jeopardize future demands for integration in the armed forces. He advised young Negroes in
Boston not to volunteer for the camp and did what he could
to prevent its establishment. In June, however, the camp
opened in Des Moines and after four months turned out
over 600 commissioned officers for the all-Negro regiments.[6]

To Trotter it was not worth the price. Spingarn had
been careful to say that he was acting as an individual, not
as NAACP board chairman, so that the whole Association
might not be drawn into the controversy. But Du Bois
supported the venture in the *Crisis*, and the NAACP board
had added its quiet approval. Consequently it was possible
for Trotter to see the Des Moines camp as a reflection of

---

[5] Johnson, *Along This Way*, p. 318; Charles Flint Kellogg,
*NAACP: A History of the National Association for the Advance-
ment of Colored People, Volume I 1909–1920* (Baltimore, 1967),
p. 251.
[6] W. M. Trotter to Roy Nash, May 16, 1917, NAACP Papers;
William Harrison, "Phylon Profile IX: William Monroe Trotter—
Fighter," *Phylon*, VII (1946), 243; Kellogg, *NAACP*, p. 254;
Johnson, *Along This Way*, p. 319.

the Association's unreliability. Further confirmation came in the summer of 1918 in a striking proposal from the *Crisis*. "Let us," Du Bois suggested, "while this war lasts, forget our special grievances and close our ranks shoulder to shoulder with our own white fellow citizens and the allied nations that are fighting for democracy." At that, Trotter exploded, calling Du Bois "a rank quitter of the fight for our rights." At the very time "when the greatest opportunity is at hand" during "the war for democracy for all others," Du Bois "has at last finally weakened, compromised, deserted the fight, betrayed the cause of his race." Clearly, Trotter was not about to close ranks with the NAACP.[7]

Nor with the federal administration. Emmett Scott had been appointed an assistant in the War Department, to specialize in racial matters. Scott, an old hand at dampening Negro dissent, could not mistake his function in the War Department: Baker advised him that "unrest among the colored people and suspicion of the Government on their part are by all means to be discouraged at a time like this." Accordingly, Scott helped George Creel (head of the Committee on Public Information) arrange a conference of black spokesmen in Washington in June 1918. "There are about forty-five of them," Creel wrote Wilson a few days beforehand, "all loyal and enthusiastic, and seeing you and hearing you is just the inspiration that they need. May I suggest Thursday afternoon?" Wilson refused to see them—"I have received several delegations of negroes and I am under the impression that they have gone away dissatisfied. I have never had an opportunity to do what I promised them I would seek an opportunity to do." Trotter, one of those "dissatisfied" Negroes, declined Scott's invitation to the conference. Almost every other important Negro leader was there: Du Bois, Robert

[7] Kellogg, *NAACP*, p. 255; *Crisis*, XVI (1918), 111; *Guardian* quoted in Cleveland *Gazette*, July 27, 1918, p. 1.

Moton, Robert Terrell, Harry Smith, Charles Anderson, Archibald Grimké, J. C. Dancy, Robert Abbott of the *Chicago Defender*, Fred Moore, Calvin Chase, and others. They heard speeches by Baker, Creel, Spingarn, and Assistant Secretary of the Navy Franklin D. Roosevelt. Then they adopted some gentle resolutions. The Negro, they agreed, "is not disposed to catalogue, in this tremendous crisis, all his complaints and disabilities; he is more than willing to do his full share in helping to win the war for democracy . . . but he is today compelled to ask for that minimum of consideration which will enable him to be an efficient fighter for VICTORY." [8]

A week later Trotter held his own National Liberty Congress in Washington. This congress, originally planned by the NERL the previous summer, did not acquiesce in the relative docility of the Creel conference. "We are the victims in many states . . . of imposition, robbery, ravishing, mob violence, murder, and massacre because of our race and color, denied protection of police, of sheriffs; denied trial by court or jury, rendered impotent to protect our daughters, wives, or mothers from violation by white men or murder by the mob." Since the United States is engaged in a war for democracy, with the assistance of her black citizens, and in order to make Wilsonian idealism a reality at home, "We do now petition you, the Congress of the United States of America, as an act of justice, of moral consistency, and to help win the war for world democracy," to pass legislation (1) to forbid segregation and discrimination in federal buildings and on federal territory; (2) to enforce equal treatment in regard to

---

[8] Newton Baker to Emmett J. Scott, November 30, 1917, in Daniel R. Beaver, *Newton D. Baker and the American War Effort 1917–1919* (Lincoln, Nebr., 1966), p. 228; George Creel to Woodrow Wilson, June 17, 1918, Woodrow Wilson Papers; Wilson to Creel, June 18, 1918, in Ray Stannard Baker, *Woodrow Wilson: Life and Letters* (8 vols., Garden City, N.Y., 1927–39), VIII, 217; Cleveland *Gazette*, July 6, 1918, p. 1.

wages, promotions, and work areas in federal buildings; (3) to eliminate discrimination on public carriers operated by the federal government; (4) to integrate the armed forces and all federally operated schools; (5) to enforce Amendments XIII, XIV, and XV; and (6) to make "mob murders" a federal crime. A Massachusetts congressman, Frederick Gillett, read the petition into the *Congressional Record*, and there it rested.[9]

The administration made one tiny concession. On July 1 Newton Baker told Wilson that Robert Moton was concerned about the lynching problem. (During May there had been nineteen mob murders.) Baker urged the President to issue an open letter on the subject. Later in the month Wilson finally made good on his 1912 promise to Villard. Anyone involved in a lynching, said Wilson, is "no true son of this great democracy, but its betrayer" for he has thereby "adopted the standards of the enemies of his country, whom he affects to despise."[10]

II

In Europe over the summer of 1918 the Allied forces won a string of victories. When members of the NERL convened in Chicago at the end of the summer it was only a matter of time before the Central Powers would seek an armistice. Consequently, Trotter could try a new approach in moral suasion. The NERL had a good meeting in Chicago, with 90 delegates from 22 states; the *Chicago Defender* called it "by far the most largely attended and truly representative convention" in the group's history. The League decided to call a National Race Congress for early January in the District of Columbia in order "to elect race petitioners to be sent to intercede for full democracy for

[9] *Congressional Record*, 65 Cong., 2 Sess., Appendix, proceedings for June 29, 1918; Washington *Bee*, July 6, 1918, p. 1; *Philadelphia Tribune*, April 7, 1932, p. 15.

[10] Newton D. Baker to Woodrow Wilson, July 1, 1918, Wilson Papers; Beaver, *Baker and War Effort*, p. 230.

Colored Americans" at the approaching peace conference. It would be under NERL auspices, Trotter explained, but "Every national organization for the rights of colored Americans shall be entitled and invited to send two delegates at-large, each such delegate to be entitled to one vote." His plan was to bring the American racial crisis to the direct attention of the world—at the actual site of the negotiations that would reconstruct the world in the interest of international democracy.[11]

He went back to Boston after the Chicago meeting and, within a few days of his arrival home, saw his wife come down with influenza. In two weeks she was dead. She had always been petite and frail, and after she died there must have been hours of agony for him as he reflected on the demands that his career had put on her and the comforts that he had not been able to provide for her. With the inevitable pangs of guilt tearing at him, he had to contend with the irrevocable loss, at once, of his wife, his co-editor, and his most dependable supporter. It was an enormous setback.

His response, and probably it came as no surprise to his admirers, was merely to pour himself back into his work. He appealed to the *Guardian*'s readers across the nation to send representatives to his National Race Congress. "Colored Americans Act," he pleaded. "The Editor of the Guardian appeals to you to be wise and to act thus in the name of his departed wife who worked for the cause." He urged Wilson to add a fifteenth item to his Fourteen Points ("the elimination of civil, political, and judicial distinctions based on race or color in all nations for the new era of freedom everywhere") and asked him to appoint a Negro to the American peace delegation. After the German sur-

[11] *Chicago Defender*, September 28, 1918, p. 1; NERL statements quoted in *New York Age*, October 12, 1918, p. 2, and in William Trotter to Woodrow Wilson, May 30, 1919, Wilson Papers.

render in November Trotter's congress was moved up to mid-December, and to publicize it he declared the week of December 8–15 to be World Democracy Week. "The earth and the heavens resound," he declared, "with the petitions of all races for freedom and democracy with the close of the World War. Every proscribed race and class is preparing to have its relief included in the world adjustment. Irish, Jew, Gentile, women, even businessmen, are arranging for representation at the Peace Conference." He invited the NAACP to cooperate in his venture. The Association's board of directors pondered a response and then decided not to acknowledge his letter.[12]

Once again it was an independent undertaking by Trotter and whatever supporters he could gather together. In Washington some 250 black people from all over the country elected eleven of their number to represent them at Versailles: Trotter, Ida Wells-Barnett, the millionaire businesswoman Madame C. J. Walker, the Reverend M. A. N. Shaw of Boston, and seven others. They claimed to speak for all American Negroes, but were received by the race with something less than unanimity. In taking the name of National Race Congress, Trotter had appropriated the title of a black group founded in Washington in 1915. Calvin Chase angrily announced that at least 50 people had come to Washington expecting to attend a meeting of the original organization. "The original Race Congress," wrote Chase, "which is incorporated under the laws of the District of Columbia, is under the auspices of Rev. W. H. Jernagin, and any other organization using the name is a fraud." And the *New York Age* observed, "This business of electing delegates to the Peace Conference at Versailles is being run into the ground. . . . It might as well be understood that there is no sense or reason in this multiply-

[12] *Guardian* fragments, November 1918 and December 7, 1918, William Monroe Trotter Papers; Minutes of Board of Directors Meetings, December 9, 1918, NAACP Papers.

ing of so-called Peace delegations that will never get as far down the harbor as the Statue of Liberty." [13]

The *Age* was prescient: Trotter's eleven delegates were not granted passports by the State Department. Du Bois was planning a Pan-African Congress to meet in Paris concurrently with the peace conference, and American Negroes who wanted to attend that congress were also denied passports. The State Department explained that the French government would not look favorably on such activity and therefore the black Americans must stay home. "To deny even the right of petition," Trotter said later, "we felt was extraordinary tyranny, flagrant enough to justify us in seeking to overcome it." Thomas Walker, financial manager of the NERL's drive to collect money to send the eleven abroad, asked that no further contributions be sent. With the money already collected, Trotter left the *Guardian* in other hands in mid-February, went down to New York, and took lodging at a roominghouse on the waterfront. He dropped his middle name ("it is an old Anglo-Saxon trait to go incognito") and as William Trotter started haunting the shipping offices. Byron Gunner and some white man vouched for him and helped him secure the necessary seaman's papers. He tried to find a berth on any ship going to Europe. For six weeks he found nothing. Finally he contacted the French-speaking cook on a small, tired freighter, the S.S. *Yarmouth*. "I knew English, but a very little French, but somehow some French came to me, I don't know where unless God gave it to me. . . ." A friend of his mother's, Mrs. Mary Gibson, came down from Boston, gave him a crash course in the elements of cooking, and at last he was hired on as a

[13] PROTESTATION DES AMERICAINS DE COULEUR ET PETITION EN FAVEUR DE LA DEMOCRATIE MONDIALE ADRESSE A LA CONFERENCE MONDIALE DE LA PAIX, 12-page mimeographed pamphlet in Mary Church Terrell Papers; Washington *Bee*, December 21, 1918, p. 4; *New York Age*, December 21, 1918, p. 4.

second cook on the *Yarmouth*. In April he was on his way to France.[14]

It was late. Du Bois, as the accredited representative of the *Crisis*, had sailed to France in December on the official press boat. He collected material for a projected history of the Negro's role in the war and, in February, organized his Pan-African Congress in Paris with black people from fifteen nations in attendance. His congress drafted a set of resolutions to be submitted to the peace conference: "Wherever persons of African descent are civilized and able to meet the tests of surrounding culture, they shall be accorded the same rights as their fellow citizens; they shall not be denied on account of race or color a voice in their own Government, justice before the courts and economic and social equality according to ability and desert"—and if this pledge should be violated, "it shall be the duty of the League of Nations to bring the matter to the attention of the civilized world." Du Bois managed to have an interview with Edward M. House of the American peace delegation, who said the resolutions should indeed be presented to the conference. Lloyd George said he would give the matter "his careful consideration." Then Du Bois returned to the United States in late March. "We got, in fact, the ear of the civilized world," he announced proudly. ". . . The world-fight for black rights is on!" [15]

Meanwhile Trotter peeled potatoes as the *Yarmouth* plowed across the Atlantic. It reached Le Havre in the first

[14] Cleveland *Gazette*, February 8, 1919, p. 2; *Crisis*, XVII (1918–19), p. 237; *Christian Science Monitor*, July 25, 1919, p. 14; Washington *Bee*, March 1, 1919, p. 4; *Guardian* fragment, August 2, 1919, Trotter Papers; *Guardian*, April 21, 1934, p. 4, Trotter Papers. In 1920 the *Yarmouth* was purchased by Marcus Garvey's Black Star Steamship Line; some members of the NERL suggested that the ship be renamed the *Monroe Trotter* (*Guardian*, January 24, 1920, p. 1, Trotter Papers).

[15] List of certified American correspondents at Versailles, January 13, 1919, Ray Stannard Baker Papers; *Crisis*, XVII (1918–19), 110, 163–164, XVIII (1919), 8, 9, 128–129.

week of May. The crew was not permitted to go ashore.
But the cook had a letter to be mailed, and Trotter, in his
work clothes, was allowed to go as far as the wharf for that
purpose. Leaving behind his good clothes and most of his
money, he left the ship, mailed his letter, and kept going.
"Ragged and hungry and in need of funds, I made my way
to Paris," finally arriving there on the afternoon of May 7.
At once he learned that the Allies had just handed a
completed draft of the peace treaty to the German delegation; there was no statement on racial equality in the draft.
His struggle to reach Paris had taken so long that the
principal deliberations were already over. Immediately he
sent protests over the lack of a racial clause to the principal
negotiators. The NERL, wrote Trotter, "protests this
awful violation of the war promises of the Entente Allies
and insists pledge should yet be kept in final peace
document." [16]

That night he presented himself at the home of an
American Negro couple living in Paris, Mr. and Mrs.
Thomas Kane. He said that his name was Clark and that
he came from Washington, D.C. Mrs. Kane assumed that
he was a friend of her husband's, so she let him in, fed
him, and prepared a bed for him. At that point he con-
fessed that his name was not Clark, that the real Clark had
given him permission to use the name in France, and that
he had come to Paris to represent black Americans at the
peace conference. "He was absolutely like a tramp," Mrs.
Kane later wrote her sister-in-law, Mrs. Fred Moore, "—in
rags, dirty, boots without soles, and he told such awful
stories. I did not sleep a wink that night." The next
morning, after a late breakfast, Trotter identified himself
to Kane, asked for a loan, and requested the use of Kane's
name in order to cable for $700 from the United States.

[16] *Christian Science Monitor*, July 25, 1919, p. 14; *Crisis*, XVIII
(1919), 254; William Trotter to Woodrow Wilson, May 9, 1919,
noting the communications of May 7, Wilson Papers.

"Of course," Mrs. Kane assured Mrs. Moore, "he would not do this as he did not believe a word of the man's story. My husband gave him a cup of chocolate and told him if he wanted to see him again to come back at half-past seven." [17]

Somehow he made friends in Paris. Living at the Hôtel du Bon Pasteur on the Rue Ste.-Anne, he started turning out petitions and news releases which the French press, intrigued by them, picked up and published. A translator named G. Collet gave him office space and secretarial assistance in his offices on the Place de la Bourse. George W. Baker, a white man also from Massachusetts, lent some assistance and wrote the *New York Age*, "Give credit to this man who came to Europe to fight for his people. He has done more good than any one else who has come over for that cause. He has reached all the leading delegates of the Convention and has received hundreds of letters approving of his conduct. Every newspaper in Paris has given him space—from one inch to one column." Black students at the university took him to dinner, as did a group of journalists headed by the editor of *Le Journal du Peuple*. A reporter for *L'Avenir* came to interview him. "Mr. Trotter has an extremely intelligent face, full of ardor," the reporter noted. Trotter described America's racial situation to him and darkly observed, according to his interviewer's report, that unless some progress was made there would be a revolution and then, at last, peace; "the peace of the world—the perpetual peace." Other black Americans in France learned of his efforts and went to see him. Mary Church Terrell found him in his office, "working like a beaver," she remembered, "trying to tell the French people the truth about conditions under which colored people live in the United States." "Colored American

[17] The only record of this incident is found in the letter of Mrs. Thomas H. Kane to Mrs. Fred Moore that Moore gleefully printed in the *New York Age*, June 28, 1919, p. 2.

laborers can help restore France," he wrote home. "Unprejudiced country." [18]

He was less successful in his overt purpose, that of influencing the proceedings at Versailles. On May 15 he sent copies of his credentials as the representative of the National Race Congress to every delegation at the conference. With his credentials he enclosed the petition he had sent to the principal negotiators on May 7 and pointedly added, "I sincerely trust you will be able to see the imperative need of recognizing this claim for democracy. Please do me the favor of acknowledging receipt of this letter." Not only was there no sign that his claim was being recognized—it was difficult, in fact, even to extract an acknowledgment of his presence. From Edward House, for example, there was no reply to his communication of May 15. Two weeks later Trotter again sent House a statement of the NERL's case. "Please do us the honor," Trotter wrote, "to peruse and weigh this petition to the Powers for whom their Colored citizens sacrificed, fought, and died in the war for world democracy . . . to the end that caste distinctions, proscriptions and mob murder shall no longer be practised against their Colored citizens. *Will you please do me the great favor of acknowledging the personal receiving of this petition.*" After a few days one of House's assistants replied, *in toto*, that "Colonel House has received your letter of May 30, 1919, and has directed me to thank you for the copies of petition by the National Equal Rights League, and other papers which you submitted to him." [19]

[18] G. W. Baker to editor in *New York Age*, September 6, 1919, clipping in Wm. Monroe Trotter folder, Schomburg Collection, New York Public Library; *Guardian*, July 12, 1919, p. 4, and December 13, 1919, p. 4, Trotter Papers; *Guardian*, December 12, 1942, p. 4; Mary Church Terrell, *A Colored Woman in a White World* (Washington, D.C., 1940), p. 341; W. M. Trotter to Edgar P. Benjamin, July 1, 1919, in Ruth Worthy, "A Negro in Our History: William Monroe Trotter, 1872–1934" (M.A. thesis, Columbia University, 1952), pp. 130–131.

[19] PROTESTATION DES AMERICAINS DE COULEUR; William Trotter to Robert Lansing, May 15, 1919, Papers of American Commis-

Wilson, no doubt, had not forgotten his encounter in 1914 with "that unspeakable fellow Tucker," and gave him no satisfaction in France. At the end of May, Trotter wrote Wilson an open letter, citing the contradictions between Wilson's Memorial Day address in Paris, a lynching back home in Missouri the day before that, and the wartime sacrifices of black American soldiers. "Will you, therefore," Trotter asked, "for their sakes and that they shall not have died in vain, grant to their kin and race at home protection of right and life in the world peace agreement? And will you not at once send a special message to Congress recommending that lynching be made a crime against the Federal Government?" The letter made interesting copy for the French newspapers, and the Associated Press cabled it to the United States. Wilson, though, was busy with other matters that he deemed more important, and he took no action on Trotter's requests.[20]

Trotter was getting nowhere at a distance, so on June 12 he asked Wilson for "a brief audience." After receiving a routine acknowledgment, but nothing more, Trotter tried to work through Wilson's secretary, Gilbert Close. Expressing "my very high appreciation for your prompt acknowledgement of the receipt of my letters and petitions to the president," Trotter requested Close to find out from Wilson "whether he will grant me an audience while he is in Paris" because "My course in the immediate future depends upon his decision in the matter." Rebuffed once more, Trotter asked Wilson to present the NERL petitions to the other principal negotiators: "Will you please have your secretary inform me of your decision in this matter at your earliest convenience, as the immediate prospect of peace makes it vital to my mission to know your decision."

---

sion to Negotiate Peace, Paris 1918–1919, State Department Papers; Trotter to Edward M. House, May 15, 30, 1919, Arthur Hugh Frazier to Trotter, June 4, 1919, Edward M. House Papers.
[20] William Trotter to Woodrow Wilson, May 31, 1919, Wilson Papers; "A Negro Delegate Who Managed to Reach the Peace Conference," *Literary Digest*, LXII (August 16, 1919), 42.

"File," someone jotted on Trotter's letter, and no answer was sent. Six days later, June 25, he tried one last time. "As the end is so near," Trotter wrote Close, "will you do me the very great favor of informing the President that my mission makes it very important and necessary that I know whether he has, or whether he will present the petition of the National Equal Rights League to the Council of Four and ascertain the facts and let me know just as quickly as possible ere all is concluded." Nothing.[21]

In the meantime he kept up a steady general fire of educational material to the French public, describing the discriminatory treatment of black soldiers in the American Army, and detailing recent cases of racial brutality in the United States for the benefit of the Council of Five and its successor, the Council of Four. After the treaty was signed in late June he sent a final appeal to the secretary general of the new League of Nations ("Despite loyalty and sacrifice is this 'Magna Charta of a new order of things' to contain no protection from the exclusion, the public segregations, the disfranchisement, from the rope and the faggot?") and then left for home, having made a greater impression on the French than on his own countrymen. Six months after he sailed back to the United States an official of the French National Museum asked the American Embassy in Paris for the address of the "délégué des citoyens américains de couleur à la Conférence de la paix, Williane [*sic*] Monroe Trotter." Joseph C. Grew of the American delegation replied that Trotter's last known address was the Hôtel du Bon Pasteur, Paris.[22]

[21] William Trotter to Woodrow Wilson, June 12, 19, 1919, to Gilbert F. Close, June 15, 25, 1919, Close to Trotter, May 30, June 12, 1919, Wilson Papers.

[22] "Negro Delegate Who Managed to Reach Peace Conference," pp. 42, 45; *New York Times*, June 23, 1919, p. 1, and July 7, 1919, p. 12; William Trotter to Sir Eric Drummond, July 3, 1919, in *Antilynching Hearings before the Committee on the Judiciary . . . on H.R. 259, 4123, and 11873 . . . January 29, 1920* (Washington, D.C., 1920), p. 34; M. Fontana to Chancelier de

III

"In the stern path of duty and with the help of God," Trotter wrote a friend from the high seas, "I got to the seat of the World Peace Conference. May it do honor to Mrs. Trotter's memory." He returned to what James Weldon Johnson called the Red Summer of 1919. It was a terrible irony that while Americans at Versailles were helping to reconstitute Europe the United States was suffering the worst outbreak of racial violence it had yet endured. From May to September there were dozens of minor flare-ups and seven major ones—in South Carolina, Texas, Tennessee, and Arkansas, but also in Omaha, the District of Columbia, and the bloodiest of all in Chicago. At the time, militant black observers perceived a new aspect to these explosions. In past racial bloodlettings, white mobs had been able to attack blacks with virtual impunity, meeting only scattered resistance from their unarmed victims. In 1919 black men were fighting back. Twenty-three Negroes died in Chicago, but so did fifteen whites.[23]

At different times since 1901 Trotter had flirted with the idea of retaliatory violence. "The lesson for our race," he wrote after a Negro was burned alive in Pennsylvania in 1911, "is to begin to unite in agitation and to organize for self-protection, yes, for self-preservation." Lynching was "a national trait, passing with as little condemnation as a Sunday school recitation," and, he warned in 1904, "What men plant that shall they surely gather. As the

l'Ambassade des Etats-Unis, Paris, January 26, 1920, and J. C. Grew to Fontana, January 30, 1920, Papers of American Commission to Negotiate Peace. Edward House, Robert Lansing, Ray Stannard Baker, and Samuel Eliot Morison all kept Versailles diaries and made no note of Trotter's activities.
[23] W. M. Trotter, aboard the *Espagne*, to Wm. H. Jackson, July 12, 1919, Trotter Papers; Johnson, *Along This Way*, p. 341; Arthur I. Waskow, *From Race Riot to Sit-In, 1919 and the 1960s* (New York, 1966), p. 12; Kellogg, *NAACP*, p. 236.

south is sowing the storm, the whirlwind it must some day reap." "We are a powerful race now," he declared at a John Brown celebration in 1909, "and we can and will take care of ourselves." For, as the *Guardian* put it in 1903, "beyond a certain point the Negro will not show his back to his pursuers."

He will turn and fight. Somewhere in the rush of white savagery against him there seems to rise up a wall in his path. It is reared by the bare instinct of self-preservation. It catches him, and he turns at bay to sell his life as dearly as possible. Is it surprising, gentle, Christian Anglo-Saxon, that he should do this? Do you think he is not merely less than man, but less than the lowest among the living creatures of God? [24]

That "certain point" seemed to have come during the Red Summer, and Trotter was grimly delighted with the new militancy. At the end of July the New York branch of the NERL sponsored a welcome-home reception for Trotter, and before two thousand supporters he spoke on the themes of self-defense and retaliation. "We have adopted the bulldog doctrine," he cried, "because the Caucasian in our midst respects nothing but fighting retaliation" and "self-preservation is the first law of nature." There can be no world peace until there is international racial democracy. "In the same week of my arrival home my heart is made to swell within me because the new spirit in my own race taught the world that they refused to be shot down in the capital of Lincoln. While they were degrading us they

[24] *Guardian:* August 19, 1911, p. 4; June 27, 1903, p. 4; March 5, 1904, p. 4; *Boston John Brown Jubilee, Faneuil Hall, Boston, Mass., December 2, 1909,* pamphlet in Trotter Papers; *Guardian,* July 18, 1903, p. 4. The literary style and the date of the last quotation suggest that it may have been the work of George Forbes. On the Pennsylvania lynching, see Eric F. Goldman, "Summer Sunday," *American Heritage,* XV (June 1964), 50–53, 83–89.

were making our boys fight for them. Unless the white American behaves, he will find that in teaching our boys to fight for him he was starting something that he will not be able to stop." [25]

In Congress, Representative James F. Byrnes of South Carolina announced that Trotter was "doing his utmost to incite riots and cause bloodshed." To illustrate the point, Byrnes read another Trotter speech into the *Congressional Record:* "We have shown how we can, and will retaliate. The other race will think twice the next time before they strike a single blow. . . . A new Negro is facing the white man to-day—one who has been aroused by a consecutive number of insults." Byrnes said that the same kind of material was being published in the *Crisis* and in the new black socialist monthly, the *Messenger*. The Negro press, said Byrnes, must be censored: "we should now prevent the I.W.W. and the Bolsheviki of Russia from using the Negro press of America to further their nefarious purposes." After all, the Negro in the South "is happy and contented and will remain so if the propagandist of the I.W.W., the Bolsheviki of Russia, and the misguided theorist of other sections of this country will let him alone." No one in Congress stood up to argue with him.[26]

A few days later, though, Trotter was allowed to bring his case directly to Congress. Through August, Henry Cabot Lodge held open hearings in his Senate Foreign Relations Committee on ratification of the Versailles treaty. Lodge did not find the treaty acceptable, and he set a leisurely pace for the hearings, giving time to a great diversity of spokesmen—even to Negroes. Trotter requested a chance to present the NERL's viewpoint and was told to appear on August 28. On that day he testified

[25] *New York Times*, July 28, 1919, p. 4.
[26] *Congressional Record*, 66 Cong., 1 Sess., 4304–4305. Byrnes later was on the Supreme Court and was Secretary of State under Truman.

with an NERL associate and two others. Trotter made the
basic point, that Negroes must be treated better if only for
the sake of law and order: "If injustice and oppression
continue to be heaped upon the people of color, our own
country may not be free from a menace to the world's
peace." Black people are as peace-loving as any other, "but
the oppression to which we in America are subjected is
such that unless national and state governments provide
guarantees against its continuance there can be no assurance that our beloved country will continue to be the land
of peace, secure from violence and insurrection." In order
to prevent that, Trotter proposed the addition of a racial
justice clause to the peace treaty. John Milholland was in
the committee room gallery and heard the presentations
delivered by Trotter and the others. "They spoke admira-
bly," Milholland wrote to Moorfield Storey. "There was
force and dignity throughout, and power in every statement. It was significant that no member of the Democratic
Party was present, but the Republican members followed
the presentation very closely. I never saw Senator Lodge
more attentive." The Republican senators listened in silence, asked no questions, and took no action.[27]

In any case, it was pointless. Wilson's treaty, with
Lodge's reservations included, was defeated in the Senate.
Trotter could take some perverse relish in Wilson's down-
fall. American racial inequities, he wrote the President,
"all constitute the greatest violation extant of your idealis-
tic pronouncements for the world." Consequently, "Your
League of Nations Covenant, void of measures or of declarations against these undemocratic conditions . . . deserved its fate." And again Trotter insisted that Wilson
use his executive powers to move against segregation, dis-

[27] John A. Garraty, *Henry Cabot Lodge: A Biography* (New
York, 1953), pp. 366–368; *New York Times*, August 25, 1919,
p. 2, and August 29, 1919, p. 2; *A.M.E. Review*, XXXVI
(1919–20), 380; John E. Milholland to Moorfield Storey, August
29, 1919, NAACP Papers.

franchisement, and lynching. And that was fruitless too.[28]

IV

Down in that volcano which Ray Stannard Baker described, the changes wrought by war were bringing a new day for black Americans. Clearly it would be a different day. There were few signs that it would be a better day. Regardless of the shape of the future, Trotter would have little impact on its direction. The trip to France was the climax of Trotter's career, and in a sense it was a microcosm of his career, distinguished by the highest principles, extraordinary diligence and perseverance of a solitary kind, and few concrete, obvious results. In 1919, at the age of forty-seven, his best years were behind him. After that it was all downhill.

[28] W. M. Trotter to Woodrow Wilson, November 25, 1919, Wilson Papers.

CHAPTER VIII

After 1919:

"You Don't Understand: You See One Side, the Public Another Side, but I See the Third Side."

T H E   E R A of the 1920s saw Trotter working as hard as ever. His sincerity and dedication remained beyond question. But it was a sad, frustrating time for him. He seemed incapable of adjusting to changes within the race. He held to his old themes and programs and was simply left behind as new black leaders took over.

I

He still hoped that the federal government might take some practical steps in the Negro's interest. In 1920, as in 1916, he returned to the Republicans and supported the GOP's presidential candidate. Warren G. Harding's campaign strategists arranged a Colored Voters Day on which their man would meet black spokesmen in Marion, Ohio, and give out assurances of his concern and democratic intentions. To ensure that it would be an agreeable occasion, though, Henry Lincoln Johnson, the Negro National Republican Committeeman from Georgia, warned Harding's aide Harry Daugherty about certain unpredictable elements within the race. "When it comes to the Equal Rights League," Johnson advised Daugherty, "it may be made up of Monroe Trotter of Boston and some other wild-eyed people like that. They may produce some embarrassment. . . . We do not want any colored people to come to see the Senator with question marks."

Trotter went to Marion on the appointed day, but, hemmed in by moderate black spokesmen, could not ask any embarrassing questions. Harding did seem to be sympathetic and declared (according to the NERL's report) that "If the United States cannot prevent segregation in its own service we are not in any sense a democracy." But later in the campaign he made no objection to segregation in the South, asking only for "race equality before the law," and denied that he would try to disturb southern racial folkways. Trotter, campaigning for Harding in the Midwest, sent the candidate a worried telegram: "LEAGUE DISTURBED REQUESTS KNOW FOR RACES INFORMATION SOLELY WHETHER ALLEGED OKLAHOMA STATEMENT AS REPORTED ILLINOIS PRESS ALTERS YOUR STATEMENTS TO LEAGUE AT MARION OR INTERPRETS THEIR MEANING PLEASE." ". . . Senator Harding directs me to state," a secretary replied, "that there was nothing in his Oklahoma speech which was not entirely consistent with his statement to the league at Marion, and that there has been no change in his attitude or position in that respect." On that and all other issues Harding was carefully vague. After Wilson's treatment of the race, however, Trotter and most Negroes had little choice but to turn on the Democrats, and they added their votes to the Republican landslide in November. With a Republican in the White House and an overwhelmingly Republican Congress, with the Dyer bill

to outlaw lynching and the Madden bill to eliminate segregated seating on interstate railroad cars both under consideration in Congress, Negroes could look on the national
scene in the spring of 1921 with more hope than they had
been able to muster in years.[1]

Once again the fight was complicated by the elusive goal
of racial unity and the precarious armistice among the
most prominent Negro leaders. The NAACP and M. A. N.
Shaw, a Boston minister who was president of the NERL,
both urged Harding to ask Congress to establish a national
race commission, an idea that Villard had pressed on Wilson without success in 1913. Harding was more receptive
and mentioned the proposal (without specifically endors-
ing it) in a special message to Congress within a few
months of his inauguration. On reflection, though, Trotter
decided that it would be foolish to lobby for a commission
just then because Congress would take the "path of least
resistance" and drop the important Dyer and Madden bills
in favor of the more innocuous commission. And, said
Trotter in the *Guardian*, there is "no one to blame for it
but outselves, especially the N.A.A.C.P." and, to a lesser
degree, the NERL and its "near responsibility." "*We
appeal to every organization, especially the N.A.A.C.P., to
realize that by lack of shrewdness and by use of terms too
general the race's cause may be sidetracked or sidestepped
virtually at our own suggestion, and to mobilize its forces
to protect our specific race measures in this overwhelmingly Republican Congress which went in with this
friendly President.*" In the interest of solidarity he assured
the NAACP that "Nothing in this editorial is censure. The
best of our people and organizations, including ourselves,

[1] Henry Lincoln Johnson to Harry M. Daugherty, August 9,
1920, in Randolph C. Downes, "Negro Rights and White Backlash
in the Campaign of 1920," *Ohio History*, LXXV (1966), 90–91,
and *ibid.*, 94, 95; W. M. Trotter to Warren G. Harding, October
18, 1920, George B. Christian, Jr., to Trotter, October 20, 1920,
Warren G. Harding Papers.

have been led into the weaker position and unless **we** quickly admit it much injury will be done the race." [2]

Since both the Association and the NERL's president had endorsed the plan for a commission, Trotter was unfair in placing most of the blame on the NAACP for the diversion of Congressional attention—unless he was willing to concede the obvious: that his own group was much less influential, and that if the government was going to heed any voice in the Negro's interest, it would be the NAACP's. Of course he would make no such admission, at least directly. He remained committed to the idea of a "racially autonomous" group, his own NERL. In the spring of 1921 he and Shaw made an extended recruiting tour through the Midwest and Rocky Mountain states, trying to build up local branches of the League. Trotter addressed the Nebraska legislature (where, the *Guardian* reported, "the legislators seemed somewhat dazed by the frankness of the address") and went as far west as Denver, the farthest he had been within the country from his citadel in Boston.[3]

Whatever this tour may have accomplished was nullified that September at the League's annual conference in Chicago. There the local branch of the NERL, in a direct challenge to Trotter's authority, tried to elect a Chicagoan, N. S. Taylor, to replace Shaw in the presidency. The conference was marred by parliamentary wrangles as charges flew back and forth: the national office was not giving a full accounting of its income, the insurgents "violated traditional procedure," the Trotterites were using fraudulent passes to pack the conference and sway all

[2] Richard B. Sherman, "The Harding Administration and the Negro: An Opportunity Lost," *Journal of Negro History*, XLIX (1964), 157; *Guardian*, May 21, 1921, p. 3, William Monroe Trotter Papers.

[3] Charles W. Puttkammer, "William Monroe Trotter: An Evaluation of the Life of a Radical Negro Newspaper Editor, 1901–1934" (senior thesis, Princeton University, 1958), pp. 57–58.

elections, the insurgents were trying to obstruct the president's authority. So it went for several days, recalling the schism of 1912 when Trotter's leadership, personal rather than constitutional, had been defied by pro-Roosevelt men. At the Chicago meeting the rebels were evidently on the verge of success, for on the next to last day of the scheduled sessions Shaw abruptly adjourned the conference without naming a time for future meetings. Then Shaw and Trotter hurried off. The Chicagoans pursued them but were ignored. Several Trotter loyalists met with their leader and formed a new executive board—without any Chicago members—and the NERL limped on, bereft of some more of its prestige and its most powerful branch outside Boston.[4]

At this point, with the NERL little more than a letter-head on his stationery, if Trotter had somehow modified his old insistence on complete independence and joined the NAACP, his later career might have been much different and probably more significant. He was starting to mellow and was no longer any more militant than the Association. Villard and other suspicious white men had ceased to control the group. Yet the white role, both in decision-making and fund-raising, was still crucial. (In contrast, the League's constitution announced its purpose to be "To organize Americans of African extraction or descent for concerted, collective action locally and nationally against every denial of justice, of liberty, of political and of civil rights . . . and to inculcate racial self-respect which calls for assertion of equal rights and privileges.")[5] Further, Trotter could not be truly reconciled with the most important black men in the Association, William Pickens, James Weldon Johnson, and especially Du Bois. And the NAACP's Boston branch was still under the firm hand of

[4] "National Equal Rights League Is Tottering," *Chicago Defender*, September 24, 1921, p. 11.

[5] NERL constitution in *Guardian*, July 14, 1923, p. 4, Trotter Papers.

Butler Wilson and his white friends.

For these reasons the NAACP would not have been hospitable even if Trotter had suddenly decided to throw his talents in with the Association men. In any event, he could not do so because of a peculiarity of his own individualistic nature. The NAACP was a well-organized institution. There were channels within which one had to operate. Major decisions were passed on by a board of directors. One man, even Du Bois or Johnson, had only so much leeway when he purported to speak for the whole group. Such an arrangement was simply impossible for Trotter. He knew it, and so did the NAACP's leaders. "Trotter was not an organization man," Du Bois said later. "He was a free lance; too intense and sturdy to loan himself to that compromise which is the basis of all real organization." Johnson wrote in the same vein that Trotter, "in many respects an able man, zealous almost to the point of fanaticism . . . . could not work, except alone; and, although there were numbers of people who subscribed to his opinions, he lacked capacity to weld his followers into a form that would give them any considerable group effectiveness." [6]

Nonetheless he persisted. During 1922 he and what was left of the NERL concentrated on the Dyer bill and in so doing inevitably collided with the NAACP's efforts. The House of Representatives passed the bill early in the year by a vote of 230–119, and it then went to the Senate Judiciary Committee, where it was stalled. Trotter exerted what pressure he could on the Judiciary's Henry Cabot Lodge. "I favor the Dyer anti-lynching bill," Lodge replied to Trotter, "and trust it may soon be reported, but I am afraid at this time with the tariff up, which occupies all the time of the Senate, even if we could secure a report

[6] W. E. B. Du Bois, "William Monroe Trotter," *Crisis*, XLI (1934), 134; *Along This Way: The Autobiography of James Weldon Johnson* (New York, 1933), p. 314.

from the committee it would be very difficult to lay the tariff aside to take up the anti-lynching bill." Shortly thereafter the bill was reported out, and Trotter promptly claimed a victory for the NERL and implied that the NAACP had been laggard in its efforts to demonstrate the bill's constitutionality. Actually Johnson at that time was trying to gain the key support of Senator William E. Borah. When the Judiciary Committee, under Trotter's prodding, approved the bill, Borah was offended by what he thought was hasty action and ended by opposing the bill —thus dealing a crucial blow to its chances of enactment. It was a minor coup for the NERL, but an important setback for the race.[7]

That fall Trotter led a group of NERL men to the White House in an effort to gain Harding's support. The President agreed "to push the Dyer Bill," said the *Guardian*, "but in his own way," and made no strong commitment either to the delegation or to the public. The NAACP mobilized its superior resources—Johnson's diplomatic lobbying, tightly argued legal briefs, petitions signed by men of power, a full-page advertisement in the *New York Times*. Nothing worked; there was no Senate vote on the Dyer bill. At the end of the year, though, Trotter reviewed the race's work for the bill and found cause for encouragement. "We are proud that so much was done by racial bodies," said Trotter, ignoring the confusion over the Judiciary Committee, "—never had any sympathy with those who complained that too many were working for the bill. . . . The time has come for consultation, conference and unity. Agreement is beginning."[8]

[7] Henry Cabot Lodge to W. M. Trotter, May 11, 1922, Henry Cabot Lodge Papers; Robert Lewis Zangrando, "The Efforts of the National Association for the Advancement of Colored People to Secure Passage of a Federal Anti-Lynching Law, 1920–1940" (Ph.D. thesis, University of Pennsylvania, 1963), pp. 184–185.

[8] *Guardian*, November 11, 1922, p. 4, and December 20, 1922, p. 4, Trotter Papers.

Perhaps it was. Early in 1923 Trotter sent letters to the four major race groups working for an anti-lynching bill, proposing that the president and secretary of each group come to a summit conference to discuss racial unity. Kelly Miller, the old mediator for the race's internecine warfare, came forward with a similar plan, Trotter pronounced him "very suitable" to lead the effort, and with that Johnson agreed to represent the NAACP at the meeting. Thus late in March the United Race Front Conference opened in New York with Trotter, Johnson, Miller, the young journalist George Schuyler from a group associated with the *Messenger* magazine, and two other Negro leaders in attendance. The theme was "Live and Let Live," and the mood was determinedly harmonious. "This conference can accomplish much," Johnson declared, "by sending out to the Negroes of the United States the inspiring news that the leaders have gotten together, allowing for differences of opinion, and are working for a common end." Trotter announced that he had renewed his membership in the NAACP. Taking his cue, Johnson gave Trotter his NERL membership fee. Trotter, chairman of the Subcommittee on Harmony, asked Johnson to draft a concordat, which the six leaders then signed:

In order to secure the most effective action and the greatest results, we must guard against the slightest loss of energy from frictions and antagonisms. . . . we are all striving for one great common goal. We deplore as harmful and injurious to the best common interests any attitude which implies that loyalty to any one of these organizations necessitates antagonism toward any of the others, or that membership in one in any way precludes membership and active interest in the others. . . . in the undertakings of these various organizations the cordial support of all shall be given. . . .

In the *Guardian* Trotter expressed his satisfaction with the new concordat.[9]

Yet it was the old story of a show of unity on the surface and the same old antagonisms beneath it. More than forty years after the Front conference in New York, Schuyler would still recall "the wrangling between the leonine Trotter from Boston and the sarcastic Kelly Miller from Washington," "a pompous pretension of representing significant memberships which they did not have," and his conclusion that "the quarrels of the liberals and the radicals did not make me hopeful." Miller, always hopeful that the race's leaders could get together, organized an enlarged version of the Front meeting—a "Negro Sanhedrin"—in Chicago in February 1924. For five days many of the race's most prominent leaders (not including Schuyler or A. Philip Randolph of the *Messenger* magazine) discussed issues and policies in an air of vague, polite harmony; Trotter presided over one panel, "The Function of Agitation in Racial Betterment." One observer of the conference noted that "Everybody seemed glad to be in the great company, but there was a notable lacking of the things you could remember after you got home. . . ." Randolph's *Messenger* dismissed the occasion as "a mere repetition of the old programs of the past" and declared that Miller "needs more of the dynamic, aggressive, militant spirit of the young Negro . . . than he does of the hesitant, cautious elder statesman."[10]

The real problem of racial unity, at least in regard to Trotter's difficulties with the NAACP, was that so long as

[9] W. M. Trotter to editor in Baltimore *Afro-American*, February 9, 1923, p. 5; *Guardian*, March 31, 1923, p. 1, and April 7, 1923, pp. 1, 4, Trotter Papers; United Race Front Concordat, March 24, 1923, copy in NAACP Papers.

[10] *Black and Conservative: The Autobiography of George S. Schuyler* (New York, 1966), pp. 150–151; "Program of the First Meeting of the Negro Sanhedrin All Race Conference," Chicago, February 11–15, 1924, NAACP Papers; Chicago *Broad Ax*, February 16, 1924, p. 1, and February 23, 1924, p. 1; *Messenger*, VI (1924), 106.

different organizations were working along parallel lines, using the same methods and seeking the same objects, there was bound to be some overlapping and friction. No concordat on paper and no polite Sanhedrin conference could alter that basic dilemma.

The issue came up again in the course of the race's campaign to free the Houston soldiers, the main federal issue of the 1920s after the struggle for anti-lynching legislation. In the summer of 1917—eleven years and a few days after the Brownsville incident—black soldiers in Houston had responded to a series of provocations by seizing their weapons and rioting through the city, killing 17 white citizens. In this case some of the soldiers were undeniably guilty, and the punishment was severe: 19 of them hanged, scores more sentenced to life imprisonment, others to lesser terms. In the fall of 1923, with the Dyer bill in legislative limbo, Trotter and the NAACP shifted their attention to seeking commutations for the 70 soldiers still in Leavenworth. Trotter and the NERL made the request in a letter to President Coolidge in September, at a White House visit in October, and again in an Armistice Day petition in November. Concurrently the Association collected signatures for a mammoth petition. Trotter published the NAACP's petition form in the *Guardian*, and at the end of November he was able to send a batch of signatures to the NAACP's New York office. But at the same time he declared that December 11, the anniversary of the first executions, would be "Houston Martyrs' Day," and that NERL members should pass resolutions asking for pardons at public meetings on that day.[11]

Walter White of the NAACP quickly advised Trotter

[11] Charles Flint Kellogg, *NAACP: A History of the National Association for the Advancement of Colored People, Volume I 1909–1920* (Baltimore, 1967), pp. 260–262; W. M. Trotter to Calvin Coolidge, September 26, November 11, 1923, Calvin Coolidge Papers; Baltimore *Afro-American*, October 12, 1923, p. 1; *New York Times*, October 7, 1923, p. 2, and November 12, 1923, p. 31; Trotter to the NAACP, November 26, 1923, NAACP Papers.

that it would be inappropriate to have pardon resolutions rain down on the White House just when the petition campaign was nearing its conclusion: "For other organizations to make themselves centers of similar campaigns simply divides the effort and lessens the effectiveness of the whole." White suggested that the NERL present its resolutions along with the Association's petition. "I cannot agree," Trotter replied, "that any one body can rightly monopolize efforts on any important general race wrong. I have, however, often thought your idea of bodies going together before public authorities, would be helpful." Trotter was as conciliatory as possible. "We purposely refrained from suggesting signatured petitions," he wrote, ". . . so as not to in any way duplicate your worthy movement. . . . The more, the better, is our idea." White responded that the NAACP of course wanted the effort to be "a non-partisan, nation-wide movement." But his group, he pointed out, had already held a "Houston Martyrs' Day" in November, and Trotter should not have appropriated the title or so much of the crusade: "I am sorry that I cannot agree with you that there is no duplication of effort. . . . We are therefore urging that all requests for pardoning be presented at the same time." [12]

Trotter went ahead and, in mid-December, issued an NERL proposal that black Americans send letters to Coolidge urging a Christmas pardon for the soldiers. To Johnson he suggested a joint audience at the White House at around Christmastime, when the League could present its resolutions and the Association its petition. "PRIOR TO RECEIVING YOUR TELEGRAM," Johnson fired back, "HAD BEGUN ARRANGING WITH PRESIDENT COOLIDGE FOR GENERAL CONFERENCE SUCH AS YOU SUGGEST WITH ALL ORGANIZATIONS CHURCHES AND OTHER BODIES REP-

[12] Walter F. White to W. M. Trotter, November 30, 1923, Trotter to White, December 3, 1923, White to Trotter, December 10, 1923, NAACP Papers.

RESENTED. AM UNWILLING TO JEOPARDIZE VITAL IN-
TERESTS OF MEN IN PRISON BY HASTY AND IMMATURE
ACTION. WILL ADVISE YOU AND ALL OTHER INTERESTED
PARTIES FULLY." Then White and the Association's press
bureau publicly criticized Trotter and the NERL for dif-
fusing the race's efforts. At that Trotter dropped the conciliatory tone and went over White's head to Johnson with
an angry complaint about "the opposition and hostile attacks" coming from the Association. "The League has not
raised a finger against anything the Asso. has proposed for
the pardons," Trotter wrote Johnson. ". . . All the attacking is by the Asso. & simply because the League is
prosecuting it's own efforts for pardons. The Asso. is
sowing public dissension by such accusations & injuring
the League." He reminded Johnson of the concordat's
pledge ("in the undertakings of these various organizations the cordial support of all shall be given") and asked
him to square it with the fact that "The Association is
conducting a race-wide publicity campaign against the
League's methods, none of which are identical with the
Association's." This was said, Trotter assured Johnson,
"in no spirit of controversy. I stand for a racial body
working on par for the race. Without a paid secretary or a
salary I cannot compete in mere controversy. . . . My
proposal would present a United Front consistent with
freedom of action & independence of & within the race,
rather than *1* channel for 15,000,000 of us. Live & let
live. My appeal is to you." [13]

Johnson, the unruffled diplomat, replied that the
NAACP "does not and will not oppose" anything the
League might do. But success in the matter "depends upon
the plans being carefully laid out and carried through one
center," and in fact the Association "did initiate and un-

[13] *New York Times*, December 16, 1923, p. 2; W. M. Trotter to
James Weldon Johnson, December 17, 1923, Johnson to Trotter,
December 18, 1923, Trotter to Johnson, December 22, 1923,
NAACP Papers.

dertake this particular piece of work. . . ." A month later Johnson told Trotter that the Association would present its petition to Coolidge at a White House appointment on February 7. Could Trotter be there to represent the NERL? Trotter asked Johnson if he could bring another NERL man with him and at the same time requested the White House for a separate appointment for the League. The White House was not agreeable, and Johnson advised Trotter that "There will be no speeches whatever. The petition will simply be presented with a brief statement by the spokesman of the delegation." [14]

Having no other choice, Trotter swallowed his resentment and joined the unity delegation organized by the NAACP. On February 7 he and Maurice Spencer of his League accompanied Johnson, Archibald Grimké, A. Philip Randolph, Robert Abbott of the *Chicago Defender*, Robert L. Vann of the *Pittsburgh Courier*, Carl Murphy of the Baltimore *Afro-American*, and others to Coolidge's office. Johnson handed over a petition with some 124,000 signatures, Trotter presented his resolutions, and that was that. "For once," the *Messenger* commented, "we presented a solid united front." Even with the prefatory bickerings, it was clearly an improvement over the bitter feuds of the Washington era. Eventually the soldiers were pardoned, and it was a good victory, mostly of a symbolic nature, for the black man. Trotter could claim at least part of the credit.[15]

[14] James Weldon Johnson to W. M. Trotter, December 26, 1923, January 23, 1924, Trotter to Johnson, January 24, 1924, Johnson to Trotter, January 25, 1924, NAACP Papers; Trotter to Calvin Coolidge, January 24, 1924, Coolidge Papers. At the last moment Trotter secured Henry Cabot Lodge's signature on the petition (see Trotter to Henry Cabot Lodge, February 1, 1924, Lodge to Trotter, February 6, 1924, Lodge Papers).

[15] *Pittsburgh Courier*, February 16, 1924, p. 1; *Messenger*, VI (1924), 69. There was an odd echo from Trotter's past in the Houston delegation: Melvin Chisum, Tuskegee's infiltrator of the Boston Suffrage League and the source of the story that Trotter had planned to kill Washington at the meeting in Cambridge in

II

But a vital question remained. Implicit in Trotter's continuing pressure on the White House was the hope that the President would have the power and the inclination to intercede with Congress in the Negro's behalf. Trotter was using an old technique, one that he had been employing since 1904: take an intense interest in national politics during a presidential election, trying to collect IOUs from politicians courting the Negro vote, and then after the election convert the IOUs into leverage on the administration in Washington. It was a traditional technique of American politics, but did not quite meet the racial situation of the 1920s.

Harding and Coolidge were no more interested in establishing racial democracy than the Presidents from earlier in the century. Harding told one Negro group that the Ku Klux Klan, on a national rampage at the time, was not really hostile to the black man; he told another group that he had made up his mind not to give any important federal appointments to Negroes in the South. When Harding called Congress into special session in the fall of 1922 Trotter asked him to endorse the Dyer bill in his special message. "As you may readily realize," a White House underling replied, "there was a most insistent pressure from many sources for the treatment of many and varied subjects in the message. In the end, however, it was found desirable to confine it to the one subject of the Merchant Marine. . . ." As Wilson had found a political priority in free wool, Harding found one in the Merchant Marine. Coolidge was no more promising. He gave no substantial help to the Dyer bill and did nothing to remove the continuing segregation in federal office buildings. "Under the Constitution," said Coolidge of Negroes in his annual mes-

November 1903, appears in the published photograph of the Houston delegates, standing next to Carl Murphy of the Baltimore *Afro-American* (see *Courier*, cited above).

sage to Congress late in 1923, "their rights are just as
sacred as those of any other citizen." But the race problem
is a southern matter, and "these difficulties are to a large
extent local problems which must be worked out by the
mutual forbearance and human kindness of each community. Such a method gives much more promise of a real
remedy than outside interference." In the face of such
presidential stolidity Trotter's endless petitions, entreaties,
and journeys to the White House were in large measure
quixotic, if not simply pointless.[16]

And while he was seeking these old goals by this old
method he was not responding fully to two vital developments within black America. Both developments sprang
from a deep vein in the American Negro's experience: the
quest for a black identity and for pride in being black.
Garveyism, under a battle cry of "Back to Africa," united
masses of Negroes in northern cities and gave unprecedented proof of the buried vitality of the black nationalist
tradition. On a different social and educational level, an
artistic renaissance in literature and music reflected the
same tradition in a different way, more literate but no less
insistent. When Langston Hughes deplored "this urge
within the race toward whiteness, the desire to pour racial
individuality into the mold of American standardization,
and to be as little Negro and as much American as possible," he spoke for a significant number of new black men
in the 1920s.[17]

"Segregation may turn out to be the Race's greatest

[16] *Guardian*, October 15, 1921, p. 4, Trotter Papers; W. M.
Trotter to Warren G. Harding, November 17, 1922, and reply,
November 22, 1922, Harding Papers; *New York Times*, December
7, 1923, p. 4; and see also Richard B. Sherman, "Republicans and
Negroes: The Lessons of Normalcy," *Phylon*, XXVII (1966),
63–79; and see n. 27 below.

[17] Langston Hughes, "The Negro Artist and the Racial Mountain," *Nation*, CXXII (1926), 692, quoted in Francis L. Broderick
and August Meier, eds., *Negro Protest Thought in the Twentieth
Century* (Indianapolis, 1965), p. 93.

blessing," one Garveyite wrote. "I know that leaders like Monroe Trotter and others, have used every possible effort to make us as acceptable as possible to white society, with only varying degrees of success so far. . . . Let us accept the situation philosophically. QUIT TRYING TO IMITATE WHITE PEOPLE, accept segregation as a blessing in disguise and capitalize the situation to our best advantage." Trotter had built his entire career on the integrationist tradition. A few of the old integrationist leaders—Bookerites such as T. T. Fortune and Wilford Smith and Niagarites such as William Ferris and J. E. Bruce—did join Garvey's crusade. Most did not. Trotter and his NERL were among Garvey's more prominent black opponents. Garveyism invoked the African heritage and urged a return to the homeland. With such a proposal Trotter had no patience. We "are Americans," he had always insisted, "not Africans, not anything else," and we must not appear "before these prejudiced white Americans as natives of Africa. We need to overemphasize our status as American citizens to the manor born because of the crusade to make us aliens and but a step removed from savages at that." He carried this attitude to the matter of racial terminology as well: since early in the century he had preferred the terms "Colored American," "Colored people," or "Afro-American" to what he viewed as the more separatist "Negro"—a term that Garvey used with insistence, both in his Universal Negro Improvement Association and in his newspaper, the *Negro World*. In 1919 the *Guardian* announced that the term would never again appear in its editorials.[18]

[18] Column by Ralph O. Gothard in *Negro World*, November 14, 1931, p. 4; *Guardian*, February 4, 1911, p. 4, and January 28, 1911, p. 4; *Guardian* editorial noted in Cleveland *Gazette*, June 7, 1919, p. 2. There was a sporadically active chapter of Garvey's UNIA in Boston, so presumably Trotter had some direct contact with the movement; see *Negro World*: April 30, 1927, p. 4; March 5, 1931, p. 2; April 16, 1932, p. 2; May 26, 1932, p. 2; June 11, 1932, p. 2.

I have found no direct comment by Trotter on Garvey, but worth

As for the artistic renaissance, Trotter had no time and probably little appreciation for such matters. He knew very little literature, and on the rare occasions when he ventured a literary allusion in the *Guardian* ("citizens to the manor born") his touch was not sure. He was an intellectual only in the broadest sense of the word. His mind was quick, inquisitive, retentive, and capable of bearing an enormous work load. But it was not imaginative, reflective, and certainly not creative. Once he said at a meeting of the Boston Literary that he had never felt the need of reading books "for amusement," but had read them "for the refinement they give." [19] That was early in 1902, when he occasionally had the leisure time to seek refinement. By the 1920s he had to be all business merely to keep himself, his paper, and his League afloat. He could not be bothered with the new literature or with the new jazz music that black performers were playing. He still urged his old programs while many Negroes were turning to different political and cultural approaches.

Yet his personality was not static, and he had changed somewhat over the decades since the ferocious era of the Boston Riot. As he wrote, a trifle sheepishly, for his college reunion in 1925, "In 1903, when young and fiery, I served a month in jail for a protest against Booker T. Washington's political conservatism." By the 1920s he

---

noting are the remarks made by Maude Trotter Steward in 1940 when she heard a premature report of Garvey's death. Mrs. Steward acknowledged that Garvey was a great mass leader who inspired considerable race pride and race consciousness. But she criticized his "petty dictatorial methods of administration and his lack of a fundamentally sound constructive political and social program" and added that "His was an essentially defeatist outlook. . . . it cannot be gainsaid that Garvey never understood the practical needs of his people" (*Guardian*, May 18, 1940, p. 4); and see Wilson Record, "Negro Intellectual Leadership in the National Association for the Advancement of Colored People: 1910–1940," *Phylon*, XVII (1956), 385 *n*.

[19] Minutes of Boston Literary and Historical Association, January 13, 1902, Trotter Papers.

thought of himself as a kind of racial elder statesman who had worked hard for the cause and therefore deserved some degree of deference. When Archibald Grimké chided him for not printing something in the *Guardian*, Trotter, in exasperation, retorted to the older man that "I thought you knew that for years I have worked as long and as hard as my physical and mental strength would allow, with no leisure, & but little bed sleep, for our race, for all of us, & without compensation."

I feel that loyal race people should think of my constant, strenuous endeavors at loss & personal sacrifice for the rights of all of us & excuse any omissions of courtesies knowing I am worked to the limit to get means to keep the Guardian going & then do personal fighting & foster racial organization for equality. . . . the Colored people are not going to have their civil rights & privileges in the North, or even in Mass. unless those still left of the Old Guard advise them along the lines of Garrison, Phillips, Sumner, Weld, Downing, Nell, Trotter & others. . . .

He had always drawn inspiration from his abolitionist heroes; in this case he gave his father—and, by extension, himself—a niche in their heritage.[20]

Responding to the general business ethos of the decade, and perhaps to Garveyism's stress on economic self-sufficiency, he gave much more editorial space to black capitalism. "Business men are builders and seers," he declared. "They represent *aggression*, *brains*, and *money*, three things that control the world. . . . Trade much with your own must be the slogan." "Study your community," he urged at another time, "then cater to a distinct need, and tend strictly to your business; make it part of yourself.

[20] *Harvard College Class of 1895: Thirtieth Anniversary Report* (Cambridge, Mass., 1925), p. 304; W. M. Trotter to Archibald Grimké, September 10, 1921, Archibald Grimké Papers.

. . . Some of our young people ought to study the art of small manufacturing." And in the last year of his life, "Industry is an established fact and we must have it." That was a remarkable modification of his remark, in 1904, that the purpose of the National Negro Business League was "to belittle political rights, which are all important, and to magnify small trade, which is of little consequence." [21]

To support black enterprise was an appropriate response to the new black consciousness of the 1920s. But to criticize Negroes, openly, harshly, even querulously, was not. The nature of Boston's Negro community changed during the decade. From 1920 to 1930 the city's black population, while remaining less than 3 per cent of the whole, grew six times faster than the white population. Migration from the South accounted for much of the jump. The southern migrants were, by and large, less skilled and less educated than Boston's native black people, and they had different life styles and values. They met a mixed reception from Boston's old Negroes. In 1921, for instance, Shaw of the NERL wrote that the League should "co-operate with all forces tending to reduce illiteracy, promote the moral welfare and better conduct on the part of our people from the South some of whom are turning their new found liberty into license." "Get down to brass tacks," Trotter suggested to the migrants, "and show us poor Bostonians what you can do. We need good business men, honest citizens, stern, clean, brilliant young men and virtuous, comely girls. Maybe we old Bostonians have grown faint with the struggle and welcome the talented blood from 'down home.' " [22]

[21] *Guardian*, July 12, 1924, p. 4, and July 28, 1923, p. 4, Trotter Papers; Puttkammer, "Trotter," p. 29; *Guardian*, June 18, 1904, p. 4.
[22] Rheable M. Edwards and Laura B. Harris, *The Negro in Boston* (Boston, 1961), p. 47; *Guardian* fragment, September 10, 1921, and *Guardian*, July 14, 1923, p. 4, Trotter Papers.

The new Bostonians—and the old Bostonians as well—
did not give him the support that he thought he deserved.
"The Colored race is trying to keep or get rights & privileges without sacrifice or personal action," he wrote
Grimké. "They feel things are wrong, but that it is up to
the whites to cease wrongs & that aside from public mass
meeting agitation & giving a dollar once or twice a year,
they have no personal duty to perform in the way of
fighting for their rights. . . . Like Harding & the G.O.P.
they use you for convenience & then forget your usefulness. . . . God will not save a race thus indifferent &
ungrateful." In the past he had expressed such opinions in
private. Now he was more outspoken, and he punctuated
his editorials with fatherly aphorisms and, occasionally,
brutal reflections on his people.

> We seem to be all tinsel and no metal, all froth and
> no liquid. It seems that like a flock of crows we sit on
> the rail and talk about our neighbors and his [*sic*]
> business. We do not seem to have any of our own to
> attend to. . . . we as a class despise ourselves by a
> constant reference to color and hair, South and North,
> West Indies and American.

> Frankly, we are beginning to wonder if the many
> things our enemies say about us are true. . . . Let us
> all wake up.

> It is a duty for us as a people to learn how to act in
> public. . . . In this country it is the whites who can
> teach us. . . . Mix and learn, don't laugh like a
> horse or make funny monkey-like noises. Observe the
> better class of people. . . . Too many of us have "tin-
> lizzy" educations and Ciceronian tongues. . . . Too
> many of us are blatant, noisy and tiresome. Every-
> body respects the telling power of silence.

> More often our stupid apathy and indifference hurts
> us more than prejudices against our skin. Many times

our brilliant minds are snapped up by the whites
because we stupidly ignore them, not through lack of
understanding, but through envy. . . . Wake up!
Wake up before it is too late! . . . Our people think
to be great is to be full of airs.

How long are we going to stand apart from the rest
of the race because of our social position and our
family tree and our lighter complexion, when we are
as ruthlessly dealt with, and as summarily, when our
racial relations are known, as any other Colored persons.

Uncouth ways are sure indications of poor blood, bad
breeding. . . .

My race is really growing up. Children willingly
mimic men because their minds have not developed.
When the mind does open up the child ceases to be
child and grows into a MAN.[23]

Perhaps he saw no contradiction between suggesting that
Negroes adopt white manners and mocking childish attempts at imitation; or between pointing out the snobbery
of invoking one's family and social position and his own
remark about "poor blood, bad breeding." As he retreated
further and further into recalling the good old days in
Boston, in the meantime issuing avuncular homilies that
somehow mingled condescension and compassion, it was
little wonder that Negroes stopped listening to him.

III

He made one last major sally onto the national stage.
During 1926, with the nation observing the sesquicenten-

[23] W. M. Trotter to Archibald Grimké, September 10, 1921,
Grimké Papers; *Guardian:* July 21, 1923, p. 4; July 12, 1924, p.
4; June 9, 1923, p. 4; July 14, 1923, p. 4; January 20, 1923, p. 4;
October 15, 1921, p. 4; January 20, 1923, p. 4; July 28, 1923, p.
4, all in Trotter Papers.

nial anniversary of the signing of the Declaration of Independence, Trotter decided to invoke that equalitarian manifesto and contrast it with the American democracy's treatment of her black citizens. He picked one of his old issues, the segregation in the federal offices in Washington. Through the *Guardian* and NERL loyalists around the country he launched an anti-segregation petition drive. As the Fourth of July approached he asked for the NAACP's help in gathering signatures—"your cooperation is especially desired for a sharp quick stroke," he wrote Johnson, "the psychological time being of paramount importance for effectiveness." After two weeks Robert Bagnall, Director of Branches for the Association, asked the local secretaries to collect signatures and send them to Trotter. That assistance, Trotter told Johnson, "manifested a noble spirit of cooperation for rights in line with our United Front Concordat, and has given us renewed spirit for the fight." He invited an NAACP representative to accompany him to the White House.[24]

In June he sent an appeal to Coolidge that played on the language of the Declaration: "For we hold it to be self-evident that consistency and national honor require that race distinction in deference to race prejudice be removed from federal executive practice in federal buildings" as the government notes the anniversary of the "Republic's first document which enunciated equality and freedom." He would have liked to present the petitions on the Fourth, but it fell on a Sunday. Accordingly, with the help of one of the Massachusetts senators he secured a White House appointment for noon on July 2. A reporter for the Baltimore *Afro-American*, wondering "What is old Trotter doing now?," went down to cover the event, treating it as a lark and "looking for humorous situations."

[24] W. M. Trotter to James Weldon Johnson, June 8, 23, 1926, and Robert W. Bagnall to NAACP branches, June 22, 1926, NAACP Papers.

Shortly before noon on the second, representatives of several race organizations gathered in a White House anteroom. Kelly Miller was there for his National Race Congress, W. H. Jernagin for the National Baptist Congress, A. S. Pinkett for the local branch of the NAACP. People from black fraternities and women's clubs filled out the delegation. Noon came and Trotter still had not arrived. He was lost in traffic outside the White House. After ten more minutes he appeared, lugging a big valise carrying petitions with 25,000 signatures, and was rebuked by the others for his tardiness. "Why, the President is Republican," he replied. "The Negro has been waiting 50 years on the Republican party; it won't hurt the President to wait a few minutes on the Negro." [25] An usher led them down a corridor into an executive office. Coolidge walked in, smiled, shook hands, and said, "Well, what are you doing down here?" Maurice Spencer presented the petitions and Trotter read a statement. Coolidge replied that the offices were being gradually integrated. He thanked them for their concern, said he would examine the petitions, and with that the interview was over. In all it took about twelve minutes. Afterward Trotter turned to the man from the *Afro-American* and asked, "Did I put it over?" [26]

He did as well as he could. On the segregation itself he had little effect. Soon he was repeating the same request, and as late as 1933 asked President Franklin Roosevelt to do something about the matter. If he could take any encouragement from his sesquicentennial petition, it was the fact that the NAACP and other groups had helped him gather the signatures. A few months later the Association's

[25] Evidently Trotter continued on occasion to use "Negro" in conversation.

[26] W. M. Trotter to Calvin Coolidge, June 10, 1926, Coolidge Papers; *Guardian*, July 14, 1928, Baltimore *Afro-American*, April 14, 1934, and *Chicago Whip*, July 10, 1926, all clippings in William Monroe Trotter folder, Schomburg Collection, New York Public Library; Cleveland *Gazette*, July 10, 1926, p. 2.

board voted to send the League $25 to help defray its petition expenses. Such cooperation was encouraging, and so were a few comments made by race men. "I have differed with him," said Kelly Miller, "and still differ in modus operandi, but his devotion, his courage and persistency demand my unlimited admiration." The *Afro-American* reporter wrote that "Men of courage and conviction, such as Trotter, by continually knocking, may eventually break down the wall of prejudice. We need more of them." "Trotter will not receive the immediate relief that he prayed," the *Chicago Whip* commented, "his efforts will not get the appreciation that they should and this noble man will not be honored, reckoned and sung but he is fighting a noble cause in a noble manner." And the *Whip* came to a sad conclusion:

> This man Trotter represents a pathetic figure bending under the weight of flying years, gazing upon a steady declination of the rights and recognition of his people, finding himself penurized by the lack of wholesome support from his own, ridiculed, sometimes ostracized, misunderstood and little appreciated, he stands undaunted, unbroken and defiant. . . . He stands as a lone figure almost in desolation, his voice comes like a hollow cry from a wilderness and only the echo returns to mock him. . . .[27]

[27] Minutes of Board of Directors Meetings, September 13, 1926, and James Weldon Johnson to B. W. Swain, September 17, 1926, NAACP Papers; *Guardian*, July 28, 1928, Baltimore *Afro-American*, April 14, 1934, and *Chicago Whip*, July 17, 1926, all clippings in Trotter folder, Schomburg Collection.
On Trotter's later work against federal segregation and discrimination, see Trotter to Calvin Coolidge, October 16, 28, 1926, August 1, 1927, March 9, 1928, Frederick H. Gillett to Coolidge, June 26, 1928, Trotter to Coolidge, June 27, 30, 1928, Trotter to Everett Sanders, June 30, July 2, 5, 1928, Coolidge to Trotter, July 5, 1928, Trotter to Coolidge, October 23, 1928, Coolidge Papers; *Chicago Whip*, August 6, 1927, clipping in Trotter folder, Schomburg Collection; Trotter to Herbert Hoover, March 7, July 1, November 11, 1929, July 3, November 12, 1931, February 15,

IV

Whatever influence he had after 1919 was in dealing with smaller, local issues back home. He gave time and *Guardian* space to desegregating a theater in Boston and removing the "Colored Only" window from the Roxbury branch of a large insurance company. He pressured a secretarial school into admitting a qualified Negro student. He secured the removal of defamatory schoolbooks from the Cambridge schools. Every year he tried to stir up enthusiasm for the celebration of Boston Massacre Day in order to honor Crispus Attucks—and, by extrapolation, black soldiers in the nation's wars.[28]

In the spring of 1921, just after he returned from his western tour for the NERL, the Shubert Theater announced that it would bring *The Birth of a Nation* back to Boston. This time Trotter was able to gather opponents to

September 28, 1932, Herbert Hoover Papers; Trotter to Franklin D. Roosevelt, June 22, 1933, Franklin D. Roosevelt Papers; Cleveland *Gazette*, July 1, 1933, p. 1. And for his other work against lynching, see Trotter to Coolidge, April 5, 1924, Maurice Warren Spencer to Coolidge, March 10, 1927, Coolidge Papers; Trotter to Hoover, April 29, 1929, November 4, 12, 20, 25, 1930, February 7, 9, 21, December 7, 1931, January 16, August 13, 1932, Hoover Papers; *New York Times*, December 1, 1931, p. 5.

On other federal matters: the proposal to send a segregated group of Gold Star Mothers to Europe, see Trotter to Hoover, February 19, 1930, Hoover Papers; the nomination of John J. Parker to the Supreme Court, Trotter to Hoover, April 1930, with enclosure, Hoover Papers; the proposed disbanding of the all-black Tenth Cavalry, Trotter to Hoover, September 5, 1931, Douglas MacArthur to Walter H. Newton, September 3, 1931, Hoover Papers; the Scottsboro case, Trotter to Roosevelt, November 20, 1933, Roosevelt Papers.

All of this is routine, perfunctory material, useful principally as documentation of Trotter's perseverance.

[28] Lillian Lewis Feurtado, "Year Leaf From the Race Work of William Monroe Trotter," *Guardian*, March 19, 1927, Trotter Papers; Ruth Worthy, "A Negro in Our History: William Monroe Trotter, 1872–1934" (M.A. thesis, Columbia University, 1952), p. 161; Adelaide Cromwell Hill, "The Negro Upper Class in Boston, Its Development and Present Social Structure" (Ph.D. thesis, Radcliffe College, 1952), p. 360; *Guardian*, May 18, 1929, p. 1, and April 21, 1934, p. 7, Trotter Papers.

the film on a broader ground than race alone. Since it glorified the anti-Catholic Ku Klux Klan, he sought and obtained a protest from the Knights of Columbus, a powerful voice in the Irish Catholic wards of Boston. He and the local NAACP demanded a hearing at City Hall before the three-man board set up by the censorship law of 1915. Six hundred Negroes looked on as Mayor Andrew Peters and the other censors heard presentations by Trotter, M. A. N. Shaw, Butler Wilson, William Lewis, and others. Trotter and one other speaker launched into an attack on Mayor Curley for his handling of the film in 1915, and "Mayor Peters advised them to keep to their present subject in further discussion," a Boston daily reported. "Do not force us to the wall," Trotter warned. After the hearing the censors suspended the Shubert's license indefinitely. *The Birth of a Nation*, this time around, could not be shown in Boston.[29]

Another local issue, also protested with success, must have hurt him deeply. Harvard University held a very special place in Trotter's memory. His undergraduate years had been in some ways the most happy and successful period in his life, a brief interlude of meeting white America on its own ground and terms and showing it what racial democracy could be. In the years after graduation he returned to Cambridge as often as he could for Phi Beta Kappa dinners and class reunions. His Harvard background helped establish his credentials with his white adversaries—Mayor Peters, for example, was a classmate— and in both spiritual and practical ways made his struggles a little easier. So it was bitterly ironic for Trotter when Harvard's President A. Lawrence Lowell and his administration ruled, in the early 1920s, that all freshmen would thereafter be required to live in the freshman dorms. That

[29] *Guardian*, May 21, 1921, p. 1, Trotter Papers; *Guardian*, February 22, 1947, p. 4; *Boston Daily Globe*, May 17, 1921, pp. 1, 2.

brought up a question: What of the white freshmen from the South who would object to living with Negro freshmen? Lowell's decision was to exclude the black freshmen from the residence halls. The issue reached the public just after the close of school in the spring of 1922 when the black students' association at Harvard made a protest. Trotter picked it up and put out an NERL statement of dismay. It was published in the *New York Times*, but nothing further came of it then.[30]

Over the summer Moorfield Storey, Robert Benchley, Lewis Gannett, and four other white alumni circulated a petition among 200 Harvard men; 142 of them signed the protest. The Harvard Corporation heard the petition that fall but was unmoved. Storey then decided to make the matter a public controversy. In December, Lowell advised Roscoe Conkling Bruce, the valedictorian of his Harvard class early in the century, that his son could not live in a dorm when he entered Harvard that fall. When this letter was published it brought Harvard some unpleasant publicity. Wrote Trotter, "If President Lowell is responsible for race exclusion in the freshman dormitory he is making Harvard turn from democracy and freedom to race oppression, prejudice and hypocrisy." "It seems to be a pity that the matter ever came up in this way," wrote a Harvard overseer, Franklin D. Roosevelt. "There were certainly many colored students in Cambridge when we were there and no question ever arose." John Haynes Holmes demanded, "What is going to be done by the graduates of Harvard to rescue the College from its betrayal at the hands of President Lowell?" In "capitulating to anti-Negro prejudice," said James Weldon Johnson for the NAACP, ". . . Harvard University affirms that prejudice and strengthens it, and is but putting into effect the pro-

[30] *New York Times*, June 9, 1922, p. 15. On Trotter and Harvard, see statement by William Harrison in *Guardian*, April 13, 1940, p. 4.

gram proclaimed by the infamous Ku Klux Klan and its apologists." The title of an article in the *Nation* summed it up: *"Fair* Harvard?" [31]

Under the pressure Lowell changed his mind. On March 26 he and the Harvard Fellows resolved that admission to the dorms should not be restricted on account of race, and the Corporation gave its unanimous approval a few weeks later. Trotter may have had some influence on the change of policy; one *Guardian* headline had proclaimed that "EX-PRES. ELIOT, GRADS, OPPOSE LOWELL POLICY," and through the League he had requested a hearing before the Corporation. The really effective work was done by others, though. An article in the *Nation*, after all, carried more weight with the Harvard administration than an outraged headline in the *Guardian*. In this case, as generally in the 1920s, Trotter supported but did not initiate, followed but no longer led.[32]

The pattern was the same in the case of what was perhaps the most difficult of the local issues, the controversy over the Plymouth Hospital. Since 1901 he had, at some cost to his local prestige, opposed many efforts by black Bostonians to create separate black institutions. "Trotter's interpretation of segregation was inconsistent and perverted," one Negro Bostonian later recalled. "He opposed anything Negroes attempted to start for themselves . . . yet, he printed a Negro newspaper!" "I am uncertain," said another, "whether he played a beneficial

[31] *Crisis*, XXIV (1922), 178–179, XXV (1922–23), 218; Lewis S. Gannett to Moorfield Storey, June 2, July 26, August 2, 1922, A. Lawrence Lowell to Storey, October 10, 1922, Moorfield Storey Papers, LC; *New York Times*, January 13, 1923, p. 5; Franklin D. Roosevelt to R. S. Wallace, February 7, 1923, in Arthur M. Schlesinger, Jr., *The Age of Roosevelt: The Politics of Upheaval* (Boston, 1960), p. 696; John Haynes Holmes to Storey, January 12, 1923, Storey Papers, LC; *"Fair* Harvard?," *Nation*, CXVI (1923), 112.

[32] *Harvard Alumni Bulletin*, XXV (1922–23), 830; *New York Times*, April 10, 1923, p. 1; *Guardian*, January 20, 1923, pp. 1, 4, 5, Trotter Papers.

role civicly or whether he helped keep the Negro back. He
was a great one for 'killing' all racial movements by the
Negroes." He did endorse black fraternal groups and,
especially in the 1920s, such business enterprises as a
chain of Negro theaters and a proposed Negro bank in
Boston. In 1907 he had advertised a "Headquarters for
real estate for Colored patrons" of his own—and was duly
accused of Jim Crowing by the *New York Age*. He *was*
inconsistent, because a few years later he was expressing
reservations about a Negro hotel in Boston. "We do not
object to Colored men doing a hotel business," he explained. His objection was to "a 'Jim-Crow' public business." He shifted on the issue of black business operations,
but remained adamant on what he called "separate Colored
institutions, of a civic nature." We must, he urged, "prevent a condition of separation from arising. Make sacrifices
to do so, even bear some less agreeable things to keep up
the affiliation. This is imperative. Once segregated there is
no end to the exclusion and injury just for color. Hence the
harm of Colored schools, Colored Y.M.C.A. branches, unnecessary surplus Colored churches created just to give
some lazy preacher a living, Colored hospitals, etc., in such
places as New England." [33]

A black physician in Boston, Dr. Cornelius N. Garland,
bought a building on East Springfield Street in 1908 and
converted it into a small hospital. It was an all-black
undertaking of both a business and a civic nature. Trotter
decided it was more of the latter and so expressed his
disapproval in the *Guardian:* Garland's hospital might do
some good "in giving colored individuals skill or jobs,"
but there would be "far more ultimate harm in causing the

[33] Statements by Mrs. Theodore Webb and Irwin Dorch in
Oswald Louis Jordan, "The Political Status of the Negro in Bos-
ton" (M.A. thesis, Howard University, 1942), p. 108; *Guardian*,
August 12, 1911, p. 1, January 10, 1920, p. 4, and November 11,
1922, p. 4, Trotter Papers; *New York Age*, October 3, 1907, p. 4;
Guardian, March 7, 1914, p. 4, in Box 7, Storey Papers, LC;
Guardian, April 28, 1923, p. 4, Trotter Papers; *Guardian*, Decem-
ber 24, 1910, p. 4.

Jim Crow lines to be drawn about us. . . ." It was characteristic of Trotter to sacrifice the short-term benefits—hospital training for Negro doctors and nurses—for the long-
term principle, the chance to integrate white hospitals.
Even in Boston that chance had no immediate prospects for
success: the general deterioration of the Washington era
had taken its effect in the medical world too, and black
medical and nursing students were not allowed to train in
Boston's hospitals. Given such conditions, Garland's hospital attracted considerable support in the black community. Trotter stuck to his principles and in 1910 tried to
persuade the Floating Hospital, a private institution, to
take Negro nurses in training. Garland still had a compel-
ling argument—the City Hospital, the largest in Boston,
supported by public money, admitted no Negroes to its
schools.[34]

For twenty years Garland kept his small Plymouth Hospital going. In 1928 he gathered a bi-racial committee,
including Moorfield Storey, to make plans for expanding
the Plymouth into a full-scale hospital, to be staffed by
Negroes, to serve the black population. It provoked a fierce
debate among Negroes, with Trotter and the *Guardian*
prominently in opposition. Storey reconsidered his support
and told Trotter, "I have resigned since I found out what
the objections to the scheme are. The more I think of them
the stronger they seem to be. . . . I don't want to take
sides in the matter." As the controversy went on, the
expansion of Garland's hospital was stalled. Those in opposition realized that their most effective argument would
be to pressure the City Hospital into accepting black train-
ees.[35]

[34] *Crisis*, XIX (1919–20), 128; *Guardian*, February 8, 1908, p.
4; Ray Stannard Baker, *Following the Color Line: American Negro
Citizenship in the Progressive Era* (Harper Torchbook edition,
New York, 1964), p. 123; Francis J. Garrison to Oswald Garrison
Villard, June 7, 1910, Oswald Garrison Villard Papers.
[35] Worthy, "Trotter," pp. 155–158; Moorfield Storey to W. M.
Trotter, February 1, 1928, Moorfield Storey Papers.

Toward that end a group of Boston's black doctors led by W. O. Taylor and William Worthy formed a committee with Trotter and other citizens. Under their auspices two local girls, graduates of the Cambridge Latin School, applied for admission to the nursing program at the City Hospital. The applicants, once their race was known, were neither accepted nor rejected; they were merely ignored. Trotter and Worthy went to see an editor of the *Boston Post*, the white daily friendliest to Negroes. The editor said that if the hospital admitted that it was discriminating on the basis of race, the citizens should press for a public hearing, and the *Post* would give it publicity. Trotter kept it out of the *Guardian* until such time as the charge of discrimination could be proved. Worthy kept badgering the hospital during the summer of 1929. "As tax-paying citizens," Worthy wrote the hospital's trustees, " . . . we are insisting on their legal rights to the same treatment accorded others in a 'School' supported by public taxes." The whole project was carried out in a spirit of polite discretion which reflected the changes in Trotter's temperament since 1901. And it worked: the trustees considered the matter and decided to admit the girls. With that push, Garland's plans collapsed. The City Hospital thereafter did not discriminate. It was a gratifying vindication of the course that had brought Trotter much unpopularity among Boston's Negroes.[36]

V

"I thank you for your 2.25," he wrote an old subscriber early in 1934, "which pays you to Feb. 1932. . . . This is the start of a very serious time for the Guardian with almost my sole dependence on such friends as you (O how few now). So if you can send another it will do a *great*

[36] William Worthy, *The Story of the Two First Colored Nurses to Train in the Boston City Hospital* (Boston, 1942), pp. 3–13; Worthy, "Trotter," p. 159. Dr. William Worthy was the father of Ruth Worthy and the journalist William Worthy.

good." After 1919 his financial troubles became an even greater burden. An attractive rival newspaper in Boston, the *Chronicle*, made steady inroads into the *Guardian*'s circulation. The *Chronicle*'s editors, more interested in journalism than in race crusading, took a more conservative line and occasionally criticized Trotter's approach, as when he competed with the NAACP's efforts on behalf of the Houston soldiers. The *Chronicle* also did not share Trotter's commitment to integration: once the paper was quoted with approval by Garvey's *Negro World* on "the wisdom of getting together." On his part Trotter was disgusted by what he called "the compromise, expediency, get the dollar, Booker Washington doctrine" of the *Chronicle*, and he angrily told Archibald Grimké that its editors "spend not a minute of time for rights here or elsewhere but are out for the dollar in policy & practise." The *Chronicle* provided reassuring news without Trotter's acerbic strictures, and it hurt the *Guardian*.[37]

He relaxed his principles enough to accept, on occasion, the advertisements for hair straighteners and skin lighteners that he used to shun. But without his wife to do the bookkeeping, his business methods grew sloppier. Friends in Boston helped out occasionally with office assistance and small contributions. In 1924 William Lewis sent a solicitation letter to the paper's many delinquent subscribers and drew this response from John Hope:

> Occasionally I do for Trotter what many other people do—send him a dollar or two. Trotter is so unbusinesslike with his bookkeeping that he makes his pa-

[37] W. M. Trotter to George A. Towns, January 23, 1934, George A. Towns Papers; Worthy, "Trotter," p. 36; Trotter to James Weldon Johnson, December 22, 1923, NAACP Papers, noting "a vituperative, yes, scurrilous attack" in the *Chronicle; Boston Chronicle* quoted in *Negro World*, August 7, 1926, p. 4; Trotter to Archibald Grimké, September 10, 1921, Grimké Papers; and see also Albert E. Pillsbury to Grimké, January 28, 1919, Grimké Papers.

trons the same way. The fact is, I do not know how
much I owe Trotter. He says I owe him $6.75.
Trotter really does not know whether I owe him
$6.75 or $16.75. And Lewis does not know, and
Hope does not know. Now here's what I am going to
do, Lewis, I am going to send a check for $5.00 with
the understanding that you and Trotter call that
square.

And without Deenie he could not do a decent job of putting
the paper together. Editorials were scribbled out in haste
and lacked their former intellectual caliber, not to mention
any touch of literary finish. "This nationally known agita-
tor undoubtedly has done some splendid things for his
people," the Negro journalist Eugene Gordon wrote in the
American Mercury, "but if he lives to twice his present
fifty-odd years he will never be a newspaper man"; the
Guardian "is one of the most poorly-written Negro sheets
in America." [38]

So he walked around Boston, stopping in to see his
advertisers, trying to collect the small sums due him. "Old
Mon" was a minor institution of the city. He always looked
the same, whatever the season: a doughty, plump, short
man, weighing perhaps 175 pounds in his last years, quite
handsome in a portly, middle-aged way, with a bushy mus-
tache and a full head of hair that was increasingly flecked
with gray. He would be wearing an old-fashioned dark suit
that generally needed pressing. He would be carrying a
bundle of his papers under one arm, and he would have an
out-of-style derby on his head. Even on the coldest winter
days he never wore an overcoat. "He is always good na-
tured," a friend observed, "carrying that smile of hope on
his lips even though he has not collected one dollar. People

[38] John Hope to William H. Lewis, May 9, 1924, in Ridgely
Torrence, *The Story of John Hope* (New York, 1948), p. 247;
Eugene Gordon, "The Negro Press," *American Mercury*, VIII
(1926), 214.

riding in automobiles pass him during this trudge and one out of a hundred will care whether he is weary or not. They wave a greeting, the car flits by and Trotter continues to trudge." [39]

That paradox—motorists waving a friendly greeting and driving by, leaving Trotter to walk—epitomized his position in the community. He was widely acquainted, and the people did come to the benefits, picnics, and dances he staged to raise money for the *Guardian*. (At least until jazz and big bands took crowds from his old-fashioned affairs. One night a jazz band lured the audience from one of his dances, leaving Trotter to say, with some bitterness, that "I have given up everything for them, they would not buy my paper; I could understand that, but now they won't even attend my dances.") Only a small circle of close friends actually gave him any help with the paper. This little group would sometimes end the working day by gathering at the home of Lillian Feurtado, a black woman who wrote for the *Guardian*. Trotter would relax in a large chair in the living room, and there would be some light chatter. "One could almost see care and fatigue fall from Monroe, like loose garments slip from one's shoulders," recalled Louis Pasco, who became president of the remains of the NERL after the death of M. A. N. Shaw in 1923. "He would address me 'Mr. President,' " and there would follow "a generous slap on the shoulder and a roaring laugh born of good will and fellowship." Yet even within this congenial little circle there were evidently moments of loneliness for Trotter when he thought about the wife who had died so quickly and prematurely. In the fall of 1930, with Deenie dead for a dozen years, he wrote that "Still acute is the pang of her going, still saddened is life by daily remembrance of her and longing for the old companionship. . . . weaker are we for the battle without her bright mind, her sense of humor, her sweet smile and cheery

[39] Worthy, "Trotter," preface; Feurtado, "Year Leaf."

laugh, her high spirit, her helping hand and encouraging support and cooperation. . . ." [40]

Practically all of his associates from his best years early in the century were dead, or retired, or out of touch. In 1932, as his sixtieth birthday approached, he wrote his old comrade Harry Smith, "Now at 60 all I ask of my race is a congratulation trial subscription to 'The Guardian,' and supplementary, a dollar membership in the National Equal Rights League, my two efforts for the race. If in your columns you can ask the race to thus lend a hand to Monroe Trotter at 60, it will encourage me more than money." Smith did praise Trotter's "splendid work for the race" in his Cleveland *Gazette*, and no doubt that was the approximate extent of Trotter's reward. Thus early in 1934, to another veteran: "I cannot give you up. No, we have been comrades too long! . . . But you are neglecting your comrade. I am in need of your help as in days gone by. Come to my rescue. . . . Save the Guardian." He still had the *Guardian*, and he clung to it. [41]

In the spring of 1934 even that was beyond him. He seemed disoriented, out of touch, pacing up and down constantly. His brother-in-law, Charles Steward, asked him why he paced like that. "To think where I'm going next," he said. Sitting in the Steward home one day, he jumped up, strode across the room, and bumped into the stove. His sister Maude Trotter Steward, who after Deenie's death would take over the paper when he was out of town, persuaded him to take a rest. "In the present emergency," she wrote in the *Guardian*, "with the editor prevailed upon by friends to let others carry the burden awhile, we do appeal to you to pay up all you owe. . . . Speedy response on your part will go far to restore him to his old

[40] Puttkammer, "Trotter," p. 114; *Guardian*, April 19, 1941, p. 4; statement by Trotter, October 1930, in *Philadelphia Tribune*, April 7, 1932, p. 9.
[41] Cleveland *Gazette*, March 19, 1932, pp. 1, 2; W. M. Trotter to "Bro. Floyd," January 23, 1934, Trotter Papers.

time vigor." To an old Trotterite she wrote, "Monroe collapsed last week & we were all frightened. The Dr. ordered him to stop all work. . . . Can you help by sending what you can in this crisis?" "Hello Pal!" another old friend wrote him. "How are you? Like thousands of others, I presume you are a little overworked, having worked hard. You know there is only one Monroe Trotter; too bad you didn't have a dozen boys to take your place. Cheer up, old boy, I am praying for you. . . ." [42]

On the night of Friday, April 6, the Stewards brought the proofs of the new issue of the *Guardian* to Trotter for his inspection. He was living at 41 Cunard Street, on the second floor of a three-story building, sharing the apartment with Mrs. Mary Gibson—the benefactress who taught him to cook in 1919—and her son Wallace. The Stewards stayed with him until about eleven o'clock. After they left he could not sleep. He went up to the flat roof of the building and, as was his custom, walked back and forth. "Monroe, lie down," said Mrs. Gibson. "I can't sleep," he said, "my burdens are more than I can bear, you don't understand, you see one side, the public another side, but I see the third side." Obviously he was distraught. One cannot say precisely what went through his mind there in the early morning hours of his sixty-second birthday as he paced on the roof and lay sleepless on his bed. It was one week after Easter weekend, and perhaps, strong Christian that he was, his thoughts turned on that theme. ("'Tis the good Easter-tide," he had written in his last editorial, "the season when Christianity hails with joy the Risen Christ. . . . His was the sacrifice extraordinary and for the multitudes. His was the sacrifice pure and unselfish and intense.") At a few minutes before five-thirty he again went to the roof. It is just possible—though improbable—that,

[42] Worthy, "Trotter," pp. 165–166; *Guardian*, April 7, 1934, p. 4, Trotter Papers; Maude Trotter Steward to George A. Towns, n.d., Towns Papers; Thomas S. Harten to W. M. Trotter, April 5, 1934, Trotter Papers.

as his family would maintain, he was merely going up for
some morning air. There was a barrier at the front edge of
the roof, sixteen inches high and three feet wide, and
perhaps, as his family later theorized, he sat down there
and simply lost his balance. . . . At five-thirty Wallace
Gibson heard a noise, awoke, saw that the door to the
stairs was open, could not find Trotter in his bedroom;
climbed to the roof, found no one there, went to the edge,
peered through the morning light, saw a form on the
sidewalk below; rushed downstairs, awakened his mother;
together they went down to the street, found Trotter
sprawled there, unconscious, his skull crushed. He died on
the way to the hospital.[43]

[43] Worthy, "Trotter," p. 167; *Guardian*, April 14, 1934, p. 1,
and May 5, 1934, p. 4, Trotter Papers; Cleveland *Gazette*, April
21, 1934, p. 1.

Epilogue

OVER THE first two decades of the twentieth century Washington, Du Bois, and (to a lesser extent) Trotter were black America's three most important spokesmen. Washington, as adviser to Theodore Roosevelt and friend to white millionaires, and Du Bois, as editor of the *Crisis*, both were most influential when they were well into middle age. Trotter, in contrast, did his most significant work before his fortieth birthday in 1912. During the second decade of the century he retained a degree of prominence mostly because of three well-publicized episodes, the Wilson encounter in 1914, the protest against *The Birth of a Nation* in 1915, and the trip to France in 1919. Thereafter he did nothing that attracted comparable attention, and his leadership position eroded steadily.

Thus the question: Why did he peak so young? If his dedication and his energies remained virtually undiminished, why did his leadership career go into that long anticlimax?

I

One must start with his personality. He was an unusual human being, austere, opinionated, and incredibly disciplined, and he was never reluctant to press his views on others. "I must say to you John," he wrote John Fairlie seven years after their graduation from college, "that you showed poor staying powers to get into the use of tobacco and of beer. It is strange to me how you fellows change your principles. Tobacco is not important, but it is important to set a good example in the matter of liquor, just as important now as it was when you were at home and at college. Liquor, commencing with ale and beer is still ruining lives and ruining character, John, and I wish you would abstain from it." And then, drawing back at the close, "I did not suppose when I started this letter I would end with this lecture, but as Dean Briggs once said, there are worse things."[1] Even as he apologized for lecturing to his friend, he pressed his case once more. And when dealing with men for whom he had no affection, and with whom he disagreed, he could be utterly obnoxious. He was capable of moods of priggishness, stubbornness, impossible arrogance, idiosyncratic independence, and cold cynicism about everyone's motives except his own. Even his best qualities could be liabilities: his independence of mind could lead to self-righteousness, and the strength of his convictions could produce an unreasoning inflexibility. For all these reasons his relations with associates were difficult, and he left behind a trail of alienated former supporters: Archibald Grimké, George Forbes, Clement Morgan, Du Bois, William Ferris, and others.

If nothing else, he was a *strong* man, persistent and not easily discouraged. Consequently it may be hard to understand how such a person could have killed himself on his sixty-second birthday. The circumstances of his death strongly imply suicide, but there can never be a final determination on the matter. It could have been simply an accident, and it freakishly might have just happened on his

[1] W. M. Trotter to John A. Fairlie, June 15, 1902, John Archibald Fairlie Papers.

birthday. If he did kill himself, the process that brought him to such a decision could be plausibly reconstructed in this way: The last fourteen years of his life brought an almost unrelieved series of frustrations and discouragements. His national importance declined inexorably, and he was not able to produce an incident or movement to restore himself to prominence. His old supporters left him or died. He missed his wife, who had helped him in so many ways. Ultimately his struggle came down to keeping the *Guardian* alive. When his health kept him from even putting out his newspaper, his spirit broke; and on his birthday, as he presumably reflected on the course his life had taken, he decided to end it.

There is a tendency, which should be avoided, to read backward from his probable suicide and thereby discover elements of neuroticism earlier in his life. On balance, he seems to have been healthy enough psychiatrically. Admittedly there were a few suggestions along the way that his furious vendetta against Washington had a demonic quality, as though he had a psychological need to spew forth his rage. "With him," Kelly Miller wrote during the Niagara Movement days, "agitation is not so much the outgrowth of an intellectual or moral comprehension of right and reprehension of wrong, as it is a temperamental necessity." The *New York Age* bluntly called him "crazy"; in 1908 the Washington *Bee* suggested that "William Monroe Trotter needs a long course of treatment at the hands of an expert on nervous disorders." Villard wrote at about this same time that "Trotter must be unbalanced." [2] All of these comments, though, came from observers who were dismayed by Trotter's methods, and their remarks derived more from exasperation over his

[2] Kelly Miller, *Race Adjustment: Essays on the Negro in America* (New York and Washington, D.C., 1908), p. 13; *New York Age*, November 25, 1905, p. 4; Washington *Bee*, September 12, 1908, p. 4; Oswald Garrison Villard to Francis J. Garrison, January 15, 1908, Oswald Garrison Villard Papers.

activities than from concern over his mental health. In his later career, when some of his early fire had left him, no one proposed that he had psychological problems.

Yet he was so much the free lance, so certain that he had a unique perception of what was true and appropriate for the race to do. When his own race group, in 1908, 1912, and 1921, tried to challenge his authority or modify the positions that he dictated, he could not bring himself to compromise. (Garrison, he would have said, never compromised either.) So he would merely slough off the dissidents and go ahead with whatever loyalists remained. In the same way he seemed unable to admit error, even in private. This could have been the mark of a towering ego —or, more plausibly, the reflection of some carefully buried insecurities.

He took himself in dreadful earnest. He was the sort of man who never, never smiled for photographs. Occasionally he gave the impression of working not just for manly principles and for the race, but for God too. Thus a cablegram from Trotter on his way home to Boston in 1919: "HAVE PRAYERS OFFERED IN ALL THE CHURCHES FOR MY SAFE RETURN. TROTTER." [3] In his most religious and egocentric moments he might even have seen his life as a divine mission, right down to his death in the Easter season—to bring manliness where he saw cowardice, to bring a spirit of sacrifice where he saw unthinking self-indulgence, to bring self-respect where he saw self-hate.

II

Hamstrung by the sort of person he was, once the anti-Washington crusade was over, his intellectual limitations kept him from making any further contribution to racial thought. His leadership approach, beyond his general militancy and insistence on integration and equal

[3] W. M. Trotter to Benjamin W. Swain in *Guardian*, July 12, 1919, p. 5, William Monroe Trotter Papers.

rights, had an episodic quality. He moved from one incident to the next, taking his strong and often courageous positions, but there never seemed to be much rationale to what he was doing. Evidently he never tried to draw up a comprehensive program for racial progress in any detail; perhaps he did not see the need for such a program.

He started his protest career by borrowing old techniques from the abolitionists, and was initially spurred on by a very personal sense of outrage. As a college undergraduate he had been able to speak comfortably about "the laboring people" and "the better class," and this smug elitism was not pricked until he realized that, despite Hyde Park and Harvard, he would still be treated like any other Negro in white America. Personal concern drove him to launch the *Guardian*, and thereafter he tended to personalize issues: in 1903 the problem was not accommodationist ideas among blacks but the specific influence of Washington; in 1914 it was not the racism of federal bureaucrats but the treachery of Wilson.[4] Personalities are generally easier to deal with than ideas or more impersonal forces, but personalities are also more ephemeral, and by focusing on them as he did, Trotter consigned the bulk of his work to merely temporary importance.

A fully developed blueprint for social change simply did not interest him. On issues outside race he was conventionally progressive. He supported prohibition and woman suffrage long before those reforms were enacted. He edged up to socialism, decided that it was "certainly a subject up for consideration by Colored Americans" and "should at least have a hearing." However, he never voted for a socialist candidate, even when confronted with the sorry choice of 1912—the year Eugene Debs polled some 900,000 votes on the socialist ticket. Probably he never moved beyond the classical economics he had learned at

[4] I am indebted to Professor Louis Harlan for his perception of the way in which Trotter personalized issues.

Harvard. "Labor, like other commodities," he explained in 1916, "is ruled by the natural laws of supply and demand, and will flow, in spite of all artificial obstructions, to the places offering the best wages, the most appreciation, the best working conditions. . . . " And while he thought women should vote, he was assuredly not a feminist. "Women follow, never lead in civilization!" the *Guardian* thundered in 1902. "Man is responsible for her elevation or degradation in every sense whatever. This talk of making women responsible for the rise or fall of a people is extremely southern, where the visible and tangible lapses of the masculine gender make it necessary, for the men of that section to place all responsibility for morality upon the women in order to save themselves." [5]

In choosing his political candidates he showed utter impartiality, shifting from Republican to Democrat, conservative to liberal, aiming only to find the man who would treat Negroes fairly. He made a minor hero out of Joseph Foraker—who was hopelessly out of touch on virtually every public issue—because the senator had the courage to press the Brownsville case. He supported Republican presidential candidates in 1904, 1916, 1920, and 1924, and Democratic candidates in 1908, 1912, 1928, and 1932; which suggests a certain flexibility but also some incongruity. He could support Bryan in 1908 and Harding in 1920, despite their widely disparate political philosophies, because each man seemed the more reasonable of the two major candidates running. Ignoring the larger context, his main interest was in how a candidate would treat the black man.

So if he had ever taken the time to write out a full statement of his social program, it could not have been

[5] For Trotter's views on prohibition, see *Guardian*, November 2, 1907, p. 4; on woman suffrage, *Guardian*, November 1, 1902, p. 4, and December 2, 1916, p. 1, Trotter Papers; on socialism, *Guardian*, March 11, 1911, p. 4; on the natural laws of labor, *Guardian*, November 18, 1916, p. 4, Trotter Papers; on why men should lead, *Guardian*, October 18, 1902, p. 4.

consistent, with everything dovetailing together neatly. On issues outside race he was unremarkable. On racial issues no major black spokesman, until Randolph's *Messenger*, stood further left on the political spectrum. Thus skewed, his social program would not have been a major new synthesis or a blueprint of real originality. It would have demanded full equality for Negroes and proposed practically nothing for the basic American economic and governmental system. It would, in fact, have been strangely conservative.

Perhaps his most damaging intellectual flaw was that he had so little capacity for growth. It would be an overstatement to say that his was a closed mind, but it certainly lacked range. Over the course of thirty years the only obvious changes in his thinking were a greater attention to black capitalism and his more frequent and public carpings at the race's failings. That was not enough to bridge the gap between 1901 and the 1920s.

III

Trotter is a more popular figure at present than he was during his lifetime. He seems to suit the contemporary racial climate better than he did his own. "A true pioneer, decades ahead of his time," Lerone Bennett, Jr., has recently written, "Trotter laid the first stone of the modern protest movement." [6] Since 1958 Trotter has been the subject of at least three undergraduate theses and an uncounted number of term papers. His 1914 encounter with Wilson was presented dramatically in Martin Duberman's popular play, *In White America*. A new elementary school named for him opened in Boston in the fall of 1969: the school is located in a black neighborhood, but, appropriately enough, it has an integrated student body and faculty.

In many ways he did anticipate the civil rights move-

[6] Lerone Bennett, Jr., *Pioneers in Protest* (Chicago, 1968), p. 221.

ment of the early 1960s. His emphasis was on integration, legal rights, and the importance of voting, and these were also the hallmarks of the civil rights movement. He ran his own protest group so that blacks would control at least one such organization, and a prominent trend of the early 1960s was toward greater black control of the NAACP, CORE, SNCC, and the NSM. His general tone was a hortatory one of crusading, with no compromise or retreat, and such also distinguished the movement. He saw the main fulcrum of power in the struggle as flowing through the federal government, and so did the movement, with its pressure for federal legislation, federal protection of civil rights workers in the South, and the climactic March on Washington of August 1963. Trotter even adopted a rudimentary form of direct action with his demonstrations and arrests at the Boston Riot and the protest against *The Birth of a Nation.*

On the other hand, from the perspective of the black assertion of the late 1960s, Trotter is a less congenial figure. His unwavering commitment to integration jars with the revival of the black nationalist tradition. Most of his values were "white," and he did not see the need of defining the peculiar nature of the black experience in America or of preserving the contributions made by the black culture from being homogenized out of existence by full integration. He opposed separate black institutions of a civic nature, and presumably would not have endorsed freedom schools in black neighborhoods or organizations that refused white members. (His NERL always had at least a few white members.[7]) His peevish lectures of the 1920s on how to behave in public and other matters of decorum sound condescending and excessively mannered today.

The difficulty with stating that Trotter, or any black leader, was ahead of or behind his times is that ideas recur

[7] *Guardian*, July 1, 1939, p. 4.

in racial thought and become more or less appropriate as the situation changes. Trotter might seem to be ahead of his own time, but he formed his ideas by drawing from the militant integrationism and techniques of agitation of the abolitionist era. He spoke occasionally of a new era for black Americans, but it would be in terms of reinstating the freedoms enjoyed during Reconstruction, or of recalling the life of the Negro elite in Boston before the age of Washington. Actually he was both behind and ahead of his times. In either case he was out of step with his times, and that accounted for part of his frustration.

IV

All these limitations made the latter part of his career a long slide downhill. And that in turn has helped to obscure his real historical importance. In the age of Washington he did more than anyone else, save Du Bois, to keep the protest tradition alive. The *Guardian* led to the Niagara Movement, which led to the Constitution League, and finally to the NAACP. He also had some influence on the race's slow liberation from its traditional allegiance to the Republican party.

He had an annoying tendency to point out the sacrifices he had made for the cause. But the important point is that he did make those sacrifices. "Trotter is the only Negro, of my knowledge, who has made a sacrifice for his race," Kelly Miller remarked after his death. "Others have had nothing to sacrifice but have gained honor, place and fortune out of the cause which they espoused. . . . His followers broke with him one by one, till he was left in pathetic loneliness." [8] He relinquished a comfortable, respectable existence and gradually took up the life of the independent racial militant. That life brought him poverty and may have helped cause the premature death of his

[8] Statement by Kelly Miller in *Guardian*, April 21, 1934, p. 1, Trotter Papers.

wife. He was ignored by most white people. He was not quite taken seriously by most black people. Nonetheless he persisted, long past the time when it was apparent that he had lost what influence he had once held.

For over thirty years he genuinely put his people's welfare above his own. And the tragedy of his life is that he died without much assurance that his dedication had been worth it.

Bibliography

Primary Materials

I MANUSCRIPT COLLECTIONS

Jane Addams Papers, Swarthmore College Library.

Papers of American Commission to Negotiate Peace, Paris 1918–1919, State Department Papers, National Archives.

Ray Stannard Baker Papers, Manuscript Division, Library of Congress.

John E. Bruce Papers, Schomburg Collection, New York Public Library.

Charles E. Chapman Collection, Moorland Room, Howard University.

Charles W. Chesnutt Papers, Erastus Milo Cravath Memorial Library, Fisk University.

Calvin Coolidge Papers, Manuscript Division, Library of Congress.

James Michael Curley Papers, Library of College of the Holy Cross.

W. E. B. Du Bois Papers, in the custody of Herbert Aptheker, New York City.

W. E. B. Du Bois Papers, notes on, by Francis L. Broderick, Schomburg Collection, New York Public Library.

John Archibald Fairlie Papers, University Archives, University Library, University of Illinois at Urbana-Champaign.

Joseph Benson Foraker Papers, Cincinnati Historical Society.

George W. Forbes Papers, Rare Book Department, Boston Public Library.

Garrison Family Papers, Sophia Smith Collection, Smith College Library.

Francis J. Garrison Papers, Schomburg Collection, New York Public Library.

Archibald Grimké Papers, Moorland Room, Howard University.

Warren G. Harding Papers, Ohio Historical Society.

Herbert Hoover Papers, Herbert Hoover Presidential Library.

Edward M. House Papers, Sterling Library, Yale University.

James Weldon Johnson Memorial Collection, Beinecke Rare Book and Manuscript Library, Yale University.

William H. Lewis Papers, in the custody of William H. Lewis, Jr., Dedham, Massachusetts.

Henry Cabot Lodge Papers, Massachusetts Historical Society.

William G. McAdoo Papers, Manuscript Division, Library of Congress.

John E. Milholland Papers, Hancock House, Ticonderoga, New York.

Freeman H. M. Murray Papers, Moorland Room, Howard University.

NAACP Papers, Manuscript Division, Library of Congress.

Orville H. Platt Papers, Connecticut State Library.

Franklin D. Roosevelt Papers, Franklin D. Roosevelt Library.

Charles Edward Russell Papers, Manuscript Division, Library of Congress.

Arthur Barnett Spingarn Papers, Manuscript Division, Library of Congress.

Joel E. Spingarn Papers, Moorland Room, Howard University.

Moorfield Storey Papers, in the custody of Charles M. Storey, Boston, Massachusetts.

Moorfield Storey Papers, Manuscript Division, Library of Congress (cited as Moorfield Storey Papers, LC).

Mary Church Terrell Papers, Manuscript Division, Library of Congress.

George A. Towns Papers, Trevor Arnett Library, Atlanta University.

William Monroe Trotter Papers, Mugar Library, Boston University.

Oswald Garrison Villard Papers, Houghton Library, Harvard University.

David I. Walsh Papers, Library of College of the Holy Cross.

Booker T. Washington Papers, Manuscript Division, Library of Congress.

Woodrow Wilson Papers, Manuscript Division, Library of Congress.

Carter G. Woodson Papers, Manuscript Division, Library of Congress.

II   NEGRO   NEWSPAPERS   AND   MAGAZINES

Alexander's Magazine.

A. M. E. Review

Baltimore *Afro-American.*

Boston *Guardian.* There is no complete file of the Boston *Guardian.* Unless otherwise noted, citations are to copies on the following microfilm reels:

> 1. One of 44 issues from July 1902 to August 1904, at the Boston Public Library, the Congregational Library in Boston, the Schomburg Collection of the New York Public Library, the Negro Collection of Howard University, and elsewhere.
>
> 2. One of 100 issues from December 1903 to November 1913, at the Boston Public Library, the Negro Collection of Howard University, and the Stetson Library of Williams College.
>
> 3. Six reels comprising a virtually complete file from January 1939 to April 1957, at the Boston Public Library. During these years the paper was edited by Trotter's sister, Maude Trotter Steward, with the assistance of her husband, Dr. Charles Steward.

Chicago *Broad Ax.*

Chicago Defender.

Chicago Whip.

Cleveland *Gazette.*

The Crisis.

Indianapolis *Freeman.*

The Messenger.

Negro World.

New York Age.

Philadelphia Tribune.

Pittsburgh Courier.

The Voice of the Negro.

Washington *Bee.*

Washington *Colored American.*

III WHITE NEWSPAPERS AND MAGAZINES

Boston Daily Globe.
Boston Evening Globe.
Boston Evening Transcript.
Boston Herald.
Boston Post.
Boston Traveler.
The Independent.
The Literary Digest.
The New Republic.
New York Times.
New York *World.*
The Outlook.
Pike County Republican (Waverly, Ohio), March 13, 1873.
The World's Work.

IV GOVERNMENT PUBLICATIONS

*Antilynching Hearings before the Committee on the Judiciary
. . . on H. R. 259, 4123, and 11873 . . . January 29,
1920* (Washington, D.C., 1920).
Congressional Record: 49 Cong., 2 Sess.; 59 Cong., 2 Sess.;
60 Cong., 1 Sess.; 65 Cong., 2 Sess.; 66 Cong., 1 Sess.
"Preliminary Report of Commission of the Constitution League
of the United States on Affray at Brownsville, Tex., August
13 and 14, 1906," *Senate Documents*, 59 Cong., 2 Sess.,
Vol. 3.

V ARTICLES

Baker, Ray Stannard. "Gathering Clouds Along the Color
Line," *World's Work*, XXXII (1916), 232–236.
Barber, J. Max. "The Niagara Movement at Harpers Ferry,"
Voice of the Negro, III (1906), 402–411.
Du Bois, W. E. Burghardt. "The Growth of the Niagara Move-
ment," *Voice of the Negro*, III (1906), 43–45.
——. "The National Committee on the Negro," *Survey*, XXII
(1909), 407–409.
——. "Of the Training of Black Men," *Atlantic Monthly*, XC
(1902), 289–297.
——. "The Parting of the Ways," *World To-Day*, VI (1904),
521–523.
——. "William Monroe Trotter," *Crisis*, XLI (1934), 134.

Ewing, Quincy. "The Heart of the Race Problem," *Atlantic Monthly*, CIII (1909), 389–397.

"Fair Play" [Kelly Miller], "Washington's Policy," *Boston Evening Transcript*, September 18, 1903, p. 8.

"George Forbes of Boston," *Crisis*, XXXIV (1927), 151–152.

Gordon, Eugene. "The Negro Press," *American Mercury*, VIII (1926), 207–215.

Hackett, Francis. "Brotherly Love," *New Republic*, II (1915), 185.

Harris, Abram L. "The Negro Problem as Viewed by Negro Leaders," *Current History*, XVIII (1923), 410–418.

Hershaw, L. M. "The Negro Press in America," *Charities*, XV (1905–1906), 66–68.

Libraries, XXXII (1927), 235–237 (obituary of George Forbes).

"Mr. Trotter and Mr. Wilson," *Crisis*, IX (1914–1915), 119–129.

"A Negro Delegate Who Managed to Reach the Peace Conference," *Literary Digest*, LXII (August 16, 1919), 42–45.

"The Opposition to Booker T. Washington," *Literary Digest*, XXVII (1903), 187–189.

Ovington, Mary White. "The National Association for the Advancement of Colored People," *Journal of Negro History*, IX (1924), 107–116.

Page, Thomas Nelson. "The Disfranchisement of the Negro: One Factor in the South's Standing Problem," *Scribner's Magazine*, XXXVI (1904), 15–24.

Roosevelt, Theodore. "The Progressives and the Colored Man," *Outlook*, CI (1912), 909–912.

Walling, William English. "The Race War in the North," *Independent*, LXV (1908), 529–534.

——. "Science and Human Brotherhood," *Independent*, LXVI (1909), 1318–1327.

Washington, Booker T. "My View of Segregation Laws," *New Republic*, V (1915–1916), 113–114.

Watson, J. B. "Recalling 1906," *Crisis*, XLI (1934), 100.

"William Monroe Trotter," *Journal of Negro History*, XIX (1934), 339–341.

VI BOOKS AND PAMPHLETS

Along This Way: The Autobiography of James Weldon Johnson (New York, 1933).

Aptheker, Herbert, ed. *A Documentary History of the Negro People in the United States* (New York, 1951).

The Autobiography of W. E. B. Du Bois (New York, 1968).

Baker, Ray Stannard. *Following the Color Line: American Negro Citizenship in the Progressive Era* (Harper Torchbook edition, New York, 1964).

Black and Conservative: The Autobiography of George S. Schuyler (New York, 1966).

Boston John Brown Jubilee, Faneuil Hall, Boston, Mass., December 2, 1909 (pamphlet in William Monroe Trotter Papers).

Brigham, W. I. Tyler. *The History of the Brigham Family* (New York, 1907).

The Celebration of the One Hundredth Anniversary of the Birth of William Lloyd Garrison, By the Colored Citizens of Greater Boston under the Auspices of the Suffrage League of Boston and Vicinity (Boston, 1906).

Celebration of the Sesquicentennial Anniversary of the Battle of Bunker Hill June 17, 1925 (Boston, 1925).

Daniels, John. *In Freedom's Birthplace: A Study of the Boston Negroes* (Boston and New York, 1914).

Du Bois, W. E. Burghardt. *The Amenia Conference: An Historic Negro Gathering* (Amenia, N.Y., 1925).

——. *Dusk of Dawn: An Essay Toward an Autobiography of a Race Concept* (New York, 1940).

——. *The Ordeal of Mansart* (New York, 1957).

——. *The Souls of Black Folk* (Chicago, 1903).

Exercises at the Dedication of the Statue of Wendell Phillips July 5, 1915 (Boston, 1916).

Ferris, William H. *The African Abroad: or His Evolution in Western Civilization; Tracing His Development Under Caucasian Milieux* (2 vols., New Haven, 1913).

Foraker, Joseph Benson. *Notes of a Busy Life* (2 vols., Cincinnati, 1916).

Hartshorn, W. N., ed. *An Era of Progress and Promise, 1863–1910* (Boston, 1910).

Harvard College Class of 1895 (Cambridge, Mass.):
 Secretary's Report, No. 1 (1898).
 Second Report (1902).
 Third Report (1905).
 Fourth Report (1910).
 Twenty-Fifth Anniversary Report (1920).
 Thirtieth Anniversary Report (1925).

The Harvard Index (Boston):
  1891–2 (1891).
  1892–3 (1892).
  1893–4 (1893).
  1894–5 (1894).
The Harvard University Catalogue (Cambridge, Mass.):
  1891–92 (1891).
  1892–93 (1892).
  1893–94 (1893).
  1894–95 (1894).
Kerlin, Robert T. *The Voice of the Negro, 1919* (New York, 1920).
A Man Called White: The Autobiography of Walter White (New York, 1948).
Miller, Kelly. *Race Adjustment: Essays on the Negro in America* (New York and Washington, D.C., 1908).
Morison, Elting E., ed. *The Letters of Theodore Roosevelt* (8 vols., Cambridge, Mass., 1951–1954).
Odum, Howard W. *Social and Mental Traits of the Negro* (New York, 1910).
Ovington, Mary White. *The Walls Came Tumbling Down* (New York, 1947).
Ransom, Reverdy C. *The Pilgrimage of Harriet Ransom's Son* (Nashville, Tenn., n.d.).
Russell, Charles Edward. *Bare Hands and Stone Walls: Some Recollections of a Side-Line Reformer* (New York, 1933).
Simmons, William J. *Men of Mark: Eminent, Progressive and Rising* (Cleveland, 1887).
Terrell, Mary Church. *A Colored Woman in a White World* (Washington, D.C., 1940).
Trotter, James M. *Music and Some Highly Musical People* (Boston and New York, 1878).
Trotter, W. M., ed. *The Two Days Observance of the One Hundredth Anniversary of the Birth of Charles Sumner . . . January Fifth and Sixth, 1911* (Boston, 1911).
The Twentieth Century Club of Boston: The Record of Twenty Years (Boston, 1914).
Villard, Oswald Garrison. *Fighting Years: Memoirs of a Liberal Editor* (New York, 1939).
[Walling, William English, ed.] *Proceedings of the National Negro Conference 1909* (New York, 1909).
Walters, Alexander. *My Life and Work* (New York, 1917).
———. *Reasons Why the Negro Should Vote the Democratic*

Ticket in This Campaign (New York, 1912).

Washington, Booker T. *The Future of the American Negro* (Boston, 1899).

———. *My Larger Education: Being Chapters From My Experience* (New York, 1911).

———. *The Story of My Life and Work* (Cincinnati, 1900).

———. *Up from Slavery* (New York, 1901).

———, et al. *The Negro Problem: A Series of Articles by Representative American Negroes of To-Day* (New York, 1903).

Washington, E. Davidson, ed. *Selected Speeches of Booker T. Washington* (New York, 1932).

Wilson, Joseph T. *The Black Phalanx: A History of the Negro Soldiers of the United States in the Wars of 1775–1812, 1861–'65* (Hartford, 1888).

Woodson, Carter G., ed. *Works of Francis J. Grimké* (4 vols., Washington, D.C., 1942).

The Works of Theodore Roosevelt (Memorial edition, 24 vols., New York, 1923–26).

Worthy, William. *The Story of the Two First Colored Nurses to Train in the Boston City Hospital* (Boston, 1942).

VII MISCELLANEOUS SOURCES

Folders of Trotter material at the Schomburg Collection, New York Public Library; Moorland Room, Howard University; Trevor Arnett Library, Atlanta University; *Boston Herald Traveler* Library, Boston; Harvard Archives, Widener Library, Harvard University.

Minutes of Boston Literary and Historical Association, Trotter Papers.

Secondary Accounts

I UNPUBLISHED DISSERTATIONS AND MONOGRAPHS

Abramowitz, Jack. "Accommodation and Militancy in Negro Life 1876–1916" (Ph.D. thesis, Columbia University, 1950).

Blaesser, Brian W. "John E. Milholland" (senior honors thesis, Brown University, 1969).

Brisbane, Robert Hughes, Jr. "The Rise of Protest Movements Among Negroes Since 1900" (Ph.D. thesis, Harvard University, 1949).

Bunche, Ralph J. "A Brief and Tentative Analysis of Negro Leadership" (memorandum for Carnegie-Myrdal study, 1940, in Schomburg Collection, New York Public Library).

——. "Extended Memorandum on the Programs, Ideologies, Tactics and Achievements of Negro Betterment and Interracial Organization" (4 vols., memorandum for Carnegie-Myrdal study, 1940, in Schomburg Collection, New York Public Library).

Daniel, James C. "Negro Leadership Minus Booker T. Washington: Depolarization and Consensus in 1916" (seminar paper, University of Maryland, 1968; typescript in Mr. Daniel's possession).

Fox, Stephen R. "William Monroe Trotter" (history honors thesis, Williams College, 1966).

Hill, Adelaide Cromwell. "The Negro Upper Class in Boston, Its Development and Present Social Structure" (Ph.D. thesis, Radcliffe College, 1952).

Jacobs, Donald Martin. "A History of the Boston Negro from the Revolution to the Civil War" (Ph.D. thesis, Boston University, 1968).

Jones, Jacqueline Lois. "The American Negro, 1877–1900, as Portrayed in the *Boston Evening Transcript*" (M.A. thesis, Howard University, 1948).

Jordan, Oswald Louis. "The Political Status of the Negro in Boston" (M.A. thesis, Howard University, 1942).

Kountze, Mabe. "A History of the Early Colored Press in Massachusetts & a Second Sketch of the Boston Guardian Weekly" (Xeroxed typescript, July 1967, Moorland Room, Howard University).

——. "Monroe Mason, Monroe Trotter & the Boston Guardian" (Xeroxed typescript, June 1965, Moorland Room, Howard University).

Lichtenstein, Nelson. "The Development of an Alliance Between White Liberals and Negro Radicals 1903–1910" (senior honors thesis, Dartmouth College, 1966).

Puttkammer, Charles W. "William Monroe Trotter: An Evaluation of the Life of a Radical Negro Newspaper Editor, 1901–1934" (senior thesis, Princeton University, 1958).

Skates, Ronald Louis. "William Monroe Trotter: The Radical Negro of Massachusetts 1900–1910" (history honors thesis,

Harvard University, 1963).

Worthman, Paul. "The Negroes' Political Realignment" (history honors thesis, Williams College, 1962).

Worthy, Ruth. "A Negro in Our History: William Monroe Trotter, 1872–1934" (M.A. thesis, Columbia University, 1952).

Zangrando, Robert Lewis. "The Efforts of the National Association for the Advancement of Colored People to Secure Passage of a Federal Anti-Lynching Law, 1920–1940" (Ph.D. thesis, University of Pennsylvania, 1963).

II ARTICLES

Abramowitz, Jack. "A Civil War Letter: James M. Trotter to Francis J. Garrison," *Midwest Journal*, IV (1952), 113–122.

Blumenthal, Henry. "Woodrow Wilson and the Race Question," *Journal of Negro History*, XLVIII (1963), 1–21.

Carter, Everett. "Cultural History Written with Lightning: The Significance of *The Birth of a Nation*," *American Quarterly*, XII (1960), 347–357.

Cripps, Thomas R. "The Reaction of the Negro to the Motion Picture Birth of a Nation," *Historian*, XXV (1962–1963), 344–362.

Downes, Randolph C. "Negro Rights and White Backlash in the Campaign of 1920," *Ohio History*, LXXV (1966), 84–107.

Grantham, Dewey W., Jr. "The Progressive Movement and the Negro," *South Atlantic Quarterly*, LIV (1955), 461–477.

Grimké, Angelina W. "A Biographical Sketch of Archibald H. Grimké," *Opportunity*, III (1925), 44–47.

Harrison, William. "Phylon Profile IX: William Monroe Trotter—Fighter," *Phylon*, VII (1946), 236–245.

James, Jacqueline. "Uncle Tom? Not Booker T.," *American Heritage*, XIX (August 1968), 50–54, 95–100.

Link, Arthur S. "The Negro as a Factor in the Campaign of 1912," *Journal of Negro History*, XXXII (1947), 81–99.

McPherson, James M. "The Antislavery Legacy: From Reconstruction to the NAACP," in Barton J. Bernstein, ed., *Towards a New Past: Dissenting Essays in American History* (New York, 1968), pp. 126–157.

Meier, August. "Booker T. Washington and the Negro Press: With Special Reference to the *Colored American Magazine*," *Journal of Negro History*, XXXVIII (1953), 67–90.

——. "Booker T. Washington and the Rise of the NAACP," *Crisis*, LXI (1954), 69–76, 117–123.

——. "The Negro and the Democratic Party, 1875–1915," *Phylon*, XVII (1956), 173–191.

——, and Elliott Rudwick. "The Rise of Segregation in the Federal Bureaucracy, 1900–1930," *Phylon*, XXVIII (1967), 178–184.

Mowry, George E. "The South and the Progressive Lily White Party of 1912," *Journal of Southern History*, VI (1940), 237–247.

Osborn, George C. "The Problem of the Negro in Government, 1913," *Historian*, XXIII (1960–1961), 330–347.

Puttkammer, C. W., and Ruth Worthy. "William Monroe Trotter 1872–1934," *Journal of Negro History*, XLIII (1958), 298–316.

Record, Wilson. "Negro Intellectual Leadership in the National Association for the Advancement of Colored People: 1910–1940," *Phylon*, XVII (1956), 375–389.

Rudwick, Elliott M. "Booker T. Washington's Relations with the National Association for the Advancement of Colored People," *Journal of Negro Education*, XXIX (1960), 134–144.

——. "The National Negro Committee Conference of 1909," *Phylon*, XVIII (1957), 413–419.

——. "The Niagara Movement," *Journal of Negro History*, XLII (1957), 177–200.

——. "Race Leadership Struggle: Background of the Boston Riot of 1903," *Journal of Negro Education*, XXXI (1962), 16–24.

——. "W. E. B. Du Bois in the Role of *Crisis* Editor," *Journal of Negro History*, XLIII (1958), 214–240.

Sherman, Richard B. "The Harding Administration and the Negro: An Opportunity Lost," *Journal of Negro History*, XLIX (1964), 151–168.

——. "Republicans and Negroes: The Lessons of Normalcy," *Phylon*, XXVII (1966), 63–79.

Smith, Willard H. "William Jennings Bryan and Racism," *Journal of Negro History*, LIV (1969), 127–147.

"Thomas Jefferson's Negro Grandchildren," *Ebony*, X (November 1954), 78–80.

Thornbrough, Emma Lou. "American Negro Newspapers, 1880–1914," *Business History Review*, XL (1966), 467–490.

——. "The Brownsville Episode and the Negro Vote," *Mississippi Valley Historical Review*, XLIV (1957–1958), 469–493.

——. "More Light on Booker T. Washington and the New York *Age*," *Journal of Negro History*, XLIII (1958), 34–49.

——. "The National Afro-American League, 1887–1908," *Journal of Southern History*, XXVII (1961), 494–512.

Tinsley, James A. "Roosevelt, Foraker, and the Brownsville Affray, *Journal of Negro History*, XLI (1956), 43–65.

Weiss, Nancy J. "The Negro and the New Freedom: Fighting Wilsonian Segregation," *Political Science Quarterly*, LXXXIV (1969), 61–79.

Wesley, Charles. "Background for Peace: Trotter Pioneered in Drive for Negro Vote," *Chicago Defender*, October 9, 1943, p. 13.

Wolgemuth, Kathleen Long. "Woodrow Wilson and Federal Segregation," *Journal of Negro History*, XLIV (1959), 158–173.

——. "Woodrow Wilson's Appointment Policy and the Negro," *Journal of Southern History*, XXIV (1958), 457–471.

III BOOKS

Aptheker, Herbert. *Toward Negro Freedom* (New York, 1956).

Baker, Ray Stannard. *Woodrow Wilson: Life and Letters* (8 vols., Garden City, N.Y., 1927–39).

Barton, Rebecca Chalmers. *Witnesses for Freedom: Negro Americans in Autobiography* (New York, 1948).

Beaver, Daniel R. *Newton D. Baker and the American War Effort 1917–1919* (Lincoln, Neb., 1966).

Bennett, Lerone, Jr. *Before the Mayflower: A History of the Negro in America 1619–1962* (Chicago, 1962).

——. *Pioneers in Protest* (Chicago, 1968).

Bontemps, Arna. *100 Years of Negro Freedom* (New York, 1961).

——, and Jack Conroy. *They Seek a City* (Garden City, N.Y., 1945).

Broderick, Francis L. *W. E. B. DuBois: Negro Leader in a Time of Crisis* (Stanford, 1959).

——, and August Meier, eds. *Negro Protest Thought in the Twentieth Century* (Indianapolis, 1965).

Chesnutt, Helen M. *Charles Waddell Chesnutt: Pioneer of the*

Color Line (Chapel Hill, N.C., 1952).

Cronon, Edmund David. *Black Moses: The Story of Marcus Garvey and the Universal Negro Improvement Association* (Madison, Wis., 1955).

Duberman, Martin. *In White America* (Signet Book edition, New York, 1965).

Edwards, Rheable M., and Laura B. Harris. *The Negro in Boston* (Boston, 1961).

Emilio, Luis F. *A Brave Black Regiment: History of the Fifty-fourth Regiment of Massachusetts Volunteer Infantry, 1863–1865* (second revised edition, Boston, 1894).

Fishel, Leslie H., Jr., and Benjamin Quarles, eds. *The Negro American: A Documentary History* (New York, 1967).

Fox, Charles Barnard. *Record of the Service of the Fifty-fifth Regiment of Massachusetts Volunteer Infantry* (Cambridge, Mass., 1868).

Franklin, John Hope. *From Slavery to Freedom: A History of American Negroes* (third edition, New York, 1967).

Garraty, John A. *Henry Cabot Lodge: A Biography* (New York, 1953).

Hawkins, Hugh, ed. *Booker T. Washington and His Critics: The Problem of Negro Leadership* (Boston, 1962).

Hirshson, Stanley P. *Farewell to the Bloody Shirt: Northern Republicans & the Southern Negro, 1877–1893* (Bloomington, Ind., 1963).

Howe, M. A. DeWolfe. *Portrait of an Independent: Moorfield Storey 1845–1929* (Boston and New York, 1932).

Hughes, Langston. *Fight for Freedom: The Story of the NAACP* (New York, 1962).

Jordan, Winthrop D. *White over Black: American Attitudes Toward the Negro, 1550–1812* (Chapel Hill, N.C., 1968).

Kellogg, Charles Flint. *NAACP: A History of the National Association for the Advancement of Colored People, Volume I 1909–1920* (Baltimore, 1967).

Link, Arthur S. *Wilson: The New Freedom* (Princeton, 1956).

———. *Wilson: The Road to the White House* (Princeton, 1947).

———. *Woodrow Wilson and the Progressive Era, 1910–1917* (New York, 1954).

Litwack, Leon F. *North of Slavery: The Negro in the Free States, 1790–1860* (Chicago, 1961).

Logan, Rayford W. *The Negro in American Life and Thought:*

The Nadir 1877–1901 (New York, 1954).

McPherson, James M. *The Negro's Civil War: How American Negroes Felt and Acted During the War for the Union* (New York, 1965).

Mathews, Basil. *Booker T. Washington: Educator and Inter-Racial Interpreter* (Cambridge, Mass., 1948).

Meier, August. *Negro Thought in America, 1880–1915: Racial Ideologies in the Age of Booker T. Washington* (Ann Arbor, Mich., 1963).

Moon, Henry Lee. *Balance of Power: The Negro Vote* (Garden City, N.Y., 1948).

Morison, Samuel Eliot. *Three Centuries of Harvard 1636–1936* (Cambridge, Mass., 1946).

Morrison, Joseph L. *Josephus Daniels: The Small-d Democrat* (Chapel Hill, N.C., 1966).

Mowry, George E. *The Era of Theodore Roosevelt* (New York, 1958).

Ottley, Roi. *The Lonely Warrior: The Life and Times of Robert S. Abbott* (Chicago, 1955).

Rudwick, Elliott M. *W. E. B. Du Bois: A Study in Minority Group Leadership* (Philadelphia, 1960).

Schlesinger, Arthur M., Jr. *The Age of Roosevelt: The Politics of Upheaval* (Boston, 1960).

Scott, Emmett J., and Lyman Beecher Stowe. *Booker T. Washington: Builder of a Civilization* (New York, 1916).

Spencer, Samuel R., Jr. *Booker T. Washington and the Negro's Place in American Life* (Boston, 1955).

Thornbrough, Emma Lou, ed. *Booker T. Washington* (Englewood Cliffs, N.J., 1969).

Torrence, Ridgely. *The Story of John Hope* (New York, 1948).

Walters, Everett. *Joseph Benson Foraker: An Uncompromising Republican* (Columbus, O., 1948).

Waskow, Arthur I. *From Race Riot to Sit-In, 1919 and the 1960s* (New York, 1966).

Woodward, C. Vann. *The Strange Career of Jim Crow* (revised edition, New York, 1965).

Index

Stephen R. Fox

Stephen R. Fox was born in Boston in 1945 and grew up mostly in Lexington, Massachusetts. He was graduated from Williams College in 1966. Since then he has been a graduate student in American Civilization at Brown University. He lives in Providence, Rhode Island, with his record player.